THE CRISIS OF 1614 AND THE ADDLED PARLIAMENT

This book is dedicated to
the memory of
Jeremy Maule (1952–1998)

Vestibus hunc igitur pullis, Academia, luge,
Et madeant lachrymis nigra feretra tuis

The Crisis of 1614 and The Addled Parliament

Literary and Historical Perspectives

Edited by

STEPHEN CLUCAS and ROSALIND DAVIES

Routledge
Taylor & Francis Group
LONDON AND NEW YORK

First published 2003 by Ashgate Publishing

Reissued 2018 by Routledge
2 Park Square, Milton Park, Abingdon, Oxon OX14 4RN
711 Third Avenue, New York, NY 10017, USA

Routledge is an imprint of the Taylor & Francis Group, an informa business

A Library of Congress record exists under LC control number: 2002024923

ISBN 13: 978-1-138-71508-0 (hbk)
ISBN 13: 978-1-138-71505-9 (pbk)
ISBN 13: 978-1-315-19777-7 (ebk)

Contents

PART III: TEXT AND TRADE

PART IV: TEXTS AND CONTEXTS

List of Figure and Tables

Notes on Contributors

Anna Beer is Lecturer in English Literature at Regent's Park College, University of Oxford. She is the author of *Sir Walter Ralegh and his Readers in the Seventeenth Century: Speaking to the People* (Macmillan, 1997) and is currently working on the first biography of Lady Elizabeth Ralegh.

Stephen Clucas is Senior Lecturer in English and Humanities at Birkbeck College, University of London. His publications include a translation of Paolo Rossi's *Logic and the Art of Memory: The Quest for a Universal Language* (Athlone Press/Chicago University Press, 2000), and two edited collections of essays, *A Princely Brave Woman: Essays on Margaret Cavendish, Duchess of Newcastle* (Ashgate, 2002) and *John Dee: Interdisciplinary Studies in English Renaissance Thought* (Kluwer Academic Publishers, forthcoming). He is currently working on a book on Henry Percy, ninth Earl of Northumberland and his intellectual circle.

David Colclough is Lecturer in English at Queen Mary, University of London. He has published articles on Renaissance rhetoric and on the poetry of John Hoskyns, and is currently working on a book on freedom of speech in early Stuart England.

John Cramsie is Assistant Professor of British, Irish and Imperial History at Union College in Schenectady, New York. He completed his BA at the University of Minnesota and his Ph.D. at the University of St. Andrews (1997). His book, *Kingship and Crown Finance under James VI & I, 1603–1625*, was published by The Boydell Press in 2002. He is currently preparing a collection of essays (with Dr Sabrina Baron) on the intersections of reading, education, and the exercise of authority in early modern Britain and Ireland. He has also begun work on a study of ethnic identity and encounters in early modern Britain.

Rosalind Davies. Following her doctoral work on the prose writings of Sir Walter Ralegh, she has published essays on Ralegh's 1603 trial, in *Renaissance Forum*, and on the Cadiz expedition of 1596 in 'War. Identities in Conflict 1300–2000', in Sutton's Themes in History series. Her biography of Francis Bacon was published in the *Dictionary of Literary Biography* (British Philosophers, 1500–1800).

Jonathan Gibson works for the Perdita Project at Nottingham Trent University. He has published essays on renaissance topics in the *Review of English Studies* and *The Seventeenth Century*.

James Knowles teaches at the University of Stirling. He has written extensively on Jonson's masques and entertainments (most notably the 'Entertainment at Britain's Burse') and he has edited a volume of essays, *Shakespeare's Late Plays, New Essays* (with Jennifer Richards). He is currently working on a monograph and editing Jonson's entertainments.

Michelle O'Callaghan is a Senior Lecturer in the English Department at Oxford Brookes University. She is the author of *The 'shepherds nation': Jacobean Spenserians and Early Stuart Cultural Politics* (Oxford University Press, 2000) and is currently working on early modern textual communities.

Joad Raymond is a lecturer in English at the University of East Anglia. He is the author of *The Invention of the Newspaper: English Newsbooks 1641–1649* (1996) and *Pamphlets and Pamphleteering in Early Modern Britain* (2003). He is presently working on a book on *Paradise Lost*.

Conrad Russell is Professor of British History at Kings College, University of London. His books include *The Crisis of Parliaments: English History 1509–1660* (1971), *The Causes of the English Civil War* (1990), *Unrevolutionary England* (1990) and *The Fall of the British Monarchies 1637–1642* (1991).

Alan Stewart is Professor of Renaissance Studies at Birkbeck College, University of London. His publications include *Close Readers: Humanism and Sodomy in Early Modern England* (Princeton, 1997) and *Philip Sidney: A Double Life* (Chatto & Windus, 2000). He co-authored *Hostage to Fortune: The Troubled Life of Francis Bacon* (Gollancz, 1998) with Lisa Jardine, and is now editor of Bacon's *Correspondence*, part of the new Oxford Francis Bacon.

Andrew Thrush has been the editor of the 1604–1629 section of the History of Parliament since 1992, and was formerly Head of History and Politics at Mill Hill School, London. He is the author of several articles on the early Stuart Navy, and with Roger Lockyer has written the third edition of *Henry VII* (Longman, 1997).

Abbreviations

Commons Debates, 1621	*Commons Debates in 1621*, ed. by Wallace Notestein, Frances Helen Relf, and Hartley Simpson, 7 vols (New Haven: Yale University Press, 1935).
Letters of John Chamberlain	*Letters of John Chamberlain*, ed. by N. E. McClure, 2 vols (Philadelphia: The American Philosophical Society, 1939).
Letters of King James	*Letters of King James VI and I*, ed. by G. P.V. Akrigg (Berkeley & London: University of California Press, 1984).
Limits of Revision	Conrad Russell, *The Addled Parliament of 1614: The Limits of Revision*, The Stenton Lecture 1991 (Reading: University of Reading, 1992).
Proceedings, 1610	*Proceedings in Parliament, 1610*, ed. by Elizabeth Read Foster, 2 vols (New Haven and London: Yale University Press, 1966).
Proceedings, 1614	*Proceedings in Parliament, 1614, House of Commons*, ed. by Maija Jansson (Philadelphia: American Philosophical Society, 1988).

1

Introduction

Stephen Clucas and Rosalind Davies

The present volume arose out of an awareness that a number of literary historians had been working on the tumultuous period between the failure of the Great Contract in the 1610 Parliament and the so-called 'Addled Parliament' of 1614. The conference *1614: Year of Crisis*, which was held at Birkbeck College, University of London in July 1998, was an attempt to bring literary historians together with constitutional and state historians to reflect on the political and ideological upheavals of 1614 from various perspectives, and the result was a series of highly focused and richly contextual papers. In the aftermath of the new historicism and 'revisionist' Stuart historiography the time seems right for the detailed study of highly specific historical moments and localities, and 1614 is particularly in need of renewed attention because few traditional historians have seriously addressed the constitutional crisis of the ill-fated parliament of that year since Conrad Russell's provocative 1991 Stenton Lecture, *The Addled Parliament of 1614: The Limits of Revision* (which attempted to 'envisage a constitutional conflict within a revisionist framework').[1] Literary historians, too, seemed to have failed to bring this significant political moment into focus, despite the fact that there were many literary interventions in contemporary debates of the period. The publication in 1988 of Maija Jansson's *Proceedings in Parliament, 1614,* which gathers together much of the remaining evidence about the turbulent proceedings of that parliament from private diaries and notebooks and the few remaining official documents (most of which James had burned after the dissolution of the session) has made an informed re-appraisal of the political issues a much less daunting task than has hitherto been the case.[2]

I

According to Thomas L. Moir – author of the only monograph to be dedicated solely to the topic – the Addled Parliament was a 'Constitutional Crisis' which 'formed one of the links in the long chain of events stretching from 1603 to 1649.'[3] Samuel R. Gardiner, who considered the parliament of 1614 as being primarily concerned with 'higher [*i.e. constitutional*] questions' rather than 'useful business', also saw in some of the proceedings 'the first dawning of the idea that, in order to preserve the rights of the subject intact, it would be necessary to make some change in the relations between the authority of the Crown and the representatives of the people.'[4] In more recent times this conflictual and proto-republican reading of the Addled Parliament has been questioned, most notably by Conrad Russell who in his

Stenton lecture argued that while the Addled Parliament 'looks superficially like one of the hardest places to sustain a revisionist thesis' (because the 'tendency of revision has been to play down constitutional conflict'), it was still possible to do so.[5]

Although Professor Russell characterises the Commons refusal to discuss the king's supply until the matter of impositions was resolved as 'an explicit pistol-point demand,'[6] his overall picture of the parliament stresses unanimity, and constitutional conservatism: 'Members did care about constitutional issues', he argues, 'but this did not make them press for change. It made them press to prevent it.'[7] MPs were not 'engaged in the pursuit of power', he suggests, but were rather 'fighting to keep something they already had.'[8] In Russell's view there was no 'battle between rival constitutional ideas',[9] but instead a profound misunderstanding on both sides about the financial needs of the Crown. 'The central disagreement of James's reign', Russell concluded,

> was about the true cost of government, and James's central failure was his failure to convince the House of Commons he needed as much as in fact he did. From that single failure, all the constitutional troubles of the reign stemmed.[10]

The mutual misunderstandings and disagreements between Commons and Crown, however, do seem to have their origins in constitutional terms of reference. If, as Russell suggests, there was 'little chance of developing a serious argument between the prerogative and the rule of law because James thought he was within his legal rights,'[11] it was precisely the inability to pursue this argument which brought the parliament to a standstill. While the issue of financial supply and its necessity was doubtless an issue fraught with mutual incomprehension, its symbolic value (at least for MPs) seems to have been more important than the fiscal details.

While Russell felt that the issue of impositions had 'a potential for creating divisions on issues of political ideas', he sees political theories as 'a consequence, rather than a cause of the dispute on impositions.'[12] He also emphasises the fact that the Addled Parliament did in fact manage to conduct some of its business, that MPs 'showed a considerable appetite for passing their own bills,' and that these bills were 'hardly the stuff of constitutional conflict.'[13] This is an issue to which Professor Russell returns in the present volume.

Despite all this, Russell does concede that 'something was clearly very badly wrong in 1614', although in his view 'the failure of the Whig analyses was not seeing that there was something wrong, but in their attempts to explain what it was.'[14] Russell sees the 1614 parliament as a 'crucial part' of a debate which was initiated by the dissolution of the 1610 parliament (which James once described as 'the House of Hell'), a debate which was re-arranging traditional relations between the king and parliament.[15] He also characterises the resistance of the Commons over the impositions debate as a gesture with more than simply fiscal ramifications. For the Commons to 'back down and meekly accept impositions,' Russell observes, 'would turn England into a monarchy in which Parliaments were not essential.'[16] It was (at least potentially) a crucial issue for the liberty of the king's subjects.

Russell also sees James's resort to dissolution as 'punitive', as the 'forging [of] a new political weapon.'[17] James's famous boast in 1624 of having 'broken the necks of three parliaments one after another' would seem to substantiate this view.[18]

While political theory (taking 'theory' in its most restricted sense) may not have been prior to the parliamentary confrontation of 1614, the implications of the House's procedural practice was not lost on James, who after the dissolution of 1610, voiced the opinion that his subjects' actions could only be motivated by 'a desiring to lay the foundations of a popular state.'[19] In conversation with the Spanish ambassador Sarmiento after the dissolution in 1614, James expressed his deepening dismay with the English parliament with surprising candour:

> The House of Commons is a body without a head. The members give their opinions in a disorderly manner. At their meetings nothing is heard but cries, shouts, and confusion. I am surprised that my ancestors should ever have permitted such an institution to come into existence: I am a stranger, and found it here when I arrived, so that I am obliged to put up with what I cannot get rid of.[20]

When James acceded in 1603, he came with a clear-cut set of constitutional ideas which he proceeded to apply to his new situation. That this caused anxieties for the Commons is clear from the drafting of the 1604 *Apology*, which set out to define the customary privileges of the institution.[21] That these initial anxieties about 'rule by strangers' did not evaporate, and continued to pervade MPs' sense of parliamentary identity, can be seen clearly delineated in the Northampton faction's promotion of the anti-Scots sentiments of Hoskins's 'Sicilian Vespers' speech in the 1614 session.[22]

The idea that parliamentary identity was at stake in the debates of 1614 is central to Maija Jansson's account of what went 'badly wrong' in 1614. In her account, Jansson sees the procedural tactics of the Addled Parliament as a practical response to a constitutional crisis, and a template for subsequent parliamentary dealings with the Crown:

> Far from being the confused do-nothing assembly of tradition, the English parliament of 1614 addressed thorny constitutional issues and anticipated the concern with procedure and privilege that is evident throughout the sessions of the 1620s.[23]

In Jansson's view the House of Commons in 1614 was primarily concerned with a defence of what they perceived to be a threat to established parliamentary rights and privileges against James's conception of prerogative power, and it was these rights and privileges which formed the pivotal point of the key debates on impositions and undertaking.[24] The stubborn refusal to address the matter of supply was, Jansson says, a 'resolve not to acquiesce in an immediate short term reconciliation with the Crown that would ultimately spell disaster for the institution of parliament.'[25]

These constitutional concerns were still (despite James's disgruntled mutterings about a 'popular state' after 1610, and Sandys's infamous speech alluding to elective monarchy) far-removed from a programmatic republicanism. 'In 1614,' Jansson observes, 'the House of Commons was not, individually or collectively, "antimonarchically" inclined [...] what the members of the Lower House desired was not a change in the structure of government but a definition of the jurisdictional authority of the courts and parliament [...].'[26]

If the Parliament was not anti-monarchical, however, it was resistant to James's conception of the absolute power of the sovereign, a point which was made forcefully by a number of MPs. Sir Edwin Sandys, for example, moved that the Commons should not allow 'the liberties of the House to run through our fingers', it was not the monetary value of impositions which was at issue, he claimed 'as that the King does take to his sole authority to impose.' In an earlier speech Sandys argued that 'If the King may impose by his absolute power then no man [is] certain what he has, for it shall be subject to the King's pleasure.'[27] In asserting the rights of parliament to be involved in the levying of imposts the Commons were, as Jansson suggests, 'self-consciously confirming the institutional identity of parliament' against a concept of kingship which they saw as alien to its traditional understanding.[28] James, for his part, saw this insistence as a 'disputation touching the prerogative of the King' – a matter for which he declared himself ready to 'die a 100 deaths'.[29] The right of imposing, as James saw it, was a matter for himself and the judges. '[T]o bar me from my right', he said in a speech before the assembled MPs on 3 May: 'To rob my crown of so regal a prerogative, to show your wills for that you cannot obtain resting in my power is mere obstinacy.[30]

The Commons for their part maintained their 'obstinacy', declaring unanimously on 12 May that 'his Majesty without parliament could not impose.'[31] Often in the 1614 session, as Jansson notes, the issue of parliament's rights 'looms as more important than the substance of the business at hand.'[32] This was expressed succinctly by Francis Ashley on 3 June, when he stated: 'Now we are at a point of the King's power and our liberty touching impositions.'[33] To concede the issue of impositions would, it was moved on the following day 'in after ages be accounted a real confirmation of the King's absolute power of imposing.'[34] If, as Russell has suggested, both Commons and king were 'prisoners of their own analysis,'[35] it was because these analyses turned upon the constitutional 'point' of the limits of regal power and the extent of parliamentary privilege. This constitutional point was destined to become the pivot on which far more momentous constitutional changes were turned in the 1640s, and as such the jurisdictional concerns of 1614 can be seen as a crisis *in utero* if not *in partum*.

Whether one agrees that there was a constitutional 'crisis' or 'conflict' or not, most historians seem to agree that something went *wrong* in the 1614 session, and that whatever it was (and the frustration of due process by dissolution was clearly a large part of this), it continued to go wrong for the remainder of James's reign and was bequeathed to his son in his turn.

While the failure of parliament in 1614 is an important focus of this volume, the events in the House are only part of the picture we hope to convey. Put bluntly, if things went wrong in parliament, it was because things were going wrong *outside* it, too. The concerns for 'liberty', jurisdictional rights and privileges in the House were symptoms of a more general malaise, and the speeches in the house (important as they are) are in many ways the product of a more general and widespread set of political expressions (in correspondence networks, and in print and scribal publication).

Most accounts of the Addled Parliament thus far have been permeated with an underlying sense of the *rumorousness* of political life in 1614, and its role in creating events.[36] The fact that the issue of undertaking, for example, was the first substantive item to be discussed on the first working day of the 1614 session, was in large part due to the fact that rumours had been wildly circulating before parliament had even been convened. While there had been discussion of rigged elections going back to the time of Richard II, Jansson has observed, 'rarely until 1614 were there such persistent rumours of rigged elections before the opening of the parliament.'[37] This was no doubt helped along by the prior circulation amongst MPs of anonymous scribal copies of Neville's 'Memorials' to the king, which (it has been plausibly suggested) was an attempt by Northampton and his faction to influence the course of the parliament.[38] The proliferation of rumours about the elections and the efficacy of Northampton's scribal publication is a marker of the growing importance of extra-parliamentary political debate and opinion in the Jacobean period.[39] Given the vital importance of the emerging public sphere of print in the events of the 1640s, it would be prudent for us to consider the genesis of this phenomenon in the 1610s and 1620s. As Annabel Patterson's work has shown, the Jacobean government (especially after 1605), was fearful of the destabilising effects of the printed word, and yet 'matters of intense social and political concern continued to be discussed in the face of extensive political censorship.'[40] If, as Professor Russell argues in his essay in this volume, 'Writing is quite a different form of theatre from parliamentary debate. They differ as artillery does from hand-to-hand combat,'[41] then we should remember that guerilla tactics can be as effective as protracted military campaigns, and in their creation of a political climate of beliefs amongst the general populace, more widespread and insidious.

II

The essays collected here address the crisis of Jacobean politics, and in the breadth of their response to the histories of a single year, 1614, they demonstrate that this crisis was not simply something that happened in parliament. The failure of parliament in 1614 saw an increase in the amount and urgency of political discussion and participation in political events: the sounding of a new culture of engagement with political life. As the work of Pauline Croft, Thomas Cogswell, Richard Cust and others has shown, this popularisation of political analysis found expression in a wide range of media – verse, libel, satire, epigram, newsletter and the transcripts of parliamentary proceedings.[42] Such materials of debate and observation make this investigation of the Addled Parliament a contextual one, going beyond the session itself to explore the perception and characterisation of the crisis.

The failure of parliament in 1614 is of value to early-Stuart scholarship because it insinuates questions about the crises of Jacobean rule. Several contributors take up the issue of freedom of speech, an aspect central to the identity of the 1614 parliament, both in contemporary analyses and subsequent historiography. Many of the essays show how this particularly heated subject was debated in the country at large, not just in the House of Commons. In this way, the constitutional crisis reflects a wider problem with voicing dissent. Some elements of the economic context of the crisis are also discussed, broadening the political focus. The Cockayne Project, initiated in the summer of 1614 to maximise customs revenues for the exchequer, is symptomatic of James's demands for remedies for the insolvency of the crown, not just at the time of the Addled Parliament but throughout his reign. A number of essays describe the presentation of advice to James and his ministers in the months following the collapse of parliament in 1614. The contributors raise questions about the status, limits and privileges of counsel. In some forms, for example, the political drama, interest in the images of government is conveyed through dramatic models of counsel and public speaking. Elsewhere, in a project such as Sir Walter Ralegh's *Dialogue betweene a Counsellor of State and a Justice of the Peace,* this takes the form of the conscious enactment of the pattern of exchange and coercion between royal prerogative and parliamentary power.

Interest in the marriage of Robert Carr, Earl of Somerset, and Frances Howard, Countess of Essex, in January 1614, suggests to several contributors that together with agitation about the legitimacy and proper place of political authority, the year 1614 saw a new level of anxiety about the person-centred government that was signalled by the rise of Somerset. Commentators saw the investment of power and influence in individuals such as Somerset, and later George Villiers, as a crisis for the Jacobean court, at the root of which lay the transgression of Elizabethan models of power relations.

Writing of his financial problems in 1607, James likened himself to a 'patient' and his ministers to 'physicians'.[43] Many 'physicians' presented themselves to the king in the aftermath of the failure of parliament in 1614, and it is this environment – in which political failure became a national event – which makes the Addled Parliament a critical topic for Stuart history and literature. Discussion in and outside of the House of Commons, of monarchy, members and the machinery of government, generated the perception of crisis and defined the identity of the parliament, not just for historians, but for James and his ministers too.

Conrad Russell's essay brings into sharp focus the range of materials and readings, contemporary and modern, which are the literary and historical remains of the 1614 parliament. In so doing, Russell confronts with great objectivity, the differences between the types of evidence that scholars like those assembled in this volume work with. In his own essay, Russell describes the intricacies of parliamentary life in the 1614 session, and the progress of bills through the House of Commons. It is an account which has been largely untold, and Russell recognises that this shift in perspective, and the records of parliamentary debate which he uses, temper the crisis of parliament with the business of parliament.

In setting out the apparatus for this analysis, Russell exemplifies the rationale behind the study of the parliamentary event and its representation in this volume, that is, to make different perspectives talk to each other. Following the statement that dialogue has no rights and wrongs, Russell compares his own work with that of another contributor, Michelle O'Callaghan, and suggests that when we look across the range of primary sources utilised in an interdisciplinary approach, we see the different emphases it contains. Places where, for example, concerns over impositions are more obvious, or less obvious; documents where political feeling is intensely stated, and documents where it is not acknowledged; official sources that are more constrained than unofficial ones, and unofficial ones that bear the marks of ideological and rhetorical ardour; verbal sources which contrast with printed; the public record with the private. As Russell says, these are all different 'forms of theatre', and they demonstrate the richness of the controversies of 1614.

III

Like Russell, John Cramsie's analysis of parliament in 1614 and afterwards provides a useful juxtaposition with other essays collected here, in which the failure of parliament is conveyed through the description and interpretation of the process of hot-tempered negotiation with James. Cramsie steers away from the parliamentary session as an 'event', concentrating instead on fiscal management as a 'genuine point of conflict'.

Cramsie refers to the junction between the subjects of crisis and crown finance in the reign of James I as 'something of a tease'. Hence this essay oversteps the long familiar financial problems of the first decades of the seventeenth century and the tussle for supply between parliament and king. Cramsie offers a view on the crisis of 1614 from the vantage point of 1621, and argues that the intersections of finance and parliament can do more for early-Stuart scholarship than point to structural weaknesses in the parliamentary system. Rather, this essay assesses how political failure in 1614 affected the course of government. This approach, as Cramsie observes, illuminates not just the Addled Parliament itself, but measures the perception of the crisis: the extent to which James and his ministers believed they had experienced a critical breakdown in relations between parliament and monarchy, and the degree to which the fiscal reforms of the following years were the result of that degeneration.

The Addled Parliament crystallised the need for a change in financial policy, and the re-establishment of proper political relationships – the effectiveness of parliament – was necessary to reform. Cramsie shows that the arguments about crown finance in 1614 point to the need for a repositioning of the traditional views of parliamentary opposition to supply an equation in which supply is dependent upon the details of good government.

The issue of finance and royal expenditure was also taken up by conciliar committees which were appointed to examine the merits of several proposed commercial projects in the period 1612–14. Sir Julius Caesar, Chancellor of the Exchequer, compiled a list of 'projects' likely to increase the royal income, one of which was the so-called 'Cockayne Project'. This initiative, which forbid the transportation of undyed cloth, and which was ratified by a proclamation in July 1614, is the subject taken up by Rosalind Davies. Davies traces the history of the rivalry between companies trading in cloth, and the regulation of the industry based on the economic importance of dyeing and dressing cloth before export. This history shows how the Cockayne Project, which was recommended as likely to be successful for James's immediate needs in 1614, had, in fact, received legislative endorsement from several monarchs from Edward III onwards. The repeated appearance and modification of these debates on England's cloth exports and industry, reveals a history in which Davies situates the economic, political and propagandist strategies of Richard Hakluyt's editing of *The Principal Navigations* (1589, 1598–1600). Davies shows how the economic theories tied to England's territorial expansion at the end of the sixteenth century, and the search for new markets which would demand finished cloth, created and promoted the trade in new draperies – a dynamism which was opposed by the arbitrary regulation of the 'project' pursued by James in 1614.

However, the origins of the parliament were not solely financial. The work of Andrew Thrush on the negotiations in 1613 and 1614 for a marriage between Prince Charles and Princess Christine, daughter of Henri IV, marshals the evidence of diplomatic correspondence which has not, until now, been sufficiently exploited. In the light of the evidence of these archives, Thrush traces the fluctuating relationship between plans for the French marriage and the summoning of parliament in 1614. Thrush's placement of the parliament in the shadow of negotiations between England and France for the marriage of Charles, reveals not just the various forms of the dynamic between the marriage and the parliamentary session, but also the different camps in the Privy Council and their agendas. The marriage and the parliament were considered by some to be mutually exclusive because the dowry claimed by James would pre-empt the need to go before the House of Commons. By February 1614 when the Council urged the king to call a parliament, it was because many of its members believed that it was the only way to prevent the marriage taking place. Thrush cites evidence that opposition to the union among privy councillors, born out of hostility to a Catholic match, was clearly recognised by some contemporaries as a reason for the failure of the parliament in 1614.

IV

1614 was a year coloured by rumour, scandal and defamation. The marriage of Robert Carr, newly created Earl of Somerset, and Frances Howard, during the Christmas festivities at court, 1613–14, attracted a good deal of attention, and fed the factional divisions in James's court. James Knowles addresses the threat to the Jacobean regime posed by Carr's marriage and his rise to power. Knowles is concerned with the masques written in celebration of the Carr–Howard marriage, and these texts, like the political verse and drama which are the subject of Michelle O'Callaghan's chapter, were charged with highly sexualised language. Knowles suggests that the marriage masques register sensitivities which were gathered around the perception of Carr's rise to power, his intimacy with James and the confusion between political and personal accessibility. In terms of the factional politics which shaped the English court and royal circle at this time, this paper makes apparent a critical point for the study of the political unrest in 1614, the move away from the authority of the privy councillor or minister to the 'bedchamber favourite'.

This patronage model and its implications for political power and alliance must also have compounded the stresses which the Addled Parliament placed upon the identity and role of that other body of 'advisers' to the king, MPs. David Colclough's paper argues that within the breakdown of communication during the short life of parliament lay the testing and defining of the role of counsel in the House of Commons. Colclough outlines five speeches delivered in the 1614 session which are notable for the discomfort they caused either king or Commons, and in which scandal was detected in variations on the themes of royal prerogative and parliamentary privilege. In one case, the reputation of members was derogated in favour of the absolute rights of the king. In another, a speaker made sinister reference to the discussion of impositions which contained a potentially threatening analogy to the king. The house was also lectured on its practices, and members were accused of slowness and disorder. In all these instances the Commons saw their freedom of speech challenged, and Colclough suggests that the desire to preserve the rights of members to deem a speech scandalous or inappropriate was the common factor in the responses provoked. This chapter sets the Addled Parliament in the context of contemporary discussions of counsel, both in the sense that this debate was going on outside, as well as inside, parliament, and in the reading and writing of humanist texts on the subject of counselling.

The place of free speech is imagined by Sir Walter Ralegh's *Dialogue betweene a Counsellor of State and a Justice of the Peace*. Anna Beer's essay sensitively presents the layers of advice in Ralegh's *Dialogue*, written in early 1615, evidently in response to the failure of parliament the year before. The Justice (as Ralegh) defends impositions and the king's prerogative powers, and asserts that a failed parliament is like a 'dangerous disease'. Yet, as Beer points out, Ralegh's apparent support for the royal prerogative is undercut by his very discussion of it, and by the resulting textual enactment of the principles of freedom of speech. In reply to the Counsellor's question as to what would be required of the king if a new parliament were called, the Justice recalls the exact terms of the 'jurisdiction over outspokenness' sought after by the House of Commons and described by David Colclough. The Justice comments that if a member of the Commons 'should speake more lardgely then of duty he ought to doe, all such offences should be pardonned and that to be of *Recorde*.'[44] In interweaving the king's freedoms with those of the subject, the *Dialogue* is a partner to the debates over the privileges and limits of counsel and the outspokenness which sent John Hoskins and others to the Tower after the dissolution of the 1614 session.

In the same batch of State Papers as Ralegh's *Dialogue* is Sir Robert Cotton's 'A Short View of the Life of Henry the Third', a text published anonymously in

1627, but composed in 1614, and distributed in manuscript in the aftermath of the collapsed parliament.[45] This work, with its observations on government and royal authority in the reign of Henry III which had application to the difficulties of 1614, is the subject of the essay by Stephen Clucas. Clucas summarises the approaches to Cotton's work made recently by Harold Love, Linda Levy Peck and Kevin Sharpe, and earlier by William Jackson, and shows that while the topicality of the text for King James in 1614 is not really in question, its relevance to 1627 has been disproportionately stressed. In the comparison between the politics of the thirteenth century, the reign of James I and the years of George Villiers's pre-eminence, Clucas describes Cotton's historical parallels, not as the fruits of antiquarianism but as an attempt to reform the practices of Jacobean rule.

Like the anxieties expressed by Ralegh about the investment of royal power in individuals like Somerset and Villiers, Clucas shows that Cotton's 'Short View' makes an unfavourable comparison between the declining powers of the Privy Council and the rise of the ambitious favourite. Cotton rehearses familiar complaints against the king's advisers, his promotion of 'straungers', and his demands on parliament for fiscal relief. Cotton's history is littered with allusions to the king as husband, at once inferring the frugal ideal, but generating profuse descriptions of the monarch as profligate, whose 'wastefull hand' has spent rewards, offices and authority. In this, the 'Short View' echoes the Lord Chancellor Ellesmere's metaphor on the subject of royal mismanagement, the 'Leakes in the Cisterne of the Treasurye.'[46]

V

Ironically, although Ralegh's *Dialogue* was written in the confines of a prison cell, in its pages the author imagined and created a place where constraints on free speech and the formulation of advice were lifted (Anna Beer suggests that the focus and content of the *Dialogue* can be partially explained by the presence in the Tower of the parliamentarian John Hoskins). One of the authors of interest to Michelle O'Callaghan, the poet George Wither, was also imprisoned in 1614, just before parliament opened. Like Beer and Colclough, O'Callaghan focuses on the 'textual communities' which were important to the transcription, circulation and multiplication of parliamentary news, and the political sensitivities of 1614, which made for a climate in which texts could be, in O'Callaghan's words, 'reconstituted through channels of rumour'. We can begin to see the way in which this arena of political debate was as responsible for the formation of the identity of the Addled Parliament as the evidence of speeches and parliamentary records.

The characterisation of the state of the nation, abuses of the court and the evils of prominent counsellors in 1614, are the materials of the writers in O'Callaghan's essay. The arrest and imprisonment of George Wither in March 1614, almost certainly indicated that Wither had fallen foul of leading members of the Privy Council and become embroiled in the scramble for office and the unsettled anticipation of the new parliament. O'Callaghan argues that Wither's arrest was probably organised by Henry Howard, Earl of Northampton, who had been the object of a defamation campaign to hinder his ambitions to become Lord Treasurer. This paper is suggestive of the cousinship of the royal prerogative and the charge of *scandalum magnatum* which Northampton brought against his detractors. Although Northampton used the law to serve his private purposes, his aggrandisement ironically made clearer the distinction between private and public spheres: Wither and others like him went on to resist the accusation of libel (an attack on a private individual), instead defending their writings as satire 'motivated by a public concern for the health of the commonwealth.' O'Callaghan situates a range of texts by Wither and his contemporaries in the battle to define the concept of public debate itself, as she says, 'how words enter the public sphere and who determines their legitimacy.'

The essays with a literary focus in this volume build up a picture of the 'oppositional' writers out-of-favour with the court. Beer and O'Callaghan argue that the work of these authors expressed grievances and generated the new 'public sphere' of print culture. Jonathan Gibson describes his work on the translation of Lucan's *Pharsalia* by Arthur Gorges, published in 1614, as a 'gloss' on the thesis of Beer and O'Callaghan, in that he isolates the dislocation common to many authors and texts following the death of their patron Prince Henry in 1612. In identifying Gorges as another 'disappointed Henrician', Gibson sees the thwarted patronage design as a means to explain the range of conservative and radical elements in Gorges's translation. The text is placed within a process of radicalisation, which occurred not only internally as Gorges made his mark on the narrative, but also through its reception in a court which no longer had Henry as a point of authority and which was defined by faction and the legacy of the failed parliament.

Gibson argues that Gorges's translation would have appeared relatively innocuous as a text dedicated to Prince Henry. Gorges's adaptations of Lucan's account of the civil war between Caesar and Pompey, his additions, sidenotes and flagging of useful *sententiae*, were instructive for a young prince with an interest in martial affairs. The appearance of the text in print in 1614, however, redirected the text's republican content, and together with Gorges's unpopularity with James, confirmed the text as subversive. The parallels between England and Rome emphasised by Gorges had contemporary resonances. Several episodes in the narrative were particularly pertinent in 1614, and Gibson says, it is not hard to find concerns shared by the republican conspirator in pre-war Rome and the observer of the troubled Addled Parliament.

VI

Alan Stewart's close reading of speeches in parliament and surrounding political publications, personalities and strategies produces an account of the mechanics of counsel in James's government. Stewart views five diverse texts – legal records, proclamations, memoranda – which followed a speech by James early in the parliament in April 1614, on the subject of a proclamation against duelling. Instead of a coherent campaign against duelling, Stewart argues that in 1613 and 1614 the personal agendas of James's leading advisers, Francis Bacon and Henry Howard, Earl of Northampton, together with the anticipation of the opening of parliament, contributed to an array of competing ambitions and advice behind the single issue of what James described as 'a lack of a law' to govern the new vogue of private combats.

Stewart uncovers the nuances of argument in the campaign, such that a contemporary observer, John Chamberlain, could detect that a discourse attached to one of the proclamations against duelling was not written by Francis Bacon as was commonly thought, but was the work of 'some higher hand', evidently that of Northampton. As well as describing the legal agendas of the various parties, this paper portrays the effects and strategies of the publications associated with the anti-duelling campaign in 1614; the timing of publications and the dependencies between texts which shaped both their construction and reception.

The role of the print media in circulating news, forming political opinion, and in particular, defining the identity of the parliament, of interest to many of the contributors in this collection, is qualified by Joad Raymond in his study of the limits of this technology for spreading news. Raymond argues that in the early decades of the Stuart regime, print, unlike the manuscript, was still an immature medium for the manipulation of public political opinion. The statistical overview in the first part of Raymond's paper shows 1614 to be a unexceptional year in terms of press output, the largest subject group among printed books being not political, but religious materials. As an important coda to the verse, correspondence, masques and satire discussed elsewhere in this volume, Raymond's essay advocates situating the public and politicised voices of 1614 in the space which, he argues, existed between manuscript culture and the evolving 'print culture'. In closer focus still, he marks the output of the press in 1614 as distinct from the representations of political turmoil later in the century, and from the development of a pamphleteering press which was capable of registering crisis. Raymond distinguishes between a 'sustained commentary' on the parliament, of which he says there was little, and the journalistic, news-telling drive, with topicality as its by-word, which was widely shared across traditional news and non-news genres. Attorney-General Bacon's judgement on duels, *The Charge of Sir Francis Bacon ... touching duells* (1614), is cited as an example of the official publication performing a 'news function'.

Several subjects raised in the parliament reappear in print. Like the business of government presented by Conrad Russell, these were subjects that were not connected to the collapse of the parliament or the negotiations of political authority surrounding it. Instead, bills about apparel, the Elector Palatine and the import of tobacco were relayed in various forms in print.

Significant for the wide-ranging excavation work around 1614 which is presented in this volume, is Raymond's view of the 'topical possibilities' of print publication; translation, editing, reprinting, even the 'campaign' that was the response to James's proclamation on duelling. We are also reminded of the way in which oral and manuscript cultures, sources fully documented in the essays collected here, occupied themselves in the elaboration, encouragement or justification of the debates brought to the boil by the parliament of 1614.

In describing the essay printed here in relation to his earlier title *The Addled Parliament of 1614: The Limits of Revision*, Conrad Russell affirms that he has 'told the constitutional story of the Addled Parliament elsewhere.' Russell's demarcation of an 'elsewhere' and a 'here' in his work, suggests an appropriate epigraph to the essays in this volume. Most of the contributors recognise the 'elsewheres' of the parliament, and it has been the editors' aim in drawing together different disciplines at the Birkbeck College conference and in this publication, to show that the crisis of 1614 *is* 'elsewhere': not in the sense that we must isolate its truest picture, but in a thoroughly expansive approach. The historical specificity (which many of the essays consciously contravene) of 'The Addled Parliament, 1614', and its simplistic and anachronistic nomenclature 'Addled' (to which we have added, in a similar tone, 'crisis'), has seemed to be one way of signalling the historiographical weight which comes with this particular subject. Reading the anxieties of the reign of James through this screen, we find ourselves over-familiar with the popular history of 1614 and dislocated from the real issues of government, power and representation.

Notes

1 Conrad Russell, *The Addled Parliament of 1614: The Limits of Revision*, The Stenton Lecture 1991 (Reading: University of Reading, 1992).

2 Maija Jansson, *Proceedings in Parliament, 1614 (House of Commons)* (Philadelphia: American Philosophical Society, 1988). On James's destruction of parliamentary documents see Samuel R. Gardiner, *History of England from the Accession of James I to the Outbreak of Civil war 1603–1642*, 10 vols (London: Longman Green and Co, 1883–4), II, 249.

3 Thomas L. Moir, *The Addled Parliament of 1614* (Oxford: Clarendon Press, 1958), p. 1.

4 Gardiner, *History of England*, II, 228.

5 *Limits of Revision*, p. 4.

6 *Limits of Revision*, p. 5.

7 *Limits of Revision*, p. 18.

8 *Limits of Revision*, p. 7.

9 *Limits of Revision*, p. 7.

10 *Limits of Revision*, p. 9. Cf. also p. 26: 'The conflict [of the Addled Parliament] did not mark a struggle for sovereignty or for rival constitutional ideas. It marked a simple, plain shortage of money [...] the central error of the Commons of 1614 was their inflexible determination to preserve a financial system which inflation and the "military revolution" had rendered obsolete.' On the Crown's financial difficulties due to the public provision of firearms, Navy and Ordnance expenses, the maintenance of garrisons and Irish subsidies see *Limits of Revision*, pp. 10–11.

11 *Limits of Revision*, p. 7.

12 *Limits of Revision*, p. 8.

13 *Limits of Revision*, p. 20.

14 *Limits of Revision*, pp. 8–9.

15 *Limits of Revision*, p. 13.

16 *Limits of Revision*, p. 17.

[17] *Limits of Revision*, p. 25.

[18] *Proceedings, 1614*, p. xviii.

[19] Public Record Office, State Papers, 14/58/26, cit. *Limits of Revision*, p. 18.

[20] Gardiner, *History of England*, II, 251.

[21] See Geoffrey Elton, 'A High Road to Civil War?' in *From Renaissance to the Counter-Reformation: Essays in honour of Garrett Mattingly*, ed. by C. H. Carter (London: Jonathan Cape, 1966), pp. 325–47.

[22] On Northampton's promotion of the 'Sicilan Vespers' speech see Gardiner, *History of England*, II, 250.

[23] *Proceedings, 1614*, p. xiii.

[24] *Proceedings, 1614*, p. xxii.

[25] *Proceedings, 1614*, pp. xxxiiii–xxxiv.

[26] *Proceedings, 1614*, pp. xix–xx.

[27] *Proceedings, 1614*, p. xxi.

[28] *Proceedings, 1614*, p. xiii.

[29] *Proceedings, 1614*, p. xxii.

[30] *Proceedings, 1614*, p. xxvii.

[31] *Proceedings, 1614*, p. xxix.

[32] *Proceedings, 1614*, p. xxxi.

[33] *Proceedings, 1614*, p. xxxiii.

[34] *Proceedings, 1614*, p. xxxiii.

[35] *Limits of Revision*, p. 18.

[36] See, for example, Gardiner, *History of England*, II, 228–30, Clayton Roberts and Owen Duncan, 'The Parliamentary Undertaking of 1614', *English Historical Review*, 93 (1978), 481–98 (pp. 490–1), Jansson, *Proceedings, 1614*, xvi–xvii, xxiii.

[37] *Proceedings, 1614*, p. xxiii.

[38] Roberts and Duncan, 'The Parliamentary Undertaking of 1614', p. 491.

[39] On the extra-parliamentary use of constitutional arguments against royal policies see Johann P. Sommerville, *Politics and Ideology in England 1603–1640* (London and New York: Longman, 1986), p. 233.

[40] Annabel Patterson, *Censorship and Interpretation: The Conditions of Writing and Reading in Early Modern England* (Madison: University of Wisconsin Press, 1984), p. 44.

[41] See *infra*, p. 25.

[42] Pauline Croft, 'The Reputation of Robert Cecil: Libels, Political Opinion and Popular Awareness in the Early Seventeenth Century', *Transactions of the Royal Historical Society* 1 (1991), 43–69; Thomas Cogswell, 'Underground Verse and the Transformation of Early Stuart Political Culture', in *Political Culture and Cultural Politics in Early Modern England*, ed. by Susan D. Amussen and Mark A. Kishlansky (Manchester & New York: Manchester University Press, 1995), pp. 277–300; Richard Cust, 'News and Politics in Early Seventeenth-Century England', *Past & Present*, 112 (1986), 60–90.

[43] 19[?] October, 1607, *Letters of King James*, p. 291.

[44] Sir Walter Ralegh, *Dialogue betweene a Counsellor of State and a Justice of the Peace* (1615; Midelburge [London], 1628), fol. 27^{r}.

[45] See Anna Beer, *Sir Walter Ralegh and his Readers in the Seventeenth Century* (Basingstoke & London: Macmillan, 1997), p. 75.

[46] Henry E. Huntington Library, Ellesmere MS 2610/1, cit. Cramsie, *infra*, p. 43.

PART I

THE ADDLED PARLIAMENT: ORIGINS AND CONSEQUENCES

2

Bishop Berkeley at Westminster

Conrad Russell

We should never forget that our perception of parliamentary life goes through a treble filter. The vast majority of items of parliamentary business are extremely tedious, and their importance is often in inverse proportion to their entertainment value. Many of our sources, especially those, like John Chamberlain, that are most fun to read, are the spiritual ancestors of Matthew Parris, Simon Hoggart and Michael Brown. They look for the entertainment value of their material. Not all of them have the x-ray eyes of John Chamberlain or Matthew Parris, which can cut through the pretensions to the revelation of the inner man, and what they record is sometimes entertaining in inverse proportion to its importance. To a lesser degree, this is true of our diarists, whose ability to report legal issues is often less than their ability to report comedy. To some extent it is true even of our Commons' Journals, especially in their reporting of speeches.

Our sources, then, are already filters. When we prepare books, articles and conference papers, we are under a duty to hold our audience, and therefore act as a further filter, to pick out the most entertaining pieces in material already pre-selected for entertainment value. Our audience, being equally human, act as a third filter. What we remember is as distilled as the best whisky. This is just as well, for in a long parliamentary day, *wie es ist eigentlich gewesen* is one long yawn. Yet it is during that one long yawn that the things which really change the lives of those subject to parliamentary legislation take place, and the best parliamentarians are those who are awake during the yawns of others and enjoy the classical parliamentarian's skill, to see all hell in a grain of sand. Indeed, one should not forget that, 'may you live in interesting times' was a curse. Political drama is very exhausting, and sometimes its absence may be a relief.

The more experienced of the members who assembled in April 1614 had had their fill of parliamentary drama. They had lived through the Apology, purveyance, the Union, Guy Fawkes Day, and the Great Contract, and, like Eric Shipton after Mount Everest, many of them wanted to get back to real mountaineering. Professor Elton has many times insisted that bills were the proper business of a parliament. This is only a half-truth. At times of profound drama, bills regularly took second place. In 1640, for example, the Commons had been sitting for three months before they sent their second bill to the Lords.[1] I have for some time had a growing suspicion that the priority given to bills in any parliamentary session is in inverse proportion to the political temperature.

What happens when we apply this thesis to the Addled Parliament? The result is a paradox. We all know that the Addled Parliament broke up in acrimony and deadlock. We know that the king, after the previous parliament, had compared it to the rotten reed of Egypt. We therefore tend, myself among others, to look at the Addled Parliament as a high constitutional story. Yet, just as Barebone's Parliament, when called to settle the English Republic, preferred to settle tithes and the Court of Chancery, so the Addled Parliament, when called to settle the king's finances, preferred to settle the Sabbath and the rules for suiting apparel to status. If there was a constitutional crisis, they preferred to think about something else.

I have told the constitutional story of the Addled Parliament elsewhere. By contrast, the story the Commons saw, which was largely one of bills, remains largely untold. That is the story of the world as the Commons liked to see it, and it may tell us something about seventeenth-century society and how they saw it. Until Bishop Neile, the seventeenth-century 'Bishop of Bolsover', threw a spanner in the works, bills were the staple diet of the Commons. Then came five days (four sitting days) in which not a single bill received a single reading. This sudden interruption of the legislative pipeline tends to confirm the thesis that there is an inverse relationship between political crisis and the progress of bills. If confirmed, this would indicate that the shock caused by Bishop Neile came out of the blue as far as most members were concerned. On 31 May, as the shock receded, the legislative flow resumed, and speeded up until the king's threat of dissolution on 3 June. From then until the end of the parliament, not a single bill received a single reading.

In the two months and two days from 5 April to 7 June, 112 bills had a First Reading moved. Of these, thirty-nine were private bills, and five were sent down from the Lords. Two bills, for preservation of timber and for brewers and alehouse keepers, were rejected on First Reading. Of the 110 bills given a First Reading, fifty-eight had a Second Reading moved. These included the five from the Lords, the naturalisation of the Elector Palatine, gold and silver thread, the naturalisations of Elizabeth Murray and of Sir Horace Vere's daughters, and the bill for the copyholders of Winslow (Buckinghamshire). Four bills were rejected. One was the bill for deceits in plastering, which was designed to preserve the demarcation between bricklayers and tilers. On the motion of Nicholas Fuller and Sir George More, the House resolved without a division, first not to commit it, and then not to engross it. The bill therefore fell. The reason, we are told, is that it left bricklayers no work in winter.[2] The second was on books printed overseas, and the record shows no reason why it was rejected.[3] The third was the bill for bankrupts, opposed by Fuller and Edward Alford, and damned with faint praise by More. Alford said it was the most dangerous bill that ever came into the House, because it gave an oath to the wife, and imprisoned her for her husband. It is hard to tell what was behind this passionate objection. The fourth, without a word spoken, was the bill for outrageous carriages.[4]

Of the fifty-four bills given a Second reading, seventeen were reported from committee. Of these, six were private, and three, the naturalisation of the Elector Palatine and of Sir Horace Vere's daughters, and the bill for gold and silver thread, came from the Lords. The survival rate, at about a third, was conspicuously lower than the survival rate of just over 50 per cent between First and Second Reading. This confirms what we know, that the committee stage was the bottleneck of the legislative process. Three of these bills were re-committed. Two of these were bills of grace, for sheriffs' accounts and for respite of homage. The third was the bill for recovery of small debts. The other fourteen were engrossed.

Of these fourteen engrossed bills, ten received a Third Reading debate – a very high rate over the last fence. One of these bills fell at the last fence. This was the bill for Sir Herbert Pelham to sell lands, and its rejection seems to mark a feeling that Acts of Parliament to break entails were being used with too much freedom. The rejection was moved by Sir Henry Poole, who said, in a plain hint at a fix, that twelve committees were all Sussex men but he, and he was the only one against it. He complained of taking away estates from infants by Act of Parliament, and was supported by Sir Dudley Digges, Sir John Saville, Glanville and Humphrey Weare. Nicholas Fuller, Francis Ashley, Browne and Richard Amherst spoke for the bill. Browne and Amherst, the only Sussex men who spoke, had been members of the committee. The bill was rejected by 201 to 133. The total of 334 voting is a large division for so small a bill, and the crowd may have come for the debate on baronets, which was about to begin.[5]

Seven bills completed three readings in both Houses. These were three out of the twelve starting in the Lords, the bills to naturalise the Elector Palatine and Sir Horace Vere's daughters, and the bill for gold and silver thread. Four out of 104 bills starting in the Commons completed their passage. They were the bill of grace for assignment of debts to the king, and three private bills, for Monmouth, Jernegan and Yew. Of these seven bills only the Bill for the Elector Palatine completed the Lords' final stage That This Bill Do Now Pass.[6] The other bills which completed their passage through the Commons were two bills of grace, for making laws in Wales and for assignment of debts to the king, and the Sabbath bill, which the Lords were never likely to pass.

This story illustrates, as usual, the lack of any controlling intelligence behind the preparation of legislation. Because there was no ordering of priorities, and no organised leadership, too many bills reached the starting gate, and too many fell in the crowds at the fences.

Bills on religion received less priority than in recent parliaments. The non-residence bill progressed as far as Report. When Fuller reported it from committee, it was considerably amended. Sir Thomas Lake, introducing the bill, said, in what may have been the voice of his brother the Bishop of Bath and Wells, that in Queen Elizabeth's time, more care had been taken to weed than to plant the church. He said ill success in previous parliaments had been because of 'not good fashion' held with the Lords of the clergy, and moved, optimistically, for a conference with representatives of the Convocation, 'if it may stand with order of the House.' Sir Edwin Sandys, Sir John Sammes and Sir George More told him bluntly that it was not possible. More, illustrating that it was possible to be an anti-clerical without being a Puritan, 'would have no clergyman of the peace.' There was never any likelihood of agreement here.[7]

The Sabbath bill was designed to stop morris dancing and bear-baiting (Glanville would have added football) on the Sabbath. An attempt by Alford to ambush it on the Third Reading failed. At the Second Reading, attempts to make it bite on carriers and lawyers, and an argument about whether it was proper to arrest on the Sabbath, indicated the scope the Lords would have had to delay the bill if they had needed it. Other religious bills, on subscription, the *ex officio* oath and so forth, made little progress. Whether this was because the House had tired of such bills because they never went through the Lords, or because Abbot had replaced Bancroft, the record does not show.[8]

I will leave aside the bills of Grace, since they are Chris Kyle's subject, and I will not put my sickle in another man's corn.[9] In general, it seems fair to say that they created sympathy but not excitement. The bills which caused most discussion seem to have been largely social and economic. The bills dealt with the moral side of economic life. One, the bill of apparel, was hotly promoted by Christopher Brooke MP for York, the man who in 1621 described silk as 'entrailes of worms'.[10] I have always wondered whether the fact that he was a witness to John Donne's marriage explains the origin of this striking phrase. The bill forbade those below the degree of knight to use gold and silver lace, and deprived men of their offices, and women of the right to take administration. The penalties were thought too severe, especially against the women. Even Nicholas Fuller, no friend to women, agreed, and Sir Robert Gardiner said juries would not convict. It is no surprise that some while later, Brooke moved for additions to the committee, and then, three days later, that the committee was *sine die*. Another committee day was fixed on 30 May, but there was no likelihood that the bill would emerge.[11] As always, apparel bills set too many economic interests against each other, and fell by the wayside. The perennial alehouses bill produced a proposal for the informer to have a quarter of the penalty.[12] Hatred of the alehouses was stronger than hatred of informers but, as always, drink against the law was an unequal contest, and there was no likelihood of the bill being completed.

A collection of economic bills gave rise to disputes about enforcement which foreshadowed the patents row of 1621. The key example is the bill against gold and silver thread, on which the committee agreed to make it a probationer, and to provide that if any letters patent were granted to make it a monopoly, it should be void.[13] One may be permitted to wonder whether so intense an anxiety illustrates an awareness that there was no other adequate method of enforcement. An intriguing minor example is Walter Earle's bill for building a pier at Axmouth. George Browne, MP for Lyme, attacked it passionately, on the ground that it was too near Lyme Regis to be necessary. Sir William Strode said Browne spoke only for fear it might damage the trade of Lyme. The bill was finally given a second reading on Glanville's pointing out that at least it relied on parliament and not a patent.[14]

One of the more interesting bills was one for the recovery of small debts which would have set up small claims courts in towns. It provoked a triangular contest between town, country and lawyers. Nicholas Fuller, MP for London and a lawyer, chaired the committee, and appears to have put his constituency interest above his professional interest. Whitson of Bristol and Brooke of York supported the bill. Sir Thomas Hoby spoke out for the gentlemen: 'many bailiffs (who so judges) fishermen. From fishing to judgement, and so back to the same.' Towse, complaining of 'ignorance of bailiffs', proposed that only citizens of towns should be subject to the bill. Sir Richard Williamson, who said it deprived the subject of the benefit of the law, was accused by Brooke of failing to declare his interest in the Council of the North. Sir Robert Phelips soothingly proposed that cases should not be tried unless the recorder or steward was present. The bill was recommitted, and did not emerge.[15] Clearly this was not a House in which bourgeois interests were well represented.

A similar town-country conflict developed on the bill against new building in London and Westminster. John Prowse, MP for Exeter, said it would thrust the poor from London into the country. Sir John Saville replied that the charge of the parish where he dwelt (presumably in London), had risen to £300 or £400, by reason of inmates, and called for a law against inmates. This tendency to sweep the poor under someone else's carpet could have come from Parliament in any century. Alford, who was certainly no Puritan, moved for a provision against the erecting of playhouses. Sir Roger Owen hopefully proposed to pull down all the suburbs. The bill disappeared into committee, where it fell asleep.[16]

A collection of transport bills of various sorts illustrated a growing concern with the issue. My favourite is the bill against outrageous carriages, preferred by Serjeant Robert Barker, whose appointment as a Serjeant occasioned Chamberlain's famous crack: 'it is good there should be one Barker amid so many byters.' This bill would have restricted axle weight to 2600 pounds – a proposal which seems to support Chartres's view that heavy road transport was increasing rapidly. The bill was rejected.[17] A bill for repairing highways, introduced by Sir John Sammes, produced a protest from Sir Jerome Horsey that no one bothered with repair of byways.[18] The bill for highways spawned a bill for the repair of bridges, which gave rise to the usual local disputes about who should pay. Francis Brakin, MP for Cambridge, said their bridge was maintained by pontage. Sir John Saville said bridges maintained at the common charge should be toll free, and Sir Robert Johnson said Monmouth was paying for five bridges already, and should not have to pay for anyone else's bridges. The Second Reading debate gave plenty of clues as to why the bill might have fallen asleep in committee.

Apart from the religious bills, only three concerned high policy. The impositions bill illustrates, once again, that bills were not a useful way of tackling issues where there was no agreement between the Houses, or between the Houses and the king. They were useful only as a device for provoking debate. The same is true of that hardy perennial, the bill against the transport of ordnance. The third was the bill for the representation of County Durham in parliament. This bill was again bogged down in the variety of local disputes which were to delay legislation until 1675, and also illustrates the weakness of the parliamentary bill as a way of solving problems. It was memorable only for the classic declaration of Sandys that people should not be bound by laws to which they were not parties.[19]

What conclusion can be drawn from this collection of bills? The sample of those discussed is pre-selected by the list of those which provoked recorded debate, so they tend to over-represent those which caused disagreement, rather than those which provoked most feeling. The absence of any bills, other than that for the naturalisation of the Elector Palatine, which progressed with particular rapidity, seems to suggest that the distortion is not great. The picture, far more than in any of the four previous sessions, is of a House of Commons getting on with mundane local business, entirely unaware that they were heading into a constitutional crisis.

The Privy Councillors who had hung their heads in 1612 when the annual deficit was announced to have risen to £160,000 would have said that that was the constitutional crisis. Perhaps they would have had a point. Bishop Berkeley was wrong: there *can* be a crisis which is not perceived, as Little Johnny Head In Air learnt the hard way.

The story also illustrates that a parliament is not a good instrument for resolving disagreements. The select committee may have succeeded in private bills, but in public bills, then as now, too much depends on the selection of the committee, as the repeated motions to force the committee on difficult bills illustrate. A parliament was a good place for ventilating arguments, but it was not a good instrument of business. Nothing changes.

How do we reconcile the evidence given in this paper with the evidence given in Michelle O'Callaghan's paper, and in her article in the *Historical Journal*, 'Talking Politics – Tyranny, Parliament and Christopher Brooke's *The Ghost of Richard III*'?[20] In this paper, we have seen a picture of members of the Commons carrying on with business as usual. They appear concerned about a variety of day-to-day questions, but give no impression of awareness that they are engaged in a major crisis. In O'Callaghan's work they appear talking among themselves about tyranny, evil counsellors and manipulation of the law. We see in O'Callaghan's work a picture of people intensely politically stirred, and feeling a good deal of anger.

In the first place, there can be no question of saying that one of these pictures is 'right' and the other 'wrong'. Both rest on a solid weight of primary sources, which no reputable scholar can dismiss. The question is not even one of priorities: these are two pieces of a jigsaw, and we must fit them together somehow. An enlargement of the canvas immediately gives a better picture. This paper has been an exercise in *Hamlet* without the Prince: it has been filling in quiet pieces of the background, rather than showing the clash of the foils over impositions. A full picture immediately narrows the disagreement. In my previous work, as in O'Callaghan's present work, the concern over impositions has always come out as a central constitutional concern, and one which caused intense alarm. The fear that a decision for the king would change the type of government known in England shows in the public record, as it does in the verses and pamphlets the protagonists were producing in private.

That this concern is more obvious in the unofficial sources than in the official ones is only what a parliamentarian should expect. Free speech in parliament, for all its obvious virtues, has a built-in restraint in that it must be uttered to one's opponent's faces. The pressure of sheer political good manners necessarily dampens the ardour of attacks on evil counsellors. Now, as then, most of us will say more in print than we will say in parliament, especially if it can be presented obliquely, without the need to spell out the personally offensive charge, or to reply to questioning designed to force one to do so. Writing is quite a different form of theatre from parliamentary debate. They differ as artillery does from hand-to-hand combat. In this way, Michelle O'Callaghan's evidence is a better guide to members' states of mind than mine. If the question is about states of mind, her evidence is to be preferred to mine in case of conflict.

Our evidence certainly provides a contrast, but does it provide a conflict? That demands an acute analysis of what each of us is not saying. I was not saying that members were anything other than deeply attached to the notion of *dominum politicum et regale*. They mostly feared and loathed any threat to that polity, and were quite capable, as early as 1614, of regarding anyone who threatened it as an evil counsellor. In confirming and strengthening these points, O'Callaghan is not confirming anything I have denied. The question is whether she is denying anything which I have affirmed. That, in the end, is a question for her to answer. My impression, for what it is worth, is that she is not. My first objective was to deny that these members were themselves setting out to destroy the existing system and erect a new, more parliamentary, version: they saw themselves as its defenders. O'Callaghan's evidence would appear to me to do more to support than to weaken that picture. My other point was to deny the traditional 'two sides' picture of politics. Here O'Callaghan has said in terms that Brooke and his poetry 'do not support a straightforward ideological and political polarisation between Crown and opposition.'[21] In this, she offers support, not criticism, of my central contention. What, perhaps, her evidence does confirm is the inability of men like Christopher Brooke to realise the non-negotiability of impositions for the king. In coupling hostility to impositions with hostility to Spain, he was taking two positions which, from an Exchequer point of view, were totally incompatible. His view of the corrupting effects of peace would only have been politically tenable if it had been combined with a determination to increase the royal revenue on a scale which would have made even impositions look trivial. His literary efforts show no more signs than his political ones that he appreciated this.

That, perhaps, fits with the main finding of this paper, that however deeply Brooke may have cared about impositions and their implications, he had no sense of the immediacy of the crisis he was running into. He behaved in the Commons like a man with plenty of time, and that was something he did not have. My central contention about the early seventeenth-century Commons has always been, not that they suffered from constitutional indifference, but that they suffered from an intense lack of financial realism. Nothing in the mental world of Christopher Brooke appears to refute this charge. There are two things which these contrasting pictures definitely do show. One is how dangerously easy it is for revision to throw out the baby with the bathwater. The other is the beginning of an interdisciplinary dialogue, which must continue.

Notes

[1] Conrad Russell, *The Fall of the British Monarchies 1637–1642* (Oxford: Clarendon Press, 1991), pp. 223–8. The one selected for haste was the Triennial Bill.

[2] *Proceedings, 1614*, pp. 85, 88.

[3] *Proceedings, 1614*, p. 293.

[4] *Proceedings, 1614*, pp. 339, 347, 101–02.

[5] *Proceedings, 1614*, pp. 318–19, 324–5. Glanville is more likely to have been John than his brother Francis. Browne may have been either George or John.

[6] This is the stage recorded in the seventeenth-century *Journals* in the word 'exped'. Bills very occasionally failed at this stage.

[7] *Proceedings, 1614*, pp. 339, 215, 220–1.

[8] *Proceedings, 1614*, pp. 171–2, 228, 308–9, 314, 316.

[9] See Michael A. R. Graves and Chris R. Kyle, '"The Kinge's most Excellent majestie out of his Gracious Disposition": The Evolution of Bills of Grace in English Parliaments 1542–1642', *Parliaments, Estates and Representatives*, 18 (1998), 27–51.

[10] *Commons Debates, 1621*, V, 497.

[11] *Proceedings, 1614*, pp. 75, 145, 158, 268, 324, 396.

[12] *Proceedings, 1614*, p. 398.

[13] *Proceedings, 1614*, p. 220.

[14] *Proceedings, 1614*, pp. 308, 313–14.

[15] *Proceedings, 1614*, pp. 289–91. The fact that Williamson introduced a bill against usury suggests the possibility that he may have failed to declare another interest. He moved the bill with more passion than his case demanded (see pp. 392, 398).

[16] *Proceedings, 1614*, pp. 401–2.

[17] *Letters of John Chamberlain*, II, 99n., 101–02, 174, J. A. Chartres, 'Road Carrying in England in the Seventeenth Century: Myth and Reality', *Economic History Review*, 30 (1977), 73–94.

[18] *Proceedings, 1614*, pp. 99, 173–4.

[19] *Proceedings, 1614*, p. 235.

[20] Michelle O'Callaghan, 'Talking Politics – Tyranny, Parliament and Christopher Brooke's *The Ghost of Richard III*', *Historical Journal*, 41:1 (1998), 97–120.

[21] O'Callaghan, 'Talking Politics', p. 119.

3

The French Marriage and the Origins of the 1614 Parliament*

Andrew Thrush

I

The Parliament of 1614 met in the shadow of negotiations between England and France for a marriage between Prince Charles, heir apparent to James I, and Princess Christine, a younger sister of Louis XIII. There was never any prospect that parliament would debate this proposed match without the king's consent, however, as it was clearly understood that the betrothal of the heir to the throne was a matter for the royal prerogative. During the Parliament members of the Commons are said by the Savoyard Agent to have desired permission to speak freely, but as this was never granted only one member of the Commons publicly alluded to the French marriage, and he did so on the day of the dissolution, during the belated debate on supply.[1] Although James was urged by some on the Privy Council to lay the subject of the French marriage voluntarily before parliament, he proved unwilling to do so because, according to the Spanish Ambassador, he feared that conciliar hostility to the match would spill over into parliament.[2] Yet if the marriage negotiations formed no part of the Westminster debate, they certainly contributed to the summoning of parliament. Gardiner recognised this long ago, but he did not fully grasp the relationship between the summoning of parliament and the French marriage, and implied that both were part of a strategy to defeat the advocates of a closer relationship with Spain.[3] More recently, Professor Conrad Russell has also directed us to conclude that the parliament and the marriage were connected. He has done so obliquely, observing that at the critical Council meeting held to decide whether to recommend the summoning of parliament to the king, some of the hotter sort of Protestants on the Council were prepared to countenance a parliament to supply the king's financial necessities if in return James would agree to abandon the marriage negotiations.[4]

The question of a marriage for Prince Charles was inextricably bound up with the state of the royal finances. Every schoolchild knows that James I summoned the Addled Parliament because of the emptiness of his coffers. What every schoolchild does not know is why James was not driven by financial necessity to

* The dates employed throughout this article are Old Style. I should like to thank Pauline Croft, Roger Lockyer, Conrad Russell and the members of the parliamentary history seminar at the Institute of Historical Research for their comments on earlier drafts.

summon it sooner than he did. The case for calling a parliament on grounds of financial necessity was put with admirable clarity by the Chancellor of the Exchequer, Sir Julius Caesar, at the end of May 1612, following the death of Lord Treasurer Salisbury. Caesar informed his fellow privy councillors that the annual deficit amounted to £160,000 and the overall burden of debt to £500,000. New projects for raising money and a retrenchment of the royal finances were, Caesar noted, expedients incapable of bridging the widening gap between income and expenditure. Elimination of the king's debts, he concluded, 'must be done by ayde of Parliament.'[5] Caesar's advice helped to fuel rumours, which had been circulating since October 1611, that a parliament would soon be called.[6] However, James was still recovering from the bruising experience of the Commons' rejection of the Great Contract in 1610 and was in no mood to summon another parliament. Instead, he preferred to retrench his finances. By March 1613 the Council had helped the treasury commissioners achieve some modest savings. Over the same period the Exchequer had benefited from various sources of windfall revenue totalling more than £309,000.[7] Despite these improvements, James's financial position continued to worsen, and by early July 1613 there was renewed talk of calling a parliament. Any hopes of fresh writs of summons, however, were soon dashed. On 4 July the Lord Privy Seal, the Earl of Northampton, reported to the king's Latin secretary, Sir Thomas Lake, that, after daily deliberations in Council lasting ten and twelve hours together, the question of whether to summon a parliament had been postponed.[8] Northampton offered no convincing explanation for this decision, but two considerations in particular are likely to have persuaded the king to accept his Council's advice. One is that James had received a recent sharp reminder of the difficulties posed in managing parliaments from across the Irish Sea, having in June been obliged to adjourn the newly assembled Irish Parliament because its members were so divided over the creation of eighty-four additional parliamentary constituencies that they had elected rival speakers.[9] The second consideration was that James was now pinning his hopes for financial relief on a French dowry.

The suggestion that the king's eldest son should marry a daughter of Henri IV of France was formally mooted in April 1612, when the French offered the hand of the six-year-old princess Christine to the then heir apparent, the eighteen-year-old Prince Henry. James was not seriously tempted by this offer, however, as Christine was absurdly young and the proposed dowry of 500,000 crowns, equivalent to £150,000, was insufficient.[10] He was preoccupied instead with a rival bid made by the Duke of Savoy, who offered 700,000 crowns, or £210,000, in return for a marriage with his daughter, the Infanta Maria. It was not until October that James's interest in a French match began to be aroused. On 28 October 1612 the ambassador to Paris, Sir Thomas Edmondes, reported that the French were so alarmed at the prospect of an English alliance with Savoy, traditionally regarded as an ally of Spain, that they had agreed to match the Savoyard offer of 700,000 crowns.[11] Edmondes viewed this offer as a promising beginning, but told James that he thought that the French could be persuaded to increase their bid still further. He had accordingly informed the French that, in view of James's financial difficulties, the king 'requyred a greater somme'. In response, he had received private assurances that the French government would eventually increase its offer to 800,000 crowns. This sum, which was equivalent to £240,000,[12] was insufficient by itself to eliminate the king's mounting debts, but viewed in parliamentary terms it was worth approximately three subsidies and one fifteenth and tenth at the rate of 1610. Taken in conjunction with measures then in hand for the sale of crown lands and other fiscal expedients, a substantial French dowry held out the hope that James would be spared the need to call another parliament.

The unexpected death of Prince Henry on 6 November 1612 did not, as one might suppose, signal the end of James's hopes for a French dowry. This was not widely appreciated at the time. In mid-November the newsletter writer John Chamberlain concluded that:

> the prince's death hath taken away the meanes of helping ourselves by his mariage, and stopping the gap of our wants for the present by that way, so that we must of necessitie have recourse to a parliament, whereof there is speach already for February.[13]

Chamberlain's reading of the situation was faulty, not because he held that parliament and a French marriage were mutually exclusive, which was perceptive, but because he did not foresee the possibility that the king's second son, Prince Charles, might step into his older brother's shoes. He assumed that Charles, then aged just twelve, was too young to be considered as a replacement for Henry. However, the desperate condition of the royal finances meant that James was quite prepared to overlook Charles's youth. Besides, the fact that Charles was much closer in age to Princess Christine than Henry increased rather than diminished James's enthusiasm for a French match. Far from contemplating a parliament in the wake of Henry's death, James lost no time in instructing Edmondes to continue the marriage negotiations, substituting Charles for the late Prince Henry.[14] After a short period of mourning, negotiations with France recommenced in December.[15]

Over the course of the next seven months the French negotiations proceeded slowly. In part this was because the English were preoccupied with the arrangements for the wedding of Princess Elizabeth to the Elector Palatine, and in part because they were distracted by preparations for the meeting of the Irish Parliament.[16] Shortly after Elizabeth was safely ensconced in Heidelberg with her new husband, towards the end of June 1613, Edmondes, aided briefly by the king's cousin, the francophile Duke of Lennox, opened the negotiations in earnest.[17] On 10 July Edmondes and Lennox were instructed to demand a dowry of 800,000 crowns, the sum which Edmondes had led James to believe that the French would eventually be willing to pay.[18] However, the negotiations with the regency government of Marie de Médici soon ran into difficulties. Leading members of her administration, including the Secretary of State for Foreign Affairs, Villeroy, inclined towards Spain and were therefore opposed to an Anglo-French marriage alliance. From the outset the French declared that the size of dowry demanded by the English was 'a condition which they could hardly satisfy.'[19] Matters were made worse by French insistence that all or most of the dowry be repaid in the event that either Charles or Christine died childless, a demand which Edmondes had earlier described as 'directlie against the custom of England.'[20] Over the remainder of the summer the French administration showed no sign of relaxing its attitude towards the size of the dowry, and at the beginning of October Edmondes reported that hispanophile ministers in the French administration had attempted to torpedo the negotiations by demanding that the English should accept just 700,000 crowns.[21] Although Edmondes subsequently reassured James that the Regent herself had privately pledged to make up the shortfall of 100,000 crowns from her own pocket if necessary, the effect of such unsettling news on James and his ministers was to reawaken discussion in the Privy Council on the merits of calling a parliament.[22] By 25 November James's patience was wearing thin. Edmondes was informed that the sum of 800,000 crowns was not negotiable and that, since the king's 'important and neer respects' required a rapid conclusion to the negotiations, he was to discover 'before the twelfth day of our Christmas' at the latest 'what is the furthest thay will be broght to.'[23]

No word was received from Edmondes by the deadline set by James. On the following day, 7 January, it was reported by one well-placed source that 'HM is now inclinable to a Parliament.'[24] James continued to look favourably on the idea of summoning a Parliament for at least the next two weeks.[25] However, just as the scales were tilting in favour of a parliament, Edmondes sent tidings that he had at last hammered out the basis of an agreement with the French. After months of prevarication, Marie de Médici had now decided that it was in her interests to bring the marriage negotiations to a swift and successful conclusion. At the beginning of January the Prince of Condé and the Huguenot Duc de Bouillon, together with their allies in the French nobility, had withdrawn from Court to eastern France in protest at the regency government's pursuit of a double marriage alliance with Spain. In response, an alarmed Marie seized upon the English negotiations in the hope that a treaty with England would be the surest way to avert civil war.[26] Edmondes was delighted at this turn of events, and hurriedly returned to England, presenting James with the terms he had negotiated on the morning of 31 January. In general, these were highly favourable to the English, although James was bound to feel irritated by the French insistence that the marriage, even if performed in England, should be celebrated by a Catholic bishop.[27] Writing on 5 February, Gabaleone, the Savoyard Agent in England, reported that 'the Queen of France had not only accepted the conditions', but 'had sent them better ones'. According to Gabaleone, whose informant was the pro-Savoyard Sir Thomas Lake, Marie de Médici had offered James a dowry of 800,000 crowns, with the promise that if he was not satisfied with this sum she would increase it to one million.[28] In fact James was offered only 750,000 crowns, although he was assured by Edmondes that, under pressure, Marie could be induced to find the extra 50,000 crowns he required.[29] Nevertheless, James declared himself so pleased with these terms that on 5 February he informed the Council that he was minded to accept them. He accordingly appointed a sub-committee of councillors to join with Edmondes and a French ambassador extraordinary, who had already been sent over, to perfect the final details.[30]

News of a breakthrough in the marriage negotiations caused dismay in the Privy Council, many of whose members were vigorously opposed to a French alliance. The Spanish Ambassador, Don Diego Sarmiento de Acuña, later ennobled as the Count of Gondomar, described seven councillors as opponents of the French marriage. These were the earls of Suffolk, Nottingham and Northampton, all members of the powerful Howard family, the Earl of Worcester, Archbishop Abbot, Lord Ellesmere and Suffolk's son-in-law, Lord Knollys. To this list should be added the Earl of Pembroke, the Earl of Somerset, who had married into the Howard clan in December 1613, and Lord Wotton. The only known favourers of a French marriage on the Council were Lennox, Viscount Fenton, Lord Zouch and Sir Julius Caesar.[31] Hostility in the Council to the French marriage stemmed in part from English unease at a policy which was thought likely to increase Scottish influence at Court. Writing at the end of January, Sarmiento shrewdly observed that a majority of the English on the Council 'cry out' against the French marriage, because 'they think the Scotts by this match (being so favored in France) will be preferred in authoritie and favor before them.'[32] English fear of Scottish domination was focused primarily on the Duke of Lennox rather than the Earl of Somerset, who, even before he married into the Howard family, regarded himself as an honorary Englishman.[33] A former ambassador extraordinary to Paris, Lennox was the leading advocate at Court of the French marriage, which he saw as a means of increasing his influence in France. It is surely no coincidence that when Lennox helped to open the formal marriage negotiations in Paris in June 1613 he simultaneously sought the command of a company of Scots in the French king's service.[34]

Opposition to a French match did not stem solely from a fear of Scottish domination. Pembroke, Abbot and Ellesmere all favoured a Protestant bride for the Prince on religious grounds. In doing so, they reflected a view which was widely shared beyond Whitehall, as popular hostility to a Catholic marriage had grown steadily since the spring of 1612.[35] Indeed, underlying resentment among members of the Commons at the king's pursuit of Catholic brides for his sons was believed by one contemporary to be a principal reason for the failure of the 1614 parliament.[36] James's boast to the Council that he would convert the young Princess Christine once she was in England is unlikely to have reassured its most Protestant members, since the draft marriage agreement allowed Princess Christine both freedom of worship and the services of four Catholic priests.[37] However, those councillors who favoured a Protestant marriage laboured under a severe disadvantage, as there was no Protestant princess available who could command the size of dowry demanded by James.

The Howards and their allies also supported an alternative marriage for Prince Charles, but with a Spanish rather than a Protestant princess. A Spanish infanta was available, and shortly after Sarmiento arrived in England in the summer of 1613 James was offered a Spanish marriage for his son, with the promise of 'such quantity of gold as should please His Majesty.'[38] However, relations with Spain were then at a low ebb, having been soured by recent disputes over the Virginia colony and the whale fisheries off Spitzbergen. As late as the beginning of 1613 the English government entertained fears of an imminent Spanish invasion. James, moreover, is unlikely to have forgotten that he had been led up the garden path by Spain in 1611, when he had pursued an offer of a Spanish bride for Prince Henry only to discover that the infanta concerned was just six years old.[39] Nevertheless, the Howards refused to abandon all hope of a Spanish marriage. At around the time that Edmondes informed James that he had extracted draft terms from the French, Somerset secretly sent Francis Cottington to implore Sarmiento to revive the offer of a Spanish match. Sarmiento was quietly delighted at this overture, and agreed to approach the king again, but as he rightly pointed out, James was unlikely to take the proposal seriously as it was so obviously timed to sabotage the plans for a French marriage.[40] His instincts were correct, for when he did finally seek an audience with James he was rebuffed, even though he had by then enlisted the aid of the queen.[41]

Faced with the king's refusal to countenance a Spanish bride for Prince Charles, the Howard camp looked instead to Savoy, which was still perceived as a satellite of Spain. In October 1612 Savoy had come within an ace of matching the Infanta Maria with Prince Henry.[42] Following Henry's death, the Duke of Savoy had offered Maria to Prince Charles on the same terms as those previously offered for Henry, and since she was already of child-bearing age he was confident of success.[43] James initially signalled his enthusiasm for a marriage treaty, either because he genuinely saw in it an alternative to a French alliance, or because he considered that a negotiation with Savoy might prove useful in persuading the French to loosen their purse-strings.[44] However, by April 1613, when Savoy's ambassador reached London to commence negotiations, James's enthusiasm for a Savoyard match had cooled. Savoyard aggression over Mantua in the spring of 1613, the perception that Savoy was a tool of Spain, and the fact that the Infanta Maria was eight years older than Prince Charles, were undoubtedly principal causes. James was also affronted that the Duke of Savoy, who was distracted by his affairs in northern Italy and thought that the English marriage might wait, had neglected to reply to his letters.[45] By September 1613, if not sooner, the Savoyard match was effectively dead, despite the evidence of French prevarication. It is true that Savoy's offer was not formally rejected until May 1614, so that Gabaleone, supported by the queen and by the Howard faction on the Privy Council, continued to advocate a marriage 'with new and greater offers'. However, as the Venetian ambassador succinctly observed in November 1613, 'he labours in vain'.[46]

In the absence of plausible alternative marriage alliances, francophobe members of the Council were reluctantly driven to the conclusion that a successful parliament was the only way to prevent a French match. The exception was the Earl of Northampton, who favoured neither a French marriage nor a parliament. The principal exponents of a parliament on the Council were the Lord Warden of the Stannaries, the Earl of Pembroke and the Lord Chamberlain, the Earl of Suffolk. By the beginning of 1614 Suffolk's recent marriage alliance with Somerset, and the declining health of Northampton, his rival for the Lord Treasurer's staff, had made him the most powerful figure at Court. It was almost certainly Suffolk who pressed the king to summon a parliament after the 6 January deadline for the completion of the marriage negotiations had elapsed. This is because the letter-writer who noted on 7 January that the king was now inclined towards a parliament also observed that Suffolk 'now guides the rudder of the state'. Suffolk did not desist from encouraging the summoning of a parliament after it became known that Edmondes had reached an agreement with the French. On the contrary, between 20 and 22 January he lavishly entertained the king at his magnificent Essex mansion, Audley End, with the result that rumours were soon rife that James had agreed to call a parliament.[47] Suffolk's advocacy of a parliament is revealed most clearly in a letter he wrote to Somerset on 12 February, the day after the Council held a marathon session to debate both parliament and the French marriage. Many councillors at this meeting had expressed themselves pessimistic about the prospect of holding a successful parliament, Suffolk wrote, 'only Pembrook and myself were the hoopfull belevers of good success.'[48] In order to win over their colleagues, the two earls volunteered to lay before them the demands that they anticipated would be made of the king in any future parliament, so that these could be offered up in the form of bills of grace in exchange for supply. This strategy was not new, as it had been suggested to the king less than two years earlier by Sir Henry Neville, who had offered to manage a parliament for James in return for a grant of the office of Secretary of State.[49] It cannot be coincidental that Suffolk was then in direct contact with Neville.

When the Council urged James in February 1614 to summon a parliament it was because a majority of its members reasoned that this was the only way left open to them to prevent a French marriage. Indeed, as has been previously mentioned, some of the more zealous Protestants on the Council even told James that if he agreed to abandon the marriage negotiations, a parliament would compensate him for the loss of the expected French dowry by a generous grant of supply.[50] The king did not share his councillors' objective of halting the marriage negotiations, of course, and expressed satisfaction at the terms negotiated by Sir Thomas Edmondes. It therefore remains to be established why he should have acquiesced in his Council's request.

The answer to this intriguing and important question is to be found in the crisis which enveloped France at the beginning of 1614. The withdrawal to eastern France of Condé and the Huguenot lords had initially worked in James's favour, as it had impelled Marie de Médici to abandon her earlier prevarication and offer generous terms to the English. However, the looming spectre of civil war now threatened to destroy the marriage negotiations altogether. The marriage treaty could not be concluded without either Bouillon, who was the principal exponent of an English alliance on the French Council, or Condé, who was second in line to the French throne, and a figure of such importance that his absence from Court in September 1613 had contributed to earlier delays in the marriage negotiations.[51] Edmondes naturally played down the significance of Condé's departure from Court at the beginning of 1614, referring to it as a routine attempt to put pressure on the regency government.[52] However, by mid-February at the latest James must have been aware that Paris was filled with the talk of war and that the rebellious nobles had begun to raise troops.[53] Indeed, a few day after Edmondes set out for England armed with the Regent's marriage proposals, Edmondes's secretary in Paris outlined in detail the extent of French military preparations.[54] The imminent prospect of a renewed outbreak of civil strife in France appalled James, who appealed for a peaceful resolution of the crisis.[55] He must have feared that the marriage negotiations would founder altogether if Bouillon and Condé were defeated; certainly he understood that no further progress could be made until French domestic difficulties had been resolved.[56] He therefore attempted to patch up the quarrel between the rival French factions.[57] Yet it was plain that a settlement was not going to be reached overnight, if at all. Thus on 19 February, precisely when it must have seemed certain that France was headed for war, James finally decided to summon a parliament.

II

The origins of the 1614 Parliament cannot be understood solely in terms of the disastrous condition of the royal finances. A critical factor which determined whether or not parliament would sit was the French marriage negotiations. Between July 1613 and February 1614 the likelihood that James would call a parliament depended largely on the fortunes of those negotiations. As these fluctuated so, in inverse proportion, did the chances that a parliament would occur. When James eventually called a parliament, it was because he feared that the marriage negotiations were about to be overtaken by events in France. Thus the turmoil which engulfed France at the beginning of 1614 not only occasioned the convening of the Estates-General but, to a considerable degree, the English parliament too. Another important reason why parliament was called is that a summons was supported by a majority on the Privy Council. This majority existed primarily because of a deep-rooted hostility towards the proposed French marriage. Since James would not consider an alternative match for Prince Charles, conciliar opponents of a French marriage were left with little alternative but to advocate a parliament. This, they hoped, would be managed so successfully that James would not need to resume the marriage negotiations once the crisis in France had passed. Principal among the opponents of a French marriage were the earls of Pembroke and Suffolk. The discovery that one of the leading advocates of a parliament was Thomas Howard, Earl of Suffolk is perhaps surprising, as it has hitherto been widely assumed that the Howards were uniformly hostile to the 1614 Parliament, and consequently that they had a large hand in spreading the rumours that were intended to wreck it. However, this picture has already been partly undermined by Professor Peck, who has demonstrated that the evidence to implicate Northampton in the breakdown of the parliament is at best circumstantial.[58] Like the importance of the French marriage itself, the role of the Howards in bringing about the parliament of 1614 deserves greater attention than it has yet received.

Notes

[1] British Library, Additional MS 32023B, fol. 252^{v}. The member was John Dackombe, MP for Corfe Castle and Surveyor-General to Prince Charles. In advocating supply, he reminded the House of James's 'power to match his son so as he shall not —.' It seems probable that the word missing from the end of this sentence is 'want'. *Proceedings, 1614*, p. 436.

[2] Public Record Office, PRO 31/3/47, fol. 243^{v}; *Narrative of the Spanish Marriage Treaty*, ed. and trans. by Samuel Rawson Gardiner (London: Camden Society, 1869), p. 285.

[3] Samuel R. Gardiner, *History of England from the Accession of James I to the Outbreak of the Civil War 1603–1642*, 10 vols (London, New York, Bombay: Longmans, Green and Co., 1896–1901), II, 227.

[4] *Limits of Revision*. p. 14.

[5] British Library, Lansdowne MS 165, fols 211–12. Caesar's memorandum is dated 1 June 1612, the day it was presented to the king. The Privy Council met on 31 May: 'The Journal of Sir Roger Wilbraham', ed. by Harold Spencer Scott in *Camden Miscellany X*, Camden Society, 3rd series (London, 1902), IV, 107–8.

[6] *The Letters of John Chamberlain*, I, 362; *Calendar of State Papers, Venetian 1610–13*, ed. by H. F. Brown and A. B. Hindes, 38 vols (London: HMSO, 1864–1947), XII, 384, 412; *Newsletters from the Archpresbyterate of George Birkhead,* ed. by Michael C. Questier, Royal Historical Society, Camden 5th Series: (London: Cambridge University Press, 1998), XII, 191. For the earlier rumours, see Clayton Roberts and Owen Duncan, 'The Parliamentary Undertaking of 1614', *English Historical Review*, 93 (1978), 481–98 (p. 483); *CSPV 1610–13*, pp. 230, 240, 276, 332; *Historical Manuscripts Commission, Report on the Manuscripts of the Duke of Buccleuch and Queensberry* (London: HMSO, 1899), I, 101–2; *HMC Report on the Manuscripts of the Marquess of Downshire*, ed. by A. B. Hindes (London: HMSO, 1938), III, 279.

[7] BL, Lansdowne MS 165, fols 223–26.

[8] PRO, State Papers 14/74/23.

[9] *Letters of John Chamberlain*, I, 456; *Limits of Revision*, p. 19.

[10] Thomas Birch, *The Life of Henry, Prince of Wales, Eldest son of King James I* (London, 1760), p. 275; BL, Stowe MS 173, fol. 142^{r-v}.

[11] PRO, SP 78/60, fols 185^{r-v}, 187^{r-v}. The Venetian ambassador thought France feared encirclement, *CSPV 1610–13*, p. 447.

[12] PRO, SP 78/62, fol. 72^{v}, 'We hold yt reasonable to demaund in dowrye the somme of 800,000 C[rowns], 6s. sterlyng to every crowne ...'. Professor Russell has mis-read this document and turned crowns into pounds, a significant error: *Limits of Revision*, p. 13. 800,000 crowns was the size of dowry to which the French were to agree in 1624.

[13] *Letters of John Chamberlain*, II, 391.

[14] The letter of instruction was dated 9 November, just three days after Henry's death: BL, Stowe MS 173, fol. 205.

[15] PRO, SP 78/61, fols 5–10^{v}.

[16] *CSPV 1610–1613*, pp. 491–2.

[17] *CSPV 1613–1615*, pp. 4–5.

[18] BL, Stowe MS 174, fol. 125.

[19] BL, Stowe MS 174, fol. 141^{r-v}.

[20] PRO, SP 78/61, fols 6^{v}, 9^{v}.

21 BL, Stowe MS 174, fol. 141^{r-v}; PRO, SP 78/61, fols 273^{r-v}, 298^{v}, 325.

22 PRO, SP 84/69, fol. 113^{v}; *HMC Downshire*, IV, 256.

23 BL, Stowe MS 174, fol. 192.

24 *HMC Downshire*, IV, 285.

25 *CSPV 1613–1615*, p. 89.

26 BL, Add. MS 32032B, fol. 184^{v} (I am grateful to my wife, Dr Helen Bradley, for translating this dispatch); *CSPV 1613–1615*, p. 89.

27 PRO, SP 94/20, fol. 241^{v}; BL, Add. MS 31111, fol. 46.

28 BL, Add. MS 32032B, fol. 187^{r-v}.

29 PRO, SP 78/60, fol. 131, mistakenly filed with papers relating to September 1612.

30 BL, Add. MS 32023B, fol. 187^{v}; PRO, SP 94/20, fol. 245; *CSPV 1613–1615*, p. 96.

31 *Narrative*, ed. by Gardiner, p. 112.

32 PRO, SP 94/20, fols 241–2.

33 Anne Somerset, *Unnatural Murder: Poison at the Court of James I* (London: Phoenix, 1998), pp. 67–8.

34 PRO, SP 94/20, fols 241–2.

35 Pauline Croft, 'The Reputation of Robert Cecil: Libels, Political Opinion and Popular Awareness in the Early Seventeenth Century', *Transactions of the Royal Historical Society*, sixth series (1991), I, 43–70 (p. 54). I am grateful to Dr Croft for valuable discussion of this point.

36 The contemporary was Arthur Wilson, a household servant of Robert Devereux, 3rd Earl of Essex: Arthur Wilson, 'The Life and Reign of James, the First King of Great Britain', in *A complete History of England: with the lives of all the kings and queens thereof; from the earliest account of time, to the death of his late Majesty King William III*, ed. by John Hughes and White Kennett, 3 vols (London, 1719), II, 696. Wilson was well acquainted with at least two members of the 1614 Parliament, Essex's half-brother, Walter Devereux, and the Earl's steward, William Wingfield.

37 BL, Add. MS 32032B, fol. 188.

38 *CSPV 1613–15*, p. 64.

39 Gardiner, *History of England*, II, 138–9, 152–3, 163.

40 *Narrative*, ed. Gardiner, p. 111; Gardiner, *History of England*, II, p. 226; BL, Add. MSS, 31111, fol. 39. For the earlier offer, see *CSPV 1613–1615*, p. 64.

41 *CSPV 1613–15*, pp. 92–3.

42 Roy Strong, 'England and Italy: The Marriage of Henry, Prince of Wales', pp. 84–6, in *For Veronica Wedgwood These: Studies in Seventeenth-Century History*, ed. by Richard Ollard and Pamela Tudor-Craig (London: Collins, 1986), pp. 59–87; Roy Strong, *Henry, Prince of Wales and England's Lost Renaissance* (London: Thames and Hudson, 1986), pp. 82–3. However, Strong's argument that the marriage treaty was finalised shortly before Henry's death is unconvincing. He asserts that the Privy Council formally declared in favour of a Savoyard marriage on 26 October, New Style (i.e. 16 October, Old Style), whereas a final resolution was not intended to be made until 27 October (o.s.) and was deferred owing to Henry's illness, *CSPV 1610–13*, p. 447. If a Savoyard match was settled by the third week of October, as Strong believes, it is necessary to explain why, on 23 October (o.s.), James instructed Edmondes to discover whether the French would be prepared to increase their original offer of 500,000 crowns, BL, Stowe MS 173, fols 174–5.

43 PRO, SP 92/1, fol. 85.

[44] *CSPV 1613–1615*, p. 490.

[45] PRO, SP 94/20, fols 137–41^{v}; *CSPV 1610–13*, p. 546; BL, Add. MSS, 31111, fol. 36. The fact that it took the Duke of Savoy more than six months to convey his condolences on the death of Prince Henry may also have caused James to reassess the value of a Savoyard match: PRO, SP 92/1, fol. 86; *CSPV 1610–13*, p. 542. I am grateful to my colleague, Dr Paul Hunneyball, for this observation, and for valuable discussions on Savoy.

[46] BL, Add. MS 31111, fol. 36; *CSPV 1613–1615*, pp. 68, 116, 122; *Narrative*, ed. Gardiner, pp. 111–12, note b.

[47] *Letters of John Chamberlain*, I, 500; *HMC Downshire*, IV, 296; *CSPV 1613–1615*, p. 89.

[48] BL, Cotton MSS, Titus F IV, fols 340–1^{r}. The letter is undated, but it refers to 'the consultation last day'. A dispatch from the French Ambassador indicates that the Council held its consultation on the 11th: PRO, PRO 31/3/47, fol. 243^{v}.

[49] Roberts and Duncan, pp. 485–7.

[50] PRO 31/3/47, fol. 244.

[51] On Bouillon's significance to the English, and to continental Calvinism generally, see S. L. Adams, 'The Road to La Rochelle: English Foreign Policy and the Huguenots, 1610–1629', *Proceedings of the Huguenot Society of London* (London: Huguenot Society of London, 1970–76), XXII, 419–29 (pp. 416–18). On Condé's earlier absence, see PRO, SP 78/61, fols. 241, 265.

[52] J. Michael Hayden, *France and the Estates General of 1614* (Cambridge: Cambridge University Press, 1974), pp. 58 n. 8, 61.

[53] Hayden, pp. 59–60.

[54] BL, Stowe MS 174, fols 226–9. Edmondes left Paris on 22 January and took ship for England on the 27th: *Memorials of Affairs of State ... from the Original Papers of Sir Ralph Winwood*, ed. by Edmund Sawyer, 3 vols (London, 1725), p. 492.

[55] Adams, 'English Foreign Policy', p. 419.

[56] *CSPV 1613–1615*, pp. 107, 113; PRO, SP 78/62, fol. 128.

[57] Hayden, *France and the Estates General*, p. 54.

[58] Linda Levy Peck, *Northampton: Patronage and Policy at the Court of James I* (George Allen and Unwin; London, Boston, Sydney, 1982), pp. 210–11.

4

Crown Finance and Reform: The Legacy of the 'Addled Parliament'

John Cramsie

This essay was originally conceived under the title 'Crown Finance in Crisis', something of a tease with respect to Jacobean finance.[1] Scholars long ago familiarised us with the acute problems of solvency which bedevilled the crown throughout the reign of James VI and I.[2] These were present whether parliament met or not. Indeed, the tide of recent scholarship has tended to emphasise the administrative handicaps under which the crown finances laboured. From the so-called revisionist standpoint, the crisis of finance under the Stuarts was as much – if not more so – the result of a 'functional breakdown' of the system as parliamentary unwillingness to vote supply.[3] The financial weaknesses of the system rather than deep-seated constitutional or philosophical conflicts were the real problem. Yet the Jacobean intersections of finance and parliament were politically important and affected the course of governance. This is particularly true of the 'Addled Parliament.' Parliamentary political failure in 1614 propelled James and his governors, by fits and starts, into a course of fiscal reform.[4] This is substantial in itself, but the convergence between reform and parliament is significant for understanding governance after 1614 as well as ongoing efforts to conceptualise politics, parliaments, and finance.[5] It is these ideas which this essay will explore.

I

The extent to which the 'Addled Parliament' affected the mindset of James and his governors, particularly whether they believed they had experienced some kind of 'crisis', is a key thread among the essays in this volume. One measure of crisis is whether anything which transpired in 1614 influenced the course of policy and governance. From this standpoint, the significance of 1614 as a year of crisis can be understood in some respects by starting in 1621, by the degree to which the parliament convened that year represents a conscious, deliberate departure from its predecessor(s). James opened parliament in 1621 on 30 January in the midst of an economic recession and confessional conflict on the continent. He informed the Lords and Commons that they were assembled to consider measures appropriate to the current circumstances and supply his financial needs – not a stunningly original agenda.[6] James's particular financial need in 1621 was driven by military assistance for his son-in-law, the Elector Palatine, in his conflict with the Holy Roman Emperor. James also needed funds for diplomatic missions aimed at preventing a European-wide war. Part of the diplomatic equation required the demonstration of England's potential for taking military action. European regimes, friends and foes alike, knew of James's failure to secure significant supply from his past parliaments (with the exception of 1606). It was essential to reverse that experience and thereby enhance the credibility of English arms.[7] Nevertheless, the king's speech in 1621 featured an interesting point of departure from previous addresses.

James was a practical-minded politician, schooled in and stimulated by the personal engagement of Scottish politics.[8] He was far from impressed with English political ritual when serious matters of governance demanded attention. Crown finance and parliamentary supply were two such entwined matters. He believed, not without good cause, that his English parliaments were inattentive to his financial needs either in accepting his necessity or in the speed with which they took up the question. At the height of his frustration following the collapse of the Great Contract in November 1610, James met with thirty members, 'private men' as he apparently termed them, to discuss supply.[9] James hoped to move discussion to a more interpersonal venue. He could participate actively at the same time effectively asking members as private men to become counsellors, willing and able to give their opinions freely outside the confines of the 'House' and its practices; he went so far as to promise them pardon for anything said in that spirit of frankness. However, James's attempt to reach a meeting of the minds in this fashion was rebuffed as meddling with members' privileges.[10] The Scottish parliament, in contrast, was a body seemingly more responsive to both his specific business and personal management.[11] Herein lay a great deal of James's frustration with English parliamentary politics, particularly what he took to be members' endless speechifying and hunting-after of esoteric precedents.[12] In 1621 this prompted the characteristically plain-spoken James to tell parliament, 'I have had less supply from my people than ever king or queen had, I know not for how many hundred years.'[13] He likened himself to a woman in travail who had laboured for the past ten years without a parliament or subsidy.[14] To James's mind, the lack of supply stood in marked contrast to the sums voted Elizabeth. While James would not publicly claim to have ruled as well as Gloriana – one suspects he believed as much, however – he did not shrink from his pride in eighteen years of peace.[15]

There had to be practical causes for parliamentary unwillingness. James took up the chief reason that past parliaments had given him, when 'some of the Lower House did boldly affirm, that they would give all they had if they knew it should come to my purse.'[16] James could have had any number of speeches in mind from past meetings. In 1606, Walter Gawyn commented that 'whereas it is moved wee should fill the Kings Cofers, it would be likewise understood whether they wilbe filled for if the bottomes be out then can they not be.'[17] Thomas Wentworth was far more explicit in 1610, offering what has become an oft-quoted complaint:

> all theise courses would be to no purpose except it would please the king to resume his pencions granted to cortiers out of the exchecquer, and to diminish his charge and expences [...] to what purpose is it for us to drawe a silver streame out of the contry into the royall cesterne, if it shall dayly runne out thence by private cocks?[18]

Similar arguments about financial mismanagement in 1614 made a direct connection between the provision of good government and supply. Henry Finch tried to sound a positive note, agreeing with members in general to 'relieve bountifully, cheerfully, and speedily', at the same time he sought to reassure members that they would also receive redress of grievances: 'Love casts out fear, our love to the King should cast fear away that the things offered should not take effect.'[19] Thomas Crew was more direct and opined that 'If the country possessed with the King's graces and that we are about them, the country will be willinger to grant.'[20]

The obvious issue is whether such statements are rhetorical or sincere: did individual members oppose supply because of financial mismanagement or the absence of good government on the king's part, were members simply unwilling to commit the purses of their localities, or both? These are interesting questions and much has been written about members' localist, parochial outlook in matters of taxation.[21] However, James's speech in 1621 makes it possible to shift the focus from the localism of members to the manner in which the king and his governors interpreted their unwillingness to vote supply. The king, known for feckless extravagance – then and now – answered members with the regime's accomplishments in *reforming* the crown finances. 'I confess', he spoke, 'I have looked narrowly into my estate within these few years and have found that there was not in it a whole piece without sores.'[22] He candidly admitted a chronic weakness in being 'loath to think there could be any corruption' but, once persuaded, James appointed commissioners who produced notable reforms which allowed him to proclaim cuts in his household, the navy, and the ordnance totalling £63,000.[23] James later affirmed his born-again reformism, saying, 'I shall be as glad to reform things amiss as you shall be willing to inform me of them.'[24] Of course, when members investigated monopolists, James – and officers involved like Francis Bacon – received more reform than they had bargained for when planning for the session. But that is moving too far afield. James's speech reveals that counsel connecting supply and good government was taken as more than rhetoric: it influenced the course of fiscal policy undertaken by James and his governors after 1614.

II

The course of fiscal policy between 1615 and 1621 allowed James with some credibility to assume the mantle of a reformer and seeker of good government. This dramatic change grew out of the divided reactions to the failure of the 'Addled Parliament'. There is no doubt that James was deeply affected by the failure of parliaments in 1610 and 1614. He wrote bitterly after the collapse of the Great Contract in 1610 of the 'repairing and clearing of our honour', musing that 'Wherein we have misbehaved our selfe here we know not nor we can never yet learn.'[25] James sometimes generalised his disaffection, but it is also clear that he did not simply equate parliament itself, or vituperative speakers, with his subjects as a whole. James had determined in 1610 to imprison the most intemperate members, Thomas Wentworth and John Hoskyns, but relented in the face of his English councillors' opposition.[26] Hoskyns and Wentworth were not so fortunate in

1614 when they, Walter Chute, and Christopher Neville (along with four non-members) were committed to the Tower while a further eleven members were ordered to remain in London.[27] Yet one of the projects to meet immediate financial needs after the 'Addled Parliament' was a benevolence, a 'free gift' solicited from the localities, following hard on the example of contributions by Archbishop Abbot and the clergy.[28] James and his governors resolved to appeal directly to his subjects, circumventing an unrepresentatively obstructive parliament, and even allowed rumours to run that the king would enact by proclamation some of the redress of grievances offered in parliament.[29] This same approach was behind a project debated in the new year to issue a proclamation and sell general pardons similar to those which usually came from the king at the end of a parliament. The new Lord Treasurer, the Earl of Suffolk, seems to have been the driving force behind this project.[30] Suffolk was among individuals advising the king who supported a direct approach to the subject as a viable alternative to parliament.[31] However, there were other voices, foremost among them Lord Chancellor Ellesmere, equally convinced this was not an appropriate or sustainable course.

The Privy Council debate over the general pardon encapsulates the wider questions about the future direction of fiscal policy.[32] Ellesmere's personal notes reveal that councillors strongly opposed the pardon on a variety of grounds including profitability and practicality, but its impact on parliament played a crucial role. Thomas Lake believed it would only confirm suspicions that James disliked parliament: it was properly pursued in that venue as part of the traditional royal thanks for supply. Edward Coke echoed Lake, but not without first saying he was 'sory for projectes etc' and decrying 'venall pardons'; Secretary Winwood equally found it dishonourable to sell the king's justice. Support for the project came from the new Chancellor of the Exchequer, Fulke Greville who 'lyked of it for necessytye' and Henry Wotton who knew of nothing more propitious while doubting another parliament would be of any use.[33] Suffolk, who first took up the project in January, asserted – in seemingly petulant fashion from Ellesmere's notes – that 'this is thought of too late' and 'yt wyll be sayed that the King must [call] a parliament.'[34] The tide of debate had already swung against the project when Ellesmere spoke and he simply opined it was presently unfit. However, Ellesmere's preparations for the debate, recorded on the same paper as his minutes of the meeting, demonstrate that he was prepared to argue against it on virtually every point.[35] There were no precedents for such pardons and present times drew into question its honour, appeal, and profitability. The people's gratitude was improbable, judging by the temper of the last parliament when bills of grace had been scorned. Finally, the project would effectively end a pardon's parliamentary utility and sever the connection between it and supply.[36]

What these policies and debates in the first year after the 'Addled Parliament' suggest is that the role of parliament in crown finance was under renewed scrutiny: in what circumstances might it be relied on to support the crown financially and using what means of persuasion? The end of the general pardon effectively brought a stalemate to the question, but the project's failure undoubtedly influenced James's decision to order a meeting of his councillors in July 1615 for the development of a more permanent financial solution.[37] Like schoolchildren before a summer holiday, there was plenty of talk, but little purposeful action. James wanted something concrete in the fall, and his councillors met again over four days in September.[38] Among several like-minded councillors, including Coke, Winwood, and Lake, Ellesmere emerged as the most focused and vocal proponent of overhauling the crown finances. What is significant is that Ellesmere and his colleagues sought reform for its obvious fiscal benefits and to restore the working political relationship between James and parliament, especially for purposes of financing the costs of governance. As Coke stated in the July meeting, 'the crowne was never maynteyned by the ordinarye but helped by parlement', an opinion with which Ellesmere agreed 'in toto' according to the Lord Chancellor's own minutes.[39] Ellesmere reflected on the ideas raised in July and spent the rest of the summer fashioning his own reform programme, titled 'Thinges to be considered before a Parliament to be called.'[40]

Ellesmere's parliamentary focus has recently been discounted by J. D. Alsop, but the Lord Chancellor consistently and explicitly made the connection between reform and parliament.[41] Ellesmere's notes had a positively parliamentary tempo when criticising importunate suitors who abused the king's bounty, the complicity of 'those who had the charge and husbandinge of the kinges treasure', and the manifold abuses of projectors who diverted most of their gains to private ends rather than serving the commonweal.[42] Ellesmere even employed the stock reference to 'Leakes in the Cisterne of the Treasurye.'[43] In one paper Ellesmere noted the importance of spending cuts, examining fraudulent and wasteful gifts and grants, reforming impositions, and addressing the balance of trade. 'And then,' he wrote, 'a parlement but not before somwhat be done in these thinges.'[44] Ellesmere's holistic perspective concluded his completed version:

> When all or some of the thinges before mencioned shall be begunne and in doinge, as namely the abatinge etc, the amendinge of the boke of Rates, the reforminge of the Imposicions etc, the putting in execucon of some of the statutes before mencioned, then yt wyll be requisite to calle a parlement, And yt is not to be doubted, but his Majestes good and lovinge subjectes, seinge this course taken by his Majestie, wylle wyllingly and cherefullye yelde large contribucon and ayde, by subsidies, tenthes, fyftenes and otherwyse.[45]

Lake, who recorded the September council meetings, reported that Ellesmere believed his proposals included some items which 'were good means to bring ye King rellief by themselves; sum others good preparations for a Parlament; and sum others fitt to be treated in a Parlement.'[46]

Ellesmere took it upon himself, in essence, to untie the Gordian knot of fiscal policy and parliament following events in 1610 and 1614. He wrote angrily of the disjunction between King, Lords, and Commons in 1610.[47] The Commons had 'growne bygge and audacious [... the] causes of callinge of the parlement, which ought to have bene first treated of, were neglected, and some mens private devises preferred, and therin much tyme mispent.'[48] They spurned the king's business, supply and Union, saying 'Pharaoes froggs were come amongst us', but their zeal to cure the 'mischiefs or inconveniences in the Comenweale' sought only the impeachment of 'his Majestes prerogative'.[49] Theirs had become an 'irregular and insolent course of procedinge' in which they would postpone all business until they had relief of their grievances.[50] Ellesmere harked back to the Elizabethan parliamentary past as he understood it, longing for the ancient course, 'that his Majesty should grant them good laws, they give him convenient relliefe, as his occasions should requyre.'[51] By 1615, Ellesmere's philosophical ire was joined by a practical-minded move to reconstruct working political relationships in parliament. He was driven to acute frustration at directionless fiscal policy and mismanagement, chastising colleagues in September for putting forward nothing 'which had not often been spoken of.'[52] Policies of inaction and waste had eroded James's estate and left him dependent upon parliament, a subversion of the proper aspect between monarchy, aristocracy, and democracy in the polity. For Ellesmere, a change in fiscal policy was crucial to restoring proper political relationships in the polity and re-establishing parliament as an effective component of finance and governance.[53]

Ellesmere and his colleagues took up these issues of politics, parliament, and fiscal reform in September 1615. After much debate, they proposed the formation of conciliar committees with each assigned a specific reform project.[54] Committees were appointed for examining gifts and grants; balancing the books with cuts in Ireland, the navy, household, wardrobe, robes, and works; reforming impositions and enhancing trade; creating a fleet of ships to contest Dutch mastery of the herring trade;[55] and developing practical means to enforce the statutes of employment, which required foreign traders to 'employ' their profits within the realm.[56] The resulting reform agenda was perhaps the most promising of the reign. Yet it was utterly abortive. James is the key. At the conclusion of the meetings, the king simply approved his councillors' agenda and began the progress to Royston.[57] James probably agreed with Ellesmere that the proposals could 'be very good for supplye and increasinge of his Majesties yerely revenewe, and wyll in tyme helpe towarde the payment of his debtes', but neither its strictures nor parliament were palatable to the king.[58] Interestingly, several committees dealing with parliamentary preparation were proposed and *not* subsequently appointed, despite James's apparent sanction. These included committees to present a public justification for James's expenses, prevent electioneering, and devise means to commit the king to spend subsidies on public expenses. The sole exception was the committee of judges and law officers appointed to examine and address past parliamentary grievances.

One factor at work in these omissions was practical. James's councillors were spread thin. The committees focused conciliar energy on reforms and projects likely to yield benefit of themselves and in setting the stage for parliament. Those omitted were more proper once the decision to summon parliament was taken. Ellesmere crabbed about projects omitted, but the programme followed his dictum that reforms should 'be begunne and in doinge' before it 'be requisite to calle a parlement.'[59] However, James remained resentful and disappointed after the acrimonious parliamentary failures in 1610 and 1614. It was James who had originally assembled his councillors for the establishment of his estate, 'as well by payment of his detts as by reducing his expenses to an equality with his revenews;

and fell uppon sum particulars in that point of abating.'[60] Parliament was not part of the king's agenda. It was only brought forward by councillors who declared the talk of spending cuts as inadequate and then not before altercations over 'the difficulties of having a Parliament.'[61] James responded warily, refusing to sanction parliament until a programme had been debated and offered to him, a reversal of 1614 in which he had acquiesced and then left his council to prepare for the session as they thought best.[62] The 'Addled Parliament' clearly haunted him, as Lake reported: 'he would not avoyd a Parliament if he might see likelyhood of comfort by it [...] on the other side he would rather suffer any extremity then have another meeting with his people and take an affront.'[63] James remained unwilling in 1615 and the moment passed for Ellesmere, who died eighteen months later.

III

Matters changed in 1617.[64] The king's progress to Scotland that year drained the Exchequer and the financial incompetence, if not outright corruption, of Suffolk became inescapable.[65] In his most decisive involvement in fiscal policy, James embraced a sweeping programme of retrenchment in the household and offices of state. It was formulated by the king's new favourite, George Villiers, and his clients Lord Keeper Francis Bacon (Ellesmere's replacement), and Lionel Cranfield, the merchant and future Lord Treasurer. These men formed a fiscal triumvirate that did not dissolve until the parliament of 1621. Cranfield is the link to Ellesmere, having provided the late Lord Chancellor with expert advice on trade and fiscal reform in 1615. It was Cranfield's project for reforming impositions that Ellesmere supported as well as his strictures for purchasing and expenditure.[66] There is even a partial copy of Ellesmere's reform programme among Cranfield's papers in his own hand.[67] Cranfield carried these shared principles of spending reform and sound management into political circumstances which made them the art of the possible: for the first time in England, James lent his full weight to the cause of reform – and the king was spurred on by Villiers, even if the favourite's motives had at least as much to do with the politics of patronage as the responsibilities of governance. This was surely the difference between the fate of the conciliar committees appointed in 1615 and the reform commissions in 1617.

Reform in 1617 was initially entrusted to the Privy Council as a corporate body, which immediately turned to the household officers for reductions. There was an understandable lack of enthusiasm on the officers' part for belt-tightening and the council did little or nothing to contest this. Playing up the officers' obstructionism and council's watery response, the triumvirate counselled James to initiate a project first outlined by Cranfield. Reform would be entrusted to independent commissions composed of junior officers, Exchequers auditors, and customs experts. Bacon and Cranfield chose the officials and drew up the commission's orders which left no doubt why the change had occurred: 'we do find what difficulties are made, and what time is lost, in disputing and devising upon the manner of doing that whereof the matter must be and is so fully resolved.'[68] 'Neither can we but see in this [...] the like event to follow in the rest upon the like reasons', they added.[69] James agreed so readily he signed the draft commission as the final instrument. Authority and oversight were taken from the council, but with characteristic Baconian subterfuge the commissioners' authority was 'to be kept in breast, and to come forth by parts.'[70] Come forth it did though, and the commissioners produced the most successful retrenchments in the reign, particularly in honeycombs of waste like the navy, household, and wardrobe.[71] Credit must go to James's consistent support, the triumvirate's determination, and the commissioners' expertise.

The reform drive produced the tangible results which allowed James in 1621 to counter members' prejudices that 'whatsoever they should give him would be miss-spent in pryvat gifts and not converted to the good of his estate' – Lake's comment in 1615.[72] How different from 1614, when Bacon bemoaned that the king had faced members as little better than a beggar.[73] And, James assumed the mantle of commonwealth reform in parliament, promising redress of grievances and beneficial legislation.[74] The first multiple subsidies since 1606 were obtained with alacrity: James's speech successfully answered immediate doubts, and voices orchestrated in the lower house persuaded members his necessities (foreign and domestic) were genuine. There also existed a strong sentiment among members that the opportunity for constructive engagement with reform was too good to lose.[75] To that end, the question of impositions, of such destructive power in 1610 and 1614, was avoided. A draft declaration stated that notwithstanding issues of high importance such as the king's prerogative and the subjects' liberties, members had 'purposely abstained from proceeding therin, least it might have hindred theire other endeavoures that were in the present most necessarie for the preservation of the weale and honour of his Majestie.' The statement was carefully drafted to add that leaving off the subject was not to 'bee taken or interrapted to theire prejudice and disadvantage in a busines of so great importance.'[76] Yet the reality was that impositions were not contested again under James. It remained for Charles I to bring that matter of principle back into the political dialogue in destructive fashion.

Finance did not addle members in 1621 as it had in 1610 and 1614, but the assembly was far from the Elizabethan model hoped for by Ellesmere and other governors after 1614. Two subsidies were far below James's needs, testimony to the tentativeness of the new-found partnership of king and Commons over supply and reform. The consensus was sorely tested by the Commons' labyrinthine pursuit of monopolists and the king's officers who approved their projects.[77] Lord Chancellor Bacon was impeached. Lord Treasurer Mandeville, Suffolk's eventual successor, just escaped the same fate and was shunted to the lord presidency of the council. The Commons' monopolies bill censured projects and the turning of the king's prerogatives to private gain. While he would not countenance such a legislative challenge to his prerogative power to issue patents, James suspended several key monopolies and turned dozens more over to the Privy Council and judges for examination, much as Elizabeth had done twenty years earlier after outspoken criticism.[78] Though lengthiness in proceeding was a life-long irritant – James gave himself the apt moniker of Baron Tell-Clock in this parliament – the king did not fall out with members over such matters of supply and grievances in 1621. James broke parliament's neck – to use another of his phrases – after members in the fall session launched into criticism of the proposed Spanish match for Prince Charles, seemingly at the king's behest, and then refused to be silenced on the subject.[79]

IV

It was a commonplace among Whig historians that parliament, the House of Commons actually, held supply hostage to visionary principles which heralded parliamentary democracy in 1688. Revisionists, foremost among them Conrad Russell, have cut the Commons' intellectual and constitutional horizons down to size, informing us that members looked for consensus, often reflected their localities' aversions to taxation, and participated in an event rather than forming an institution. Yet we should not lose sight of the fact that financial mismanagement and fiscal policies, especially impositions and monopolistic projects, were issues of good government of genuine concern to members, *both* as local representatives and as participants in a national event. The reluctance of members in this respect was only partly parochial while their criticisms and counsel were interpreted by James and his governors from a decidedly national or central perspective. They responded to denunciations of fiscal policy and management as a genuine point of conflict, one which, at least to them, explained a great deal about why parliaments failed the king financially.[80]

The 'Addled Parliament' looms especially large in this dynamic. While some governors proposed to directly present subjects with the king's financial needs, others like Ellesmere rejected such an approach. They became acutely aware that mismanagement was an issue which blocked the effectiveness of parliament as a tool of governance and left crown finance in crisis. Ellesmere articulated a vibrant programme of fiscal reform which laid the basis for James's one great success with reform during his English reign, a success which favourably affected the parliament of 1621. However, much changed in the five years after Ellesmere composed his 'Thinges to be considered before a Parliament.' Parliamentary revenue became no longer simply a question of fiscal policy, management, and the king's necessity. Parliamentary politics moved away from these familiar intersections with crown finance. European diplomacy and its volatile religious implications emerged as the *cause célèbre* of parliamentary politics. James – and later Charles I – proved far less willing to accept parliamentary counsel on those subjects than on fiscal reform, a dynamic which produced its own years of crisis through the 1620s.

Notes

[1] I am grateful to Dr Stephen Alford, Professor John Guy, and Dr Natalie Mears for their comments on the original draft of this paper as well as those of my fellow conference participants at Birkbeck College in July 1998.

[2] The standard works are Frederick C. Dietz, *English Public Finance 1558–1641* (New York: Century, 1932) and Menna Prestwich, *Cranfield: Politics and Profits under the Early Stuarts* (Oxford: Clarendon Press, 1966); also Conrad Russell, *Parliaments and English Politics 1621–1629* (Oxford: Clarendon Press, 1979), pp. 35–70.

[3] Russell, *Parliaments*, pp. 64–70.

[4] The term governor is used here in the early-modern sense of those who assisted rulers in governing their realms, from counsellors and ministers to local crown officers and regional magnates.

[5] See John Cramsie, *Kingship and Crown Finance under James VI & I, 1603–1625* (Woodbridge: Boydell Press, 2002).

[6] There are several reports of the king's speech in *Commons Debates, 1621*.

[7] Thomas Cogswell, *The Blessed Revolution: English Politics and the Coming of War, 1621–1624* (Cambridge: Cambridge University Press, 1989), pp. 18–20; Russell, *Parliaments*, pp. 87–91.

[8] Jenny Wormald, 'James VI & I: Two Kings or One?', *History*, 68 (1983), 187–209; Jenny Wormald, 'James VI and I, *Basilikon Doron* and the *Trew Law of Free Monarchies*: The Scottish Context and the English Translation', in *The Mental World of the Jacobean Court*, ed. by Linda Levy Peck (Cambridge: Cambridge University Press, 1991), pp. 36–54; Cramsie, *Crown Finance*, Chapter 3.

[9] *Proceedings, 1610*, II, 337–8.

[10] *Proceedings, 1610*, II, 342 n. 7.

[11] Jenny Wormald, *Court, Kirk, and Community: Scotland 1470–1625* (London: Arnold, 1981), pp. 156–8.

[12] Stanford E. Lehmberg, 'The Role of Parliament in Early Modern England – A Reconsideration', in *The Swedish Riksdag in an International Perspective*, ed. by Nils Stjernquist (Stockholm: Olaf Palme Gotta, 1989), pp. 75–87.

[13] *Commons Debates, 1621*, II, 7.

[14] *Commons Debates, 1621*, II, 8.

[15] *Commons Debates, 1621*, II, 7.

[16] *Commons Debates, 1621*, II, 8.

[17] *The Parliamentary Diary of Robert Bowyer 1606–1607*, ed. by David Harris Willson (Minneapolis: University of Minnesota Press, 1931), p. 77.

[18] *Parliamentary Debates in 1610*, ed. by Samuel Rawson Gardiner (London: Camden Society, 1862), pp. 11–12.

[19] *Proceedings, 1614*, p. 66.

[20] *Proceedings, 1614*, p. 67.

[21] Russell, *Parliaments*, pp. 5–34, 49–53, 64–70, and Michael J. Braddick, *Parliamentary Taxation in Seventeenth–Century England: Local Administration and Response* (London: Boydell, 1994) are particularly important.

[22] *Commons Debates, 1621*, II, 8.

[23] *Commons Debates, 1621*, II, 8–9.

[24] *Commons Debates, 1621*, II, 12.

[25] Hatfield House Library, Salisbury MS 147, fol. 162^{v} (7 December 1610).

[26] Public Record Office, State Papers, 14/58/54, fols 109^{r}–110^{r} (2 December 1610); PRO, SP, 14/58/62, fol. 122^{r} (6 December 1610); HHL, Salisbury MS 147, fol. 162^{r}.

[27] Theodore K. Rabb, *Jacobean Gentleman: Sir Edwin Sandys, 1561–1629* (Princeton: Princeton University Press, 1998), pp. 203–4.

[28] *Historical Manuscripts Commission, Downshire*, IV, 431 (17 June 1614); PRO, SP, 14/77/53, fol. 107^{r} (30 June 1614).

[29] *Acts of the Privy Council 1613–1614*, p. 492; PRO, SP, 14/77/58, fol. 114^{r} (7 July 1614).

[30] Oxford, Bodleian Library, Carte MS 121, fols 1^{r}–20^{v}.

[31] This subject is treated fully in Cramsie, *Crown Finance*, Chapter 6.

[32] Henry E. Huntington Library, Ellesmere MS 445 [unfoliated; June 1615 (my dating)]; the notes of the meeting were made by Ellesmere. The dating is established by a letter of 15 June 1615 in which John Chamberlain informed Dudley Carleton that the pardon project had finally been dismissed. PRO, SP, 14/80/115, fol. 181^{r}.

[33] HL, Ellesmere MS 445; *HMC Downshire*, V, 120 (26 January 1615) and 131 (14 February 1615).

[34] HL, Ellesmere MS 445.

[35] HL, Ellesmere MS 445.

[36] HL, Ellesmere MS 445.

[37] HL, Ellesmere MS 441 [unfoliated].

[38] British Library, Harleian MS 4289, fols 224^{v}–30^{v}; reprinted in *The Letters and Life of Francis Bacon*, ed. by James Spedding, 7 vols (London: Longman, 1861–1874), V (1869), 194–207.

[39] HL, Ellesmere MS 441.

[40] HL, Ellesmere MS 2610.

[41] J. D. Alsop, 'The Privy Council Debate and Committees for Fiscal Reform, September 1615', *Bulletin of the Institute of Historical Research*, 68 (1995), 191–211 (p. 198).

[42] HL, Ellesmere MS 2610/1 [Ellesmere's pagination].

[43] HL, Ellesmere MS 2610/1 [Ellesmere's pagination].

[44] HL, Ellesmere MS 2507; Ellesmere completed only five points.

[45] HL, Ellesmere MS 2610/11.

[46] BL, Harleian MS 4289, fol. 230^{r}.

[47] HL, Ellesmere MS 2599; BL, Cotton MSS, Titus F IV, fols 333^{r-v}.

[48] HL, Ellesmere MS 2599, fols 1^{v}–2^{r} [Ellesmere's foliation].

[49] HL, Ellesmere MS 2599, fols 3^{v}, 5^{r}.

[50] HL, Ellesmere MS 2599, fol. 7^{r}.

[51] BL, Harleian MS 4289, fol. 229^{v}.

[52] BL, Harleian MS 4289, fol. 229^{v}.

[53] For Ellesmere's concerns about mismanagement already at the end of Elizabeth's reign, see Louis Knafla, *Law and Politics in Jacobean England: The Tracts of Lord Chancellor Ellesmere* (Cambridge: Cambridge University Press, 1977), p. 35.

[54] HL, Ellesmere MS 2614 [unfoliated]; Alsop, 'Fiscal Reform', pp. 201–5.

[55] John Cramsie, 'Commercial Projects and the Fiscal Policy of James VI & I', *Historical Journal* 43:2 (2000), 345–364.

[56] HL, Ellesmere MS 2614 [unfoliated].

[57] BL, Harleian MS 4289, fol. 230^{v}.

[58] HL, Ellesmere MS 2610/7.

[59] HL, Ellesmere MS 2610/11.

[60] BL, Harleian MS 4289, fol. 224^{v}.

[61] BL, Harleian MS 4289, fol. 224^{v}.

[62] Linda Levy Peck, *Northampton: Patronage and Policy at the Court of James I* (London: Unwin, 1982), pp. 205–8.

[63] BL, Harleian MS 4289, fol. 224^{v}.

[64] The ensuing discussion is based on Cramsie, *Crown Finance*, Chapter 7.

[65] PRO, SP, 14/93/73, fols 94^{r-v} (30 August, 1617); Spedding, *Letters and Life*, VI, 254–6.

[66] Knafla, *Law and Politics*, pp. 101–2.

[67] Centre for Kentish Studies, U269/1, OE1528 [Cranfield MSS, 2330; unfoliated].

[68] Spedding, *Letters and Life*, VI, 280.

[69] Spedding, *Letters and Life*, VI, 280.

[70] Spedding, *Letters and Life*, VI, 284.

[71] Prestwich, *Cranfield*, pp. 199–252 is an effective summary of the programmes if not the political milieu.

[72] BL, Harleian MS 4289, fol. 225^{r}.

[73] Spedding, *Letters and Life*, V, 184–8.

[74] *Commons Debates, 1621*, II, 12–13 and 22–3.

[75] *Commons Debates, 1621*, II, 4–94.

[76] PRO, SP, 15/42/44, fol. 79^{r} [1621].

[77] Russell, *Parliaments*, pp. 98–116 discusses the attention to patents.

[78] PRO, SP, 14/121/124, fols 231^{r}–32^{v}; *Commons Debates, 1621*, III, 416; David Dean, *Law-making and Society in Late Elizabethan England: The Parliament of England 1584–1601* (Cambridge: Cambridge University Press, 1996), pp. 85–92.

[79] Cogswell, *Blessed Revolution*, p. 19.

[80] Russell, *Parliaments*, p. 49.

PART II

ARENAS OF POLITICAL DEBATE IN 1614

5

'Better Becoming a Senate of Venice'? The 'Addled Parliament' and Jacobean Debates on Freedom of Speech

David Colclough

I

In his opening speech to the 1614 parliament, James I declared that:

> a king [as opposed to a tyrant] knows his subjects can never have so good access unto him, speak so freely and safely, and have means to lay open the just complaints and griefs of his subjects as in parliament; and this parliament, I hope, shall be called the parliament of love.[1]

He went on to promise that he would speak to the Commons directly and not through the intermediaries of the Speaker or his servants. Despite his friendly words and good intentions, though, the parliament was distinguished by a failure of communication not only between the king and the Commons but between members of the Lower House themselves. Less than two months later, in the face of paranoia about the misreporting of speeches and threats of dissolution, John Hoskyns pointed out that 'this was titled a parliament of love but the arguments that are made are rather of fear.'[2] Many of his fellow MPs made speeches that seriously suggested James was acting more like a tyrant than a king and that they were in danger of being enslaved.

In this chapter I hope to show that this breakdown of communication centred around the desire of many MPs to counsel the king, and the incompatibility of this desire with the king's intentions for the session. It was a session notable for a series of speeches that excited the displeasure of either king, Lords, or Commons, and I want here to place the handling of these speeches in the context of contemporary discussions of counsel and its limits and privileges. The Parliament may have been no parliament at all but an assembly, and the threats to their powers perceived by some of its members may have been exaggerated or even illusory, but the debates concerning freedom of speech and its limits were to become increasingly typical of discussions in and outside parliament during James's reign. In those debates the need for frank yet decorous counsel to counterbalance the supposed evil influence of those who had the king's ear would be more and more vigorously asserted.

II

When, amid the hasty dissolution of the parliament, James sent John Hoskyns, Thomas Wentworth, Christopher Neville and Sir Walter Chute to the Tower for their outspokenness in the last days of the session, Sir Henry Wotton acerbically described their speeches as 'better becoming a Senate of Venice, where the treaters are perpetual princes, than where those that speak so irreverently are so soon to return (which they should remember) to the natural capacity of subjects.'[3] Wotton's comments seem to indicate (albeit ironically) that the speeches of 1614 could be considered from the perspectives of constitutional debate and political theory: MPs were perhaps challenging the absolute distinction between their parliamentary privileges and the duties of 'subjects'. Such issues were indeed being raised, I shall argue, and they were intimately linked to questions of parliamentary privilege and procedure. It is the details and the wider implications of these questions as they relate to parliamentary free speech that I will be discussing in the rest of this chapter.

Matters which addressed the freedom of speech properly to be accorded to MPs arose repeatedly during the brief life of the parliament, and I will begin by offering a short survey of what I take to be the most significant of these. There are, it seems clear, five specific speeches or sets of speeches considered to be scandalous by the Commons or the king – or at least noted to have caused considerable discomfort. The first was Richard Martin's speech on 17 May. Martin was in the Commons to speak as counsel for the Virginia Company, along with a delegation from the Lords, but (as the anonymous diarist notes), 'he, contrary to all men's expectations, beginning with Virginia, came into another subject both in taxing the House in general and also some particular men.'[4] Chamberlain describes Martin 'taxing [the Commons] for their slow proceeding, for their disorderly carriage, and schooling them what they should do, with divers odd glances'[5] – rather touching evidence of the Commons' attachment to procedure appears in the fact that despite this speech being the 'most offensive and injurious to the House' that Sir Edward Montagu had ever heard, Martin was 'not interrupted because it was agreed by the House before he came in to hear him in silence.'[6]

The second scandalous speech was only heard at second-hand in the Commons, but despite – or it may be because of – this caused even more upset than Martin's brainstorm. It in fact consisted of two separate comments by Bishop Richard Neile of Lincoln, uttered on 21 and 23 May respectively, that a joint conference of Lords and Commons should not be entertained because – as Mervyn reported him –

> to question the King's prerogative in imposing was like a disease called *noli me tangere* and in touching that matter we did not only cut off a branch but strike at the root of the imperial crown [. . .] he said he knew our spirits and thought it not fit to hear us, for the Lords should hear nothing but undutiful and seditious speeches of us.[7]

A committee was quickly, and predictably, selected to investigate and report on the matter.

On 21 May, the same day that Bishop Neile was applying his horticultural analogies to the Commons, Thomas Wentworth – described by Wotton as a 'silly and simple creature'[8] – applied some distinctly uncomfortable scriptural passages to the discussion of impositions, notably Daniel 11:20 ('Then shall stande up in his place in the glorie of the kingdome, one that shall rayse taxes: but after fewe dayes hee shall bee destroyed, neither in wrath, nor in battell'), and referred to the murder of Henri IV.[9] These comments seem, indeed, to have provoked Neile's second outburst. Wentworth ended, in either a hapless attempt to prevent analogical reasoning or an even more sinister ultimatum, depending on the drift of one's interpretation, by saying 'but by far be it from my Lord the King that aught so should befall him.'[10] Unsurprisingly, neither James nor the French ambassador found the speech to their liking.

The fourth speech was delivered by Sir Walter Chute on 1 June, and suggested there were multiple financial abuses which acted as a drain on the 'main cistern' of the king's coffers as well as declaring that 'they that practiced with the King to have no parliament would also labour to dissolve it' and suggesting that supply and dissolution should come only after redress of grievances.[11] The last set of speeches are the most notorious, and came on 3 June: Christopher Neville borrowed from Bishop Neile's horticultural thesaurus, asking 'would the King take from us the cedars of freedom and liberty under which the subjects of England were shadowed, and shroud us with these shrubs of bills of grace'?, and went on to describe Neile himself as one of a fearsome mongrel species: 'their master's spaniels but their country's wolves.'[12] John Hoskyns' notorious speech attacking James's Scottish favourites and hinting at a massacre through a reference to the Sicilian Vespers followed soon after, and four days later the session was over.[13]

This is a mere list, and the speeches are by no means intended to be regarded as characteristic of the session or its members at large: they were a very heterogeneous group, and, moreover, Professor Russell has rightly reminded us to be as alert to the 'silences of conciliation' as to the 'speeches of conflict'.[14] Staying with the speeches, we need to ask what response they provoked from the Commons as well as how they were regarded by the king. All these responses had one important factor in common, and that was the Commons' desire to ensure that it was they who could deem a speech excessive or scandalous and, if necessary, punish the speaker. Martin's speech was in no sense an assertion of any right to freedom of speech, but it *was* regarded as an insult to the House and he was censured by the Commons and called to the bar to be admonished and to excuse his actions.[15]

The Neile affair was, similarly, a case of an insult by a non-member, but was treated much more seriously, both because it was transmitted by rumour and because of the threat it offered to friendly relations between two of the three components of parliament, the Lords and Commons. Discussions in and out of committee went on until the end of the session, with the main point of debate being whether Neile should be investigated by the Lords, acting on advice from the Commons, or by the king. Certainly one of these had to be relied upon, since the

Lower House had no jurisdiction over the Upper, nor vice versa. On 26 May the volatile Edwin Sandys, noting that the case was 'as weighty as any ever came here concerning the liberties of this and the higher House of Parliament', argued that 'to go immediately to the King wrongs the liberties of the Upper House', while Sir Roger Owen worried that 'if the King may punish him now for an offense to our House, so he may do one of ours.'[16] The committee's vote finally went narrowly in favour of going to the king, but not before many hot-tempered verbal attacks on both the Bishop's person and on his office, and a decision on the part of the committee to forbear any other business until a satisfactory message had been received from the Lords.[17] Neile had slighted the Commons' good intentions in their discussion of impositions and was thus likely, Hoskyns thought, to 'make discord between the king and his people.'[18]

Wentworth, meanwhile, having provoked the Bishop by his speech on 21 May, made his apology on the day that the latter's remarks were first discussed in the Commons: apologising for his remarks, he was cleared 'by a general acclamation' of the House.[19] He was nonetheless investigated by the Council at the end of the session and briefly imprisoned, possibly to placate the French ambassador.[20] Here, as with the speeches on 3 June, a conflict between the king's and the Commons' jurisdiction over outspokenness becomes apparent. The day before the dissolution Sir Guy Palmes brought a motion effectively to assert and shore up this jurisdiction, saying that:

> since it was said the parliament should be so soon dissolved, in respect of some reports cast forth that divers of the House should be called into question after the parliament, he wished if there were any that could accuse any member of the House to have spoken any unbeseeming words of the King that they might here be charged with them, and either purge themselves or receive punishment.[21]

The Speaker thought this dubious, since nobody was actually named, but Hoskyns acknowledged that 'it concerned him in particular'; Sir John Saville reminded the House that 'the ancient course in parliament was that if any man's speech had been excepted against, the Queen sent to the House and accused the party, and the House punished him.'[22] Wotton then attempted, it seems, to bring this discussion to some sort of conclusion, and to do so in the Commons while it was still possible, asking Hoskyns to explain what he meant by referring to the Sicilian Vespers.[23] Hoskyns's reply hardly sounds satisfactory: he said that 'he had no private intent in it and he thought the story was known to many and he meant it general.'[24] Later, he was to amplify this excuse, claiming that he had been working entirely from a script given to him by Lionel Sharp and Sir Charles Cornwallis: when he was investigated by the Privy Council after the end of the session and asked to explain his reference to the Sicilian Vespers, he said he had a 'hint thereof, and afterwards a general information, from Dr *Lionel Sharp of Cambridge.*'[25] Chamberlain, in addition, asserted that 'Hoskins was embroucht, abetted, and indeed plainly hired with monie to do that he did.'[26] This seemed to implicate Sharp and Cornwallis's patron, the Earl of Northampton, who certainly had some interest in seeing the Parliament fail (and who notoriously drove through London in triumph when it was dissolved), but Northampton's involvement has been effectively questioned by Linda Levy Peck.[27] However lame his explanation, Hoskyns was then cleared upon the question put to the House. Neville and Sir Edward Giles went on to reply to rumours of accusations against them, but their replies do not survive in any of the records. Of course, none of these manoeuvres was successful in keeping these speeches a matter for and in the House, and the four members were soon incarcerated.

To illustrate that what we are seeing here was not another peculiarity of this peculiar session, we should note that this desire to keep the punishment of outspoken members a parliamentary matter was also apparent in the next parliament, of 1621. Looking back then to the conclusion of the previous session, and with an eye to the proclamation of December 1620 'against lavish and licentious speech of matters of state', several MPs were concerned to ensure both that their liberty of speech would not be infringed and that they should be dealt with properly if they were deemed to break decorum. On the first day of business in parliament, Monday 5 February 1620/1, Sir Edward Giles 'moved for a petition to the king for freedom of speech, and that those that spake extravagant in the House might be punished by the House and not after Parliament, in regard of the late proclamation'; a motion that was seconded by Sir Robert Phelips.[28] The session was the occasion of just such punishments for what was considered to be 'extravagant speech': the first was of an MP named Shepherd, for speaking against petitions for banishing Catholics. Later in the year, the House, which had by that time rediscovered judicial muscles it hardly knew it possessed, took it upon itself to punish a non-member, Floyd, for insulting the King and Queen of Bohemia – James's son-in-law and daughter. Having no jurisdiction over non-members, this was a gamble – but it paid off.

III

Such concern about parliamentary procedure and privilege is familiar to the student of the Jacobean parliaments, but what does it have to do with free speech? It is clear that MPs were not trying to use their supposed jurisdiction to let fellow members get away with outrageous speeches, nor would this have come within the compass of the liberty of free speech requested and granted at the beginning of each session, as it was regarded by the vast majority of the Commons.[29] Nor is such attention to procedure a symptom of some lust for power. Rather than seeking *new* powers, the members saw themselves as, in Professor Russell's phrase 'fighting to keep something they had already.'[30] This 'something' was not generally conceived in terms of a range of ancient rights of a hazy sepia-tinted 'ancient constitution' sort – though such terms were used – but with what MPs saw as the very real and vital function of counselling the king.[31] It was the forthright exercise of this duty, and of the free pursuit of parliamentary business, that were provided for by the four parliamentary liberties of freedom from arrest, freedom of speech, access to the king and benign interpretation of speeches and proceedings in the Commons. We also need, then, to ask how MPs perceived the threats to these liberties; what form did assaults on them take? Here concentration on the language of the common law and ancient constitution seems inadequate as a mode of explanation, as has often been argued. More satisfactory explanations have, however, been harder to find. In the Commons' near-desperate attempts to retain their freedom to counsel and their jurisdiction over misdemeanour we can perceive, I think, the serious concern with the possibility of becoming enslaved that Quentin Skinner has recently identified.[32] In Skinner's analysis, MPs, far from depending on the language of the common law (the distinction, for example, between bondmen and free men), were at this point turning to descriptions of freedom and unfreedom as offered in Roman law – drawing on the Digest, and also on Cicero, Livy and Sallust. These texts suggested to the Jacobean MPs that it was the very *existence* of prerogative powers, not their exercise, that deprived subjects of their liberty.[33] The debates and complaints of 1614 so often sound paranoid to our ears – as they did to James I – because the classical language of freedom and slavery has been drowned out. In fact, the frequent references to the necessity of counselling, to the perilous state of freedom and to the primacy of the *salus populi* can be seen to derive directly from this way of thinking, and make a great deal more sense when read in that context.

In the face of James's increasingly desperate need for money, many MPs were determined to assert parliament's conciliar function, to present it as their right as well as their duty to advise the king. On 5 May 1614 Hoskyns declared that the parliament had been 'called to give counsel not to give money'; giving supply, he pointed out, was not mentioned in the writ of summons as one of parliament's functions; [34] on 12 April Sir George More had reminded his fellow members that they were 'sent hither from all the commons of the kingdom; our principal care to speak for the commonwealth that continually speaks to us', and that there was 'health' in 'the multitude of counsellors',[35] and in his speech on the afternoon of 4 May the king himself had agreed that 'there is not in the world so great a counsel as yours, both in the quantity and quality.'[36] Even when emphasising in his opening speech that this parliament was 'principally called to relieve my wants' (whatever Hoskyns might have wished), James went on to say:

> so I trust to meet with you at Michaelmas, at which time I will promise you to ask you nothing (and so assure your countries) but say: my masters come, let us consult what is good for the commonwealth and what laws are fit either to be added, amended, or taken away and you in all humble manner to inform me what is amiss and fit to be amended in the commonwealth.[37]

Although the parliament never saw Michaelmas, this is evidence of James's awareness both of his MPs' desire to fulfil a conciliar role and of the importance of at least attempting the appearance of patience. In the next parliament, seven years later, Peter Alford declared to the House that 'we are the Counsell of the land, where Counsell fayles, the people perish.'[38]

Throughout the considerable body of literature on counselling being written and read in the early modern period, liberty of speech is considered to be essential: if the prince does not actively encourage frankness then his or her counsel will be worthless, and he or she will become the object of flattery framed as counsel, rather than of constructive advice. At the same time, the counsellor will become both slavish (by acting like a flatterer) and enslaved (because where the prince can punish a counsellor's free speech at will there is no freedom). Enslaved counsellors are not envisaged merely as having their freedoms taken away but as having their very ability to imagine frank counsel curtailed by living in a condition of servitude.[39] Lipsius, in his *Sixe Bookes of Politics or Civil Doctrine*, placed liberty of speech second only to piety in his list of five precepts for counsellors; and while discussing the other side of the counselling relationship in his chapter on 'how a prince ought to behave him selfe in hearing counsel' advised him to 'love those that are free of speech, and Hate flatterers which are hurtfull.'[40] At the beginning of his 'To Nicocles', a hugely influential classical text for the sixteenth and seventeenth centuries, Isocrates noted that while the education of private individuals included 'freedom of speech [*parrhesia*] and the privilege which is openly granted to friends to rebuke and enemies to attack each others faults,' kings are deprived of this privilege.[41] The same points are made in a range of humanist texts concerning the duties of a monarch's counsellors and the monarch's duties to those counsellors, including More's *Utopia*, Erasmus's *Education of a Christian Prince*, Starkey's *Dialogue*, Sir Thomas Smith's *Discourse*, William Cavendish's *Discourse Against Flatterie* and Bacon's celebrated essay 'Of Counsel'.[42]

Counselling is in essence a deliberative process, and is thus also essentially rhetorical.[43] As well as carrying out the business of supplying the king's wants and handling legislation, parliament was supposed to deliberate and advise on specific matters of political moment, and to persuade the monarch toward or away from a particular course of action. Parliamentary speeches, though it is often difficult to discern now in their fragmentary state, were rhetorical performances, and in those that were intended to offer frank counsel or friendly admonition we can often see the strategies associated with the rhetorical figure of *parrhesia* or free speech being deployed.[44] The figure was defined as of use when speaking out to one's superiors, and it was recommended as a way of exciting the emotions; its potential for being used deceitfully was often acknowledged, but by the late sixteenth century it was almost indistinguishable from the apology for frankness with which it was supposed to be prefaced.[45] On 25 May 1614, Hoskyns began his attack on Bishop Neile by asking pardon 'if transported with the zeal of the liberty of England.'[46]

A key part of effective persuasion was, of course, decorum – ensuring that one's words were appropriate to time, place and person. In the context of parliamentary outspokenness this also involved ensuring that one was within the bounds allowed for by the rather vague terms of the formal request for and granting of parliamentary liberties.[47] In 1614 Speaker Crew had put his request thus:

> since in this great council there be many things of weight and consequence to be consulted of, which by the freedom of speech and debate may be best discerned and understood, we are likewise humble suitors to your Majesty for your gracious allowance *ut in libero senato loquemur libere*, not doubting but that we shall confine and circle ourselves within those lasts and limits of duty and moderation as shall be fit.[48]

Lord Chancellor Ellesmere replied that the king would grant the request:

> assuring himself you will speak with that reverence and duty to his Majesty as becomes subjects, with such judgement and discretion as becomes councillors [...] Let me tell you the property of councillors which is to speak *rara, vera, et ponderosa*.[49]

Many would find it hard to discern any of those properties in the more voluble MPs of the session; but it should not be doubted that they often felt that they were indeed speaking with as much 'judgement and discretion' as was fit. The question was one of definitions, and of who had the power to define a given contribution as appropriate, excessive but excusable, or seditious. Much of the Commons' energy seems to have been put into claiming this power of definition for themselves, or at least maintaining a show of co-operation between themselves and the king, who was of course acknowledged as having ultimate jurisdiction. The instability of evaluative terms is evident in Wotton's explanation of Hoskyns's imprisonment: he was, he wrote,

> in for more wit, and for licentiousness baptized freedom. For I have noted in our House, that a false or faint patriot did cover himself with the shadow of equal moderation, and on the other side, irreverent discourse was called honest liberty; so as upon the whole matter, 'no excesses want precious names.'[50]

Liberty and licentiousness had an alarming tendency to merge into one, just as a 'forebearance' of business could be indistinguishable from a 'cessation' if one were James I, while they were utterly distinct if one were Sir Edward Montagu.[51] Unfortunately, by this point even the debate over the definition of the role of parliament seemed at an impasse, since the institution was unwilling to accept James's account of both his hardship and its principal purpose (he announced in his opening speech that 'this parliament is principally called to relieve my wants'), while he would not accept the interpretation they wished him to place upon their actions, specifically their attempts to bargain hard for the grant of supply.[52] What seemed to James like new, efficient ways of getting his income (impositions are the most obvious example here) seemed to many MPs like frontal assaults on their status as free men: if the king could impose duties at will, then in what sense was a subject's property his own? And if his property was not his own, then in what sense was he free? In these terms, servitude was only around the corner.[53] The lines of communication were thoroughly addled, and one can understand James's frustration when, with the wolf (and, no doubt, the spaniel) at the door, Sir Edwin Sandys spent time not voting for subsidies but noting that:

> It was the resolution of the last parliament that it is in the King's power to call a parliament, but when they are assembled it is freely to consult of what they shall determine themselves; for if they should be bound to treat of what the King list, there is no freedom.[54]

James was not speaking the same language as Sandys and his fellow MPs, as should by now be evident. As historians, however, we surely need to understand both languages. It would be a bitter irony if we did not recognise why to many in 1614 there really did seem to be a crisis of liberty, and if we failed to comprehend Sandys's conviction that even if he was not imprisoned, to be 'bound to treat of what the King list' would place him and his fellow MPs in a condition of bondage as harsh as that suffered by Hoskyns and his companions in the Tower, and much more enduring.

Notes

[1] 5 April, 1614; *Proceedings, 1614*, p. 19.

[2] 3 June; *Proceedings, 1614*, pp. 422–3.

[3] Wotton writing to Sir Edmund Bacon; Logan Pearsall Smith, *The Life and Letters of Sir Henry Wotton*, 2 vols (London: Oxford University Press, 1907), II, 37 (hereafter *Life and Letters*).

[4] Anonymous notes, MS 0.2.7, Trinity College, Cambridge; *Proceedings, 1614*, p. 279.

[5] *Letters of John Chamberlain*, I, 531, quoted in *Proceedings, 1614*, p. 271.

[6] *Proceedings, 1614*, p. 276. No complete copy of Martin's speech appears to have survived; see *Proceedings, 1614*, p. 271, n. 25.

[7] *Proceedings, 1614*, p. 348.

[8] Wotton, *Life and Letters*, II, 37.

[9] *Proceedings, 1614*, pp. 313, 316, 317; Geneva Bible version of Daniel 11:20 quoted from Thomas L. Moir, *The Addled Parliament of 1614* (Oxford: Clarendon Press, 1958), p. 116.

[10] *Proceedings, 1614*, p. 316.

[11] *Proceedings, 1614*, p. 408.

[12] *Proceedings, 1614*, p. 420. On Neville's speech, see Quentin Skinner, 'The Greek and Roman Classics as the Cause of the English Civil War', Neale Lecture, University College London, 3 March 2000. I am grateful to Professor Skinner for allowing me to refer to his unpublished lecture.

[13] *Proceedings, 1614*, pp. 422–3; on this speech see the perceptive comments of Conrad Russell, *Limits to Revision*, pp. 23–5, esp. p. 25. On Hoskyns's involvement in this parliament, see Baird W. Whitlock, *John Hoskyns, Serjeant-at-Law* (Washington: University Press of America, 1982), pp. 427–68.

[14] See Conrad Russell, 'Parliamentary History in Perspective, 1604–1629', in *Unrevolutionary England, 1603–1642* (London: Hambledon Press, 1990), pp. 31–57 (pp. 52, 53).

[15] See *Proceedings, 1614*, pp. 271–87.

[16] *Proceedings, 1614*, pp. 355–357.

[17] See Moir, *Addled Parliament*, p. 125.

[18] 25 May; *Proceedings, 1614*, p. 349.

[19] 25 May; *Proceedings, 1614*, pp. 340; 348–9.

[20] Sir Henry Wotton wrote to Sir Edmund Bacon that the ambassador had lodged a complaint about Wentworth's speech (8 June, 1614; Wotton, *Life and Letters*, II, 37. *Proceedings, 1614*, p. 313, wrongly cites p. 32), while Chamberlain wrote to Carleton on 30

June that Wentworth 'had leave this Whitsontide to go home to his wife for five or sixe dayes, but is now returned to the Towre, where he hath the libertie of the place, and stayes more to satisfie the French ambassador then any thinge els' (*Letters of John Chamberlain*, I, 540).

[21] *Proceedings, 1614*, p. 426.

[22] *Proceedings, 1614*, p. 428.

[23] *Proceedings, 1614*, p. 428.

[24] *Proceedings, 1614*, p. 428.

[25] Quoted in Whitlock, *John Hoskyns*, p. 459.

[26] *Letters of John Chamberlain*, I, 540.

[27] Linda Levy Peck, *Northampton: Patronage and Policy at the Court of James I* (London: George Allen and Unwin, 1982), pp. 208–10.

[28] *Commons Debates, 1621*, I, 17.

[29] On the Speaker's requests for privileges, see n. 47 below.

[30] Russell, *Limits to Revision*, p. 7.

[31] On the Commons' desire to counsel and its relation to freedom of speech, see Conrad Russell, 'The Nature of a Parliament in Early Stuart England', in *Unrevolutionary England*, pp. 1–29 (pp. 8–9); Norman Jones, 'Parliament and the Political Society of Elizabethan England', in *Tudor Political Culture*, ed. by Dale Hoak (Cambridge: Cambridge University Press, 1995), pp. 226–42 (pp. 236–7). A rather different reading is offered by Kevin Sharpe, 'Introduction: Parliamentary History 1603–1629: In or out of Perspective?', in *Faction and Parliament: Essays on Early Stuart History*, ed. by Kevin Sharpe (Oxford: Clarendon Press, 1978), pp. 1–42 (pp. 37–42). For a thorough reinterpretation of the language of the ancient constitution in early seventeenth-century parliamentary debates, see Alan Cromartie, 'The Constitutionalist Revolution: The Transformation of Political Culture in Early Stuart England', *Past & Present*, 163 (1999), 76–120.

[32] See Skinner, 'The Greek and Roman Classics'; see also, Quentin Skinner, 'John Milton and the Politics of Slavery' *Prose Studies*, 23:1 (2000), 1-22, which deals with much of the same complex of ideas in the period immediately after 1649. I am grateful to Professor Skinner for allowing me to read a typescript of this article prior to its publication.

[33] These arguments later coalesce around complaints about the king's dependence on the Negative Voice; see Skinner, 'John Milton and the Politics of Slavery', esp. 7–9.

[34] *Proceedings, 1614*, p. 152.

[35] *Proceedings, 1614*, p. 64.

[36] *Proceedings, 1614*, p. 140.

[37] *Proceedings, 1614*, p. 19.

[38] 30 May 1621, reported by Barrington; *Commons Debates 1621*, III, 354.

[39] See Skinner, 'The Greek and Roman Classics', and 'John Milton and the Politics of Slavery', esp. 13–18.

[40] Justus Lipsius, *Sixe Bookes of Politics or Civil Doctrine*, trans. by William Jones (London, 1594), sigs. [Giv] – [Giv]^{v}; sig. Hii^{v}.

[41] Isocrates, 'To Nicocles' in *Isocrates, With an English translation by George Norlin*, 3 vols. (London: William Heinemann, 1928–45), I, 40–71(pp. 41, 43).

[42] This subject will be dealt with in detail in my forthcoming book, *Freedom of Speech in Early Stuart England*. On counsel, see John Guy, 'The Henrician Age', in *The Varieties*

of British Political Thought, 1500–1800, ed. by J. G. A. Pocock, with the assistance of Gordon J. Schochet and Lois G. Schwoerer (Cambridge: Cambridge University Press, 1993), pp. 13–46; John Guy, 'The Rhetoric of Counsel in Early Modern England', in *Tudor Political Culture*, ed. by Dale Hoak (Cambridge. Cambridge University Press. 1995), pp. 292–310; Glenn Burgess, 'The Impact on Political Thought: Rhetorics for Troubled Times', in *The Impact of the English Civil War*, ed. by John Morrill (London: Collins & Brown, 1991), pp. 67–83; F. W. Conrad, '"A Preservative Against Tyranny": Sir Thomas Elyot and the Rhetoric of Counsel', in *Reformation, Humanism, and 'Revolution'. Papers Presented at the Folger Institute Seminar 'Political Thought in the Henrician Age, 1500–1550'*, ed. by Gordon J. Schochet with Patricia E. Tatspaugh and Carol Brobeck (Washington: Folger Institute, 1990), pp. 191–206; F. W. Conrad, 'The Problem of Counsel Reconsidered: The Case of Sir Thomas Elyot', in *Political Thought and the Tudor Commonwealth. Deep Structure, Discourse and Disguise*, ed. by Paul A. Fideler and T. F. Mayer (London: Routledge, 1992), pp. 75–107; Linda Levy Peck, 'Kingship, Counsel and Law in Early Stuart Britain', in *The Varieties of British Political Thought*, pp. 80–115; J. G. A. Pocock, *The Machiavellian Moment. Florentine Political Thought and the Atlantic Republican Tradition* (Princeton: Princeton University Press, 1975), pp. 338–48.

[43] I am very grateful to Markku Peltonen for discussions of this point.

[44] On the problems attendant on using parliamentary reports as evidence, see John Morrill, 'Reconstructing the History of Early Stuart Parliaments', *Archives*, 21:91 (1994), 67–72; John Morrill, 'Paying One's D'Ewes', *Parliamentary History*, 14:2 (1995), 179–86, and the debate between Morrill and Maija Jansson: Maija Jansson, 'Dues Paid', *Parliamentary History*, 15:2 (1996), 215–20; John Morrill, 'Getting Over D'Ewes', *Parliamentary History*, 15:2 (1996), 221–30.

[45] *Parrhesia*, from Greek πας (all) + ρησις (speech). See Diane Parkin-Speer, 'Freedom of Speech in Sixteenth Century English Rhetorics', *Sixteenth Century Journal*, 12:3 (1981), 65–72; David Colclough, '*Parrhesia*: The Rhetoric of Free Speech in Early Modern England', *Rhetorica*, 17:2 (1999), 177–212.

[46] *Proceedings, 1614*, p. 341.

[47] On the earlier history of the Speaker's request for freedom of speech and a discussion of the *de facto* exercise of such speech in Parliament, see J. S. Roskell, *The Commons and their Speakers in English Parliaments 1376–1523* (Manchester: Manchester University Press, 1965), Chapter 2, 'The Speaker's Protestation, and the Problem of Freedom of Speech in the Lower House', pp. 31–58; G. R. Elton, *The Parliament of England 1559–1581* (Cambridge: Cambridge University Press, 1986), pp. 341–9.

[48] *Proceedings, 1614*, p. 28.

[49] *Proceedings, 1614*, p. 29.

[50] Wotton, *Life and Letters*, II, 37.

[51] 27 May; *Proceedings, 1614*, pp. 374–5.

[52] *Proceedings, 1614*, p. 19.

[53] See Skinner, 'The Greek and Roman Classics'.

[54] 5 May; *Proceedings, 1614*, p. 159.

6

'Now thou may'st speak freely': Entering the Public Sphere in 1614

Michelle O'Callaghan

WILLY: Then now thou may'st speak freely, there's none hears,
But he whom I doe hope thou do'st not doubt.

ROGET: True; but if *dores* and *walles* haue gotten *eares*,
And *Closet-whisperings* may be spread about:
Doe not blame him that in such *causes* feares
What in his *Passion*, he may blunder out:
In such a *place*, and such strict *times* as these,
Where what we speak is tooke as *others* please.[1]

This exchange between William Browne and George Wither, thinly disguised as the shepherds Willy and Roget, is set in the Marshalsea where Wither had been imprisoned in March 1614. The prison is the physical manifestation of the constraints on speaking freely; such restrictions have spread beyond the confines of the prison walls to become a condition of the times. *The Shepherds Hunting* is one of a group of texts that appeared in 1614 and early 1615 that includes William Browne's *The Shepheards Pipe*, published together with eclogues by Wither, Christopher Brooke, and John Davies of Hereford, Brooke's *The Ghost of Richard the Third*, and Wither's *A Satyre: Dedicated to His Most Excellent Majestie.* One thing that these texts have in common is their characterisation of 1614 as a year in which England descended into tyranny. They did not go to the extent of branding James a tyrant king, but rather were drawing on an anti-court tradition in which tyranny is the condition of court life itself. Wither gave a particular inflection to this theme through his identification with the slandered David of the *Psalms*. As Anne Lake Prescott points out, to write about the *Psalms* was to engage in a political drama which has at its centre the abuse of public language. The *Psalms* present an image of court life in which tyrants are served by evil counsellors and, in doing so, place particular emphasis on the ways in which the channels of counsels, in which ideally words should serve the interests of the commonwealth, are being corrupted.[2] For Wither, the counterpart of the abuse of counsel was censorship; evil counsellors took advantage of the corruption of the times to silence the faithful for their own ends. The writers involved in these volumes do see culture in distinctively oppositional terms. And yet they were not alone in their sense that public language had been subjected to unusual pressures in recent years, to the extent that one can characterise 1614 as a year when the question of who had the authority to speak became particularly heated.

1614 was a year beset by rumour and 'such discoursing'.[3] Although much of this talk focused on the new parliament, the marriage of Robert Carr, the newly created Earl of Somerset, and Frances Howard, the daughter of Thomas Howard, Earl of Suffolk, celebrated during the Christmas festivities at court 1613/14, also attracted a great deal of attention. Just as Frances Howard's first marriage to Robert Devereux, third Earl of Essex, had been intended to reconcile factions at court, King James and Suffolk had hopes that, since this match had proved unhappy and divisive, her divorce and remarriage to James's favourite Robert Carr would bring an end to these tensions. Considerable efforts were made at the marriage festivities to bring together the Howard family and their main rivals at court, William Herbert, Earl of Pembroke, and his brother Philip Herbert, Earl of Montgomery.[4] Those hostile to the influence of the Howards did not put such a favourable construction on this marriage between the royal favourite and a member of the Howard family, and rather saw it as a cynical manoeuvre by Suffolk and his brother, Henry Howard, Earl of Northampton, to seize advantage at court and so sideline Pembroke and Montgomery and marginalise further those identified with the old Essex circle, such as Henry Wriothesley, Earl of Southampton. Libellous verses attacking the couple had been circulating since rumours of a divorce in August 1613.[5] This campaign of defamation may have gained impetus from the flood of libels generated by the death of Robert Cecil, Earl of Salisbury, in May 1612 which continued late into 1613. These libels had a precedent in a smear campaign against his father, William Cecil, Lord Burghley, organised by Robert Devereux, second Earl of Essex, and his followers in the 1580s and 1590s. Burghley seems to have counter-attacked in 1599 when Essex was beset by libels during his ill-fated Irish campaign.[6]

These libelling campaigns may have had their origins in the political manoeuvring at the court, but they spread beyond the confines of the court into a broader oral, manuscript, and print culture. Pauline Croft, in her study of the mass of libels occasioned by Salisbury's death, has argued that libels should be studied as 'spontaneous expressions of popular culture': 'By the early seventeenth century, public interest in current affairs was easily sufficient to generate a multitude of spontaneous political libels.'[7] The Essex circle and their supporters clearly had an interest in undermining the reputation of Carr and Howard; the honour of the Earl of Essex had been sullied at the divorce trial when it was argued that the marriage had not been consummated due to his impotence. The Somerset libels also had a vigorous life outside court circles and continued to be copied and circulated long after the Overbury trial. Like the Cecil libels, they tended to employ a language of corruption that was culturally intelligible and accessible due to the way that it was highly formalised. The equation of libels with popular culture is misleading if the term popular is being used in opposition to elite. Because of their formulaic language and use of simple verse forms, verse libels crossed social boundaries and attracted audiences from a range of social classes, including the non-literate. They were widely disseminated socially and geographically; verse libels were copied or read aloud in private or public, circulated amongst friends and associates, and through these channels radiated from London out to the provinces and, as the correspondence of John Chamberlain testifies, to the continent.[8] The formulaic language of corruption deployed by these verse libels may have lacked political and historical specificity, but it is precisely because of this looseness that it was able to provide a flexible and dynamic framework for comprehending, talking about, and linking events in terms of their effect on the health of the commonwealth.

The marriage celebrations offered the supporters of the Earl and Countess of Somerset a public opportunity to combat the verse libels and to defend the couple's reputation. Two of the marriage masques were published in 1614: Thomas Campion's *Somerset Masque*, performed on the wedding night, and *The Masque of Flowers*, put on by Gray's Inn and sponsored by Sir Francis Bacon. George Chapman's epithalamion for the couple, *Andromeda Liberata, or the Nuptials of Perseus and Andromeda*, was intended to confront the slanders and rumours head-on. The volume was licensed by four members of the Privy Council who had supported the marriage: Frances's father, the Earl of Suffolk, Esmé Stuart, Earl of Lennox, John Erskine, Earl of Mar, and Julius Caesar.[9] This unusual step may have been because senior members of the Stationers' Company responsible for licensing books were anxious about the status of the work, whether it would cause offence to the Earl of Essex, or perhaps even the Earl and Countess of Somerset. Chapman's epithalamion demonstrates the way in which the oral and manuscript cultures in which rumours and libels circulated were not distinct from print cultures but were interconnected through a range of practices. The prefatory material to the poem, the epistle 'To the prejudicate and peremptory Reader' and the dedicatory verse 'To the Right Worthily Honored, Robert Earle of Sommerset, etc. and his most Noble Lady the Ladie Frances', gives the volume a topicality by reconstructing the immediate context in which the text was making an intervention, in this case, the rumours and gossip that surrounded the divorce and wedding. These slanderous rumours have their source both in court faction and vulgar, '*Plebeian*' opinion.[10] Chapman clearly indicated that it was the Countess's reputation that had come under particular attack:

> And you, (most noble) Lady as in blood
> In minde be Noblest, make our factious brood
> Whose forked tongs, wold fain your honor sting
> Convert their venomd points into their spring:
> Whose owne harts guilty, of faults faind in yours.

The epithalamion itself stages the rescue of Andromeda–Frances by Perseus–Robert from the monstrous whale which is another figure for the slanderous rumours circulating in the period.[11] The dedicatory verse similarly characterises the situation in terms of the triumph of stoic aristocratic virtue, embodied in the Earl and Countess, over the forces of court faction and '*Opinions* prou'd / By vulgar *Voices*.'[12] Yet, because of the effort required to combat vulgar opinion, it seems to dominate the volume, leaving the impression that the couple have not been and cannot remain entirely unaffected. Chapman's attitude towards publicness is ambivalent; the volume sets out to reform public perception of the marriage by combating the rumours through the mechanisms of print, hence engaging in a battle over the public sphere, while advising the Earl and Countess to withdraw from a public sphere which is populated by scandal, envy, and opinion. The verse makes a complex equation of stoic withdrawal with the *arcana imperii*:

> And as, the Royall Beast, whose image you
> Beare in your armes, and aires great Eagle too;
> Still as they goe, are said to keepe in close
> Their feres, and Tallons, lest their points shold lose
> Their useful sharpnes, when they serve no use.[13]

Yet, the direction of the analogy is unclear: stoic withdrawal itself becomes a site of contamination as Chapman advises the reader to look inside 'Our owne fowle bosomes [...] before / We ransacke others,' this advice then has to be quickly distanced from the Countess as irrelevant to her situation, 'leave / These Rules to them they touch.'[14] The distinctions that the poem needs to maintain between public opinion and private withdrawal, truth and opinion, panegyric and scandal often seem in danger of collapsing under the weight of the task it has set itself.

Chapman's public defence of the couple's reputation, rather than putting pay to rumour, generated further controversy. Soon after *Andromeda Liberata* appeared, he felt compelled to publish *A Free and offenceles justification of a lately publisht and most maliciously misinterpreted Poeme: Entituled Andromeda liberata*, complaining that 'the violent hoobub, setting my song to their owne tunes, have made it yeeld so harsh and distastefull as sound to my best friends, that my Integritie, even they hold, affected with the shrill eccho thereof, by reflexion.'[15] Chapman paints a vivid picture of the circulation of rumour, talk, and scandal in which his own poem has been appropriated by popular opinion, 'the violent hoobub', and assimilated to its practices. Images of contamination dominate the defence: he denies that he had any intent to mix the 'noble [...] with the grosse substance of the vulgar'[16] in *Andromeda Liberata* and counters accusations that he is 'a *Satyrist* or *Libeller*' who plays 'with worthie mens reputations.'[17] The defence takes the form of a dialogue between Pheme and Theodines. Pheme, the representative of public opinion, the 'Peoples god-voice', claims Chapman's *Andromeda Liberata* has 'scandald' Somerset,[18] and calls on Theodines–Chapman to defend passages in his poem that have caused particular offence, such as the 'Homicides' and the barren rock – precisely those aspects of the poem that were felt to cast aspersions on Essex's virility. The debate between Theodines and Pheme is a contest between contrasting models of a public sphere, one idealized, elite, and exclusive, the other satirized, plebeian, and open:

> THEO: O thou with peoples breaths and bubbles fild,
> Ever delivered, evermore with childe:
> How Court and Citty burnish with thy breede
> Of newes and nifles? seasoning all their feede
> With nothing, but what onely (drest like thee)
> Of surfet tasts and superfluitie? [...]

[...] On the cloven feete
Of thy *Chymaera* tost from streete to streete;
Our *Perseus* skornes to skuffle with the prease
Or like th'inconstant Moone be, that like these
Makes her selfe readie by her glasse the seas
The common *Rendes vous* of all rude streames:
And fed in some part, with our common *Thames*
As that is hourely serv'd with sewers and sinckes.

Panegyric, championed by Theodines, functions to magnify the virtue of the patron, to put in circulation an image that would evoke admiration, awe, and deference, and relies for its effect on a hierarchical public sphere that is dependent on the monarch's or the aristocratic patron's grace. Chapman describes the situation in 1614 as a time when panegyric although it 'skornes to skuffle with the prease' is nonetheless forced against its better judgment to walk to another tune, and rub shoulders with satire, libel, and rumour.

Andromeda Liberata was forced to walk to another tune in a copy of a libel on the Somersets, 'A proper new ballad to the tune of why do me no harme good man or the cleane contrary way' ('There was an old ladd rode on an old padde'), in a miscellany owned by an Inns of Court man, Richard Roberts. This version differs from others in that it includes details of its 'publication' and an explanatory note which wittily sketch out a context for the ballad in the 1616 trial of the Somersets for the murder of Sir Thomas Overbury:

> Imprinted in Poules church yard at the signe of the yellow Band and Cuffes by Adam Arsincke for Robert Roseare, and are to be sould at the Andromeda Liberata in Turnbull streete. Andro: Liberata was the title of a booke made by George Chapman dedicated to the earle of Essex wife from whom she was divorst causa frigidatatis.[19]

This parody of the imprimatur which authorised the printed book seems to revel in the liberties that can be taken when publishing verses through manuscript channels as opposed to print. Yet, at the same time, it does not hold to a clear-cut opposition between the worlds of manuscript and print, and instead gives an impression of creative and sometimes antagonistic dialogue between the two media and an environment in which books and texts in manuscript were traded, exchanged, and read alongside one another. *Andromeda Liberata* is once again caught up in the language of scandal and libel and its notoriety is such that it has become a recognisable symbol of the battle for reputation and textual authority that was currently being waged through the medium of print, manuscript, and talk.

Both *Andromeda Liberata* and its defence, *A Free and offenceles justification*, were published by Laurence Lisle. In the same year, he also published *Sir Thomas Overbury, His Wife*. It has been argued that this volume was part of the defamation campaign against the Earl and Countess of Somerset.[20] Sir Thomas Overbury, who opposed the marriage, had been confined to the Tower where he died on 15 September 1613. On 13 December, just under two weeks before the wedding on 26

December, Lisle entered *Sir Thomas Overbury, His Wife, Now a Widowe* in the Stationers' Register. Lisle clearly had an interest in the Somerset marriage, but it is an open question as to whether he was politically or commercially motivated. *Sir Thomas Overbury, His Wife* appears to have been put together by Lisle with an eye to a market with a taste for satirical sketches.[21] The 'News' and 'Characters', on the whole, are general satires that draw heavily on a language of corruption. The volume was very popular in 1614: five impressions appeared during that year and the fourth impression, *A Wife, Now the Widdow of Sir Thomas Overburye*, advertised that it was enlarged and the letter of the 'Printer to the Reader' is dated 16 May 1614. The rumours and talk surrounding the Somerset marriage may have given life to the generalised satire of the various 'News' and 'Characters', that often have a misogynistic or anti-court edge, even if the volume was not intended as part of an organised campaign. The ninth edition, published in 1616 following the trial of the Earl and Countess of Somerset for the murder of Sir Thomas Overbury, *Sir Thomas Overbury, His Wife, with New Elegies upon his (now knowne) vntimely death*, is more suggestive of a volume produced with a specific objective in mind and includes new elegies which see the Overbury murder as symbolising the degeneracy of the court.

Frances Howard's uncle, Henry Howard, Earl of Northampton, also seems to have been the target of a defamation campaign in this period. Late in 1612, he moved quickly against one of Prince Henry's chaplains, Bayley, for a sermon preached at St Martins just over a week after the prince's death. Soon after, he brought Henry Vernon, Sir Richard Cox, Thomas Lake, Serjeant Mynours, Thomas Goodrick, and James Ingram before the Star Chamber where they were arrested and fined for circulating rumours of a rift in the Privy Council between Archbishop Abbot and Northampton, that since Northampton had been made Lord Warden of the Cinque Ports more priests had entered than before, and that he had written to Cardinal Bellarmine telling him to ignore his book against Father Garnet and the Gunpowder plotters as it was only written to appease James. Linda Levy Peck has argued that this was part of an organised campaign against Northampton to prevent him from becoming Lord Treasurer. Late 1612 was certainly a turbulent time at court; Prince Henry's court was in the process of being dissolved, and there was much jostling for office and a flood of rumours speculating on candidates.[22] Yet these attacks on Northampton were not just about his fitness for office, but fed into a wider discoursing on court corruption and rumours of a Papist conspiracy to overthrow the Protestant religion. When Bayley was called upon to justify himself, Chamberlain reported that he did so 'so soundly' and with 'a very great audience' that he succeeded in making the matter more plain, while other preachers 'begin to speake freely' on the same matter and 'they make themselves understoode though they kepe within compasse.'[23] Northampton's attempts to silence his detractors through the Star Chamber proved counterproductive. The rumours continued throughout 1613 and into 1614. Henry Wotton wrote to Sir Edmund Bacon in May 1613 of a case Northampton had brought against Sir Peter Buck for a letter he had written 'containing this news "that some of the Lords had kneeled down to the King for a toleration in religion", besides some particular aspersion in the said letter of my Lord Privy Seal, whom likewise of late a preacher or two have disquieted.'[24] Again, in February 1614, Northampton brought a case against Sir Stephen Proctor before the Star Chamber. Proctor had suggested that Northampton and Wotton had suppressed evidence and discredited witnesses in the case of two Yorkshire knights suspected of involvement in the Gunpowder plot. Much to Northampton's annoyance, the councillors were divided over the sentencing, and he was reported as complaining 'that he neded not to have ben so nice, having precedents of some great persons that have geven sentence in causes that concerned themselves.'[25]

January 1614 was a highly unsettled time at court which may have added to Northampton's sensitivity to rumour. Chamberlain wrote to Dudley Carleton of the scramble for office: 'for here is such discoursing, such working, plotting and supplanting, that what stands right to day is awrie to morrow, and every day brings new alterations.'[26] Talk also began in earnest in late January that a parliament would be called before Easter and there were rumours of packing even before it had been opened. By early March, Chamberlain prophesied that all this talk and activity would disturb the new parliament: 'Here is much bustling for places in parlement, and letters flie from great personages extraordinarilie, wherin me thinckes they do the King no great service, seeing the world is apt to conceave that yt is a kind of packing.'[27] On 20 March, George Wither was arrested. As David Norbrook has pointed out, the timing of Wither's arrest during the elections for parliament was significant. His imprisonment was almost certainly organised by Northampton who may have seen himself satirised in the 'Man-like monster' of Wither's *Abuses Stript, and Whipt*.[28] Northampton had opposed a new parliament due to concern that it would provide a platform for whipping up public opinion against Spain and so may have wanted to discourage potential troublemakers like Wither.[29] *Abuses Stript, and Whipt* was highly popular and went into eight editions between 1613 and 1617, five of those in the first year. There was even a pirated edition that came to the attention of the authorities on 20 February 1614.[30] Wither complained in a new passage incorporated into the 1615 edition of *Abuses Stript, and Whipt* that the popularity of his satire had led to his downfall:

> [...] heere's the reason they my labour like,
> *They thinke I meane him they suppose I strike.*
> So shall my well-meant lines become to be
> A wrong to others, and a plague to me.
> Heaven shield me from such monsters: for their breath
> Is worse than blasting, and their praise is death.[31]

Pritchard comments that he 'may have suffered as much from the enthusiasm of admirers who persisted in reading personal satire on Northampton into *Abuses* and thus gave the work a dangerous reputation.'[32] It may have been the case that the text became part of a defamation campaign against Northampton, irrespective of Wither's own intentions. That said, in both *Abuses Stript, and Whipt* and his *Prince Henries Obsequies*, he does attack specific, if unnamed courtiers on the basis of their sympathy with Spain and Catholics, even to the extent of urging Prince

Charles to purge his court of such men when he is created Prince of Wales. What this passage also indicates is that once published, a printed book could take on a life outside of its own pages. As Chapman had lamented in relation to his *Andromeda Liberata*, books could be 'talked up', reconstituted through channels of rumour, and in this way achieve a circulation that was not solely dependent on the number of printed copies in circulation.

As we have seen earlier, Wither turned his arrest into a battle over the public sphere. In *The Shepherds Hunting* and *A Satyre: Dedicated to his Most Excellent Majestie*, those responsible for his imprisonment were evil counsellors, abusers of public language, who have led England into tyranny. Northampton's sensitivity to slander and care for his reputation was related to his absolutist sense of the public sphere as identifiable with the king and his peers. Wither does not seem to have been brought before the Star Chamber, instead his warrant was signed by privy councillors at Northampton House where meetings were held during Northampton's illness.[33] The Privy Council could function as a court in a similar way to Star Chamber and it did not keep records. In the case of Stephen Proctor earlier in the year, Northampton had invoked the power of ministers to imprison at will in the name of the Privy Council and since the death of Salisbury he had dominated the Council. The charge of *scandalum magnatum* used by Northampton in his defamation cases brought before the Star Chamber was an extension of the royal prerogative and part of the rhetoric of the divine right of kings.[34] The way that Northampton was using *scandalum magnatum* was perceived by contemporaries as unprecedented, even tyrannical, in that it served his own private purposes rather than the preservation of public order as it was originally intended. Chamberlain wrote that:

> howsoever these fines be executed or no (as most men beleve they will not, but that only yt was don *in terrorem*) yet the precedent is thought straunge, and the Lord hath got no great advantage, but only this, that men must learne not to speake of the great ones *ni en bien ni en mal*.[35]

Wotton commented on the case that Northampton brought before the Star Chamber in May 1613 that 'he hath been moved, besides his own nature and (as some think also) besides his wisdom, to call these things into public discourse, *quae spreta exolescunt*, if ancient grave sentences do not deceive us.' The passage is from Tacitus and refers to the 'prosecution of Cremutius Cordus upon the novel and till then unheard-of charge of publishing a history, eulogising Brutus, and styling Cassius the last of the Romans'; the supposed crime was not covered by law of treason and therefore the charge was an act of despotism.[36]

Wither's defence in *A Satyre: Dedicated to his Most Excellent Majestie* rests on the conventional distinction between libel and satire. The subject of satire is general vice and it is motivated by a public concern for the health of the commonwealth. Libel, by contrast, is directed at particular individuals and motivated by private malice. The anonymity of libel and its association with court faction meant that it could be seen as an abuse of public language. By insisting on the distinction between satire and libel, Wither elevates satire as a literary form, identifying it with the language of counsel. In corrupt times, satire rather than panegyric is the representative genre of the public sphere and, tellingly, *A Satyre* opens with the Juvenalian complaint '*Tis a hard thing not to write Satyrs*, now.'[37] Wither has a strong sense of the writer's public duty to condemn vice that is shaped by Foxe's *Acts and Monuments* and so is expressed in oppositional terms. The poet as Protestant martyr is characterised by heroic acts of resistance to corrupt and hostile authorities and by speaking boldly in defence of truth in spite of the consequences.[38] His imprisonment in 1614 was therefore a confirmation of his poetic vocation. From now on, his poems are dramas of contestation which play out a conflict between tyrannical authorities and the poet, the lone defender of Truth. His justification of his satire uses similar strategies to the Martin Marprelate pamphlets. In *An Epistle*, Marprelate challenged the authorities to prove 'my book to be a libell' and boasted that he had 'prevented you of that advantage in lawe, both in bringing in nothing but matters of fact, which may easily be prooved, if you dare denie them: and also in setting my name to my booke.'[39] Wither is similarly careful to point out that he brought his satires into 'open view' and insists on the absolute truth of his satire. Defamation was a particularly unstable offence and to a certain extent reversible in that those accused could claim to have been themselves the victim of a slander by insisting that their words were true or misrepresented and that the charge against them was itself motivated by malice.[40] This is Wither's defence but, like the Marprelate pamphlets, he places further pressure on the already unstable concept of libel by using it to provoke discussion over the concept of public debate itself – how words enter the public sphere and who determines their legitimacy. Wither explicitly links libel laws with censorship through his account of a conspiracy to close down public debate on issues affecting the commonwealth.

Wither's attitude to libel and its sphere of circulation is, however, marked by certain inconsistencies as the implied equation between his own writings and '*Closet-whisperings*' in the opening quote from *The Shepherds Hunting* suggests. *A Satyre* encourages, while distancing itself from, interpretive practices associated with verse libel.[41] Like Chapman, he is troubled by the way that words are entering a public sphere where the relationship between words and authorial intention is highly unstable. Their anxiety over the mobility of words is symptomatic of the growth and vitality of a market for rumour and verse libels in this period. Wither distances himself from this market but then sets out a hypothetical case in his *A Satyre* which leaves the reader with the strong impression that his 'Man-like Monster' is to be read as referring to a particular individual at court.[42] The difference between satire and libel then is not its subject, whether it is general or particular, or even necessarily its words, but rather its intent, in that satire is motivated by the public good and not malice, and its mode of publication, as satire is public and authored while libel is private and anonymous. These slippages between satire and libel point to broader conceptual problems in formulating the relationship between libel and the public sphere. Pauline Croft has argued for political libels as the expression of 'an active public opinion', while Tom Cogswell, drawing on the work of Robert Darnton, speaks of the oral and scribal production and circulation of verse libels in terms of an '"underground" market [that] arguably was as close to a mass media as early Stuart England ever achieved.'[43] The question arises as to what kind of public we are talking about since these 'closet-writings' and Cogswell's 'underground market' cannot easily be mapped onto a Habermasian model of the public sphere which relies on a civic and print-based notion of publicness. One answer is that there were different kinds of public and concepts of publicness available in this period so that the early modern public sphere was not singular and homogeneous but multiple and heterogeneous, and therefore can be conceived of in terms of a 'plurality of competing publics', in the words of Nancy Fraser, existing within a stratified society.[44] Wither has a civic and print-based understanding of publicness. The entrance of *Abuses Stript and Whipt* into this 'underground media' is a cause of anxiety for Wither, but rather than close this public down, he seems to want to reform it by turning libels into satires and bringing them into 'open view'.[45]

William Browne's *The Shepheards Pipe* was entered in the Stationers' Register while Wither was still in the Marshalsea. Wither appears as Roget in the first eclogue as well as contributing his own eclogue to the volume. His presence means that the volume's anti-court stance takes on a contemporary specificity, and readers could find an analogue for the shepherds defending the 'country' values of liberty and free speech in the situation of the imprisoned Wither and his poet friends. This is certainly the way that one contemporary responded to the volume. Richard Brathwaite in his *A Strappado for the Divell* (1615) commends Wither, Browne, John Selden, and Brooke as a group of poets that are able to counsel the court on its failings 'freely, (as full well they may)', even though some 'have bin mew'd up for't', and contrasts their free speaking to the constraints imposed by patronage in such corrupt times, when poets 'write not for respect, or due esteeme, / Had to their profession, but to gaine / The favour of a great one.'[46] Wither's *The Shepherds Hunting* was entered in the Stationers' Register in late October 1614 by the same bookseller, George Norton, who had published *A Shepheards Pipe* and had acquired the copyright to *Abuses Stript, and Whipt* in 1614. Wither's collection of eclogues is a sequel to *The Shepheards Pipe*, and assimilates the earlier volume to a pro-Wither campaign. The poets involved in *The Shepheards Pipe* re-appear in *The Shepherds Hunting* as his loyal friends who are visiting him in the Marshalsea. At the beginning of the second eclogue, he has Cuddy/Brooke inform the reader that his cause is being spread abroad so that 'at all meetings where our *Shepheards* be, / Now the maine Newes that's extant is of thee.'[47] His cause is no longer a private concern but 'Newes' circulating in the public domain through talk and, implicitly, texts such as *The Shepheards Pipe*, *The Shepherds Hunting*, and his defence *A Satyre: Dedicated to his Most Excellent Majestie*.

The Shepheards Pipe is not just a defence of Wither, but stages its own intervention in literary culture. The collection is a conscious revival of the genre of pastoral satire that was stimulated, in part, by the recent Somerset marriage. As Chapman's situation testifies, because the couple's reputations were deeply compromised and tainted by scandal, poets confronted in a clear-cut way 'the deep-seated problems of panegyric or epideictic art.'[48] Browne's dedicatory verse to Lord Edward Zouche is in danger of subverting itself as the poet draws a clear dividing line between those poets who engage in undiscriminating flattery and his own language of praise, ending tersely 'I scorn to flatter but the men I hate.'[49] The seventh eclogue of Browne's *The Shepheards Pipe* is a veiled satire on the Somerset marriage. The eclogue is a type of anti-epithalamion which relates Palinode's attempts to dissuade his friend, Hobinoll, from marriage with Phillis, and has a satiric sharpness and specificity that calls for contemporary analogues. It functions in a similar fashion to the verse libels by opening the divorce and marriage to public speculation. Browne and Brooke will contribute elegies to the 1616 volume *Sir Thomas Overburie His Wife with new Elegies upon his (now knowne) untimely death* condemning the leniency shown to the Earl and Countess of Somerset following their conviction for Overbury's murder.

The second eclogue in the collection similarly appears to be playing out divisions in the political culture of Jacobean London in the wake of the Somerset marriage and the following build up to the 1614 'Addled' parliament. It mobilises a satiric 'court'/'country' opposition that pits Willie/Browne and his friends, Jockie and Weptol, against a swineherd, and the eclogue closes with the shepherd community vowing to produce satires to 'rid him fro our plaines.'[50] Jockie and Weptol also appear to be pastoral pseudonyms, possibly for John Selden, whom Brathwaite included amongst this group, and John Powlet or Poulett, a student of the Middle Temple and member for Somerset in the 1610 and 1614 parliaments.[51] The eclogue locates itself within the environment of the Inns of Court and tavern societies, with the swineherd usually to be found loitering at the 'Ale-house door'.[52] Kathleen Tillotson has argued that the swineherd is a pun on Bacon. Bacon was no friend of Brooke and his fellow MPs: in 1613, when exploring means of controlling parliament to James's advantage, he had delighted in the apparent collapse of opposition from the previous 1610 parliament, and prematurely announced Brooke's death.[53] Early in the 1614 parliament, a dispute had arisen over his membership of the House while remaining the king's Attorney General which was fuelled by rumours that members were being approached to manage the House in the king's personal interests. Moreover, Bacon's Inn, Gray's Inn, had recently produced the *Masque of Flowers*, which he had sponsored, for the Somerset marriage. There may have been some tension between the Inns over this event as they appear to have had distinct, if changing, political and factional allegiances.[54]

Both *The Shepheards Pipe* and *The Shepherds Hunting* participate in the circulation of talk by narrativising contemporary events, such as Wither's imprisonment, through the medium of anti-court satire which itself relies on a politicised language of court corruption. *The Shepherds Hunting*, in particular, stages itself as an event, taking place at a particular historical moment, by reconstructing the circumstances and conditions behind its production. At the same time, these volumes conceptualise by their very form the type of public sphere that would make such public debate possible. The print community they describe gives the impression of an actual community that exists just beyond the text. The pastoral metaphor of the shepherd poet could be said to have become metonymic: as Joan

Grundy has noted, Willy is William Browne, Cuddy is Christopher Brooke, Roget is George Wither.[55] Through this type of deixis, these eclogues are located in a recognisable London environment, that of the Inns of Court and tavern societies. This print community has a materiality, in that it is constituted by actual social relationships and practices, but it is also an imagined community that relies on cultural fictions. The predominant language of community employed by these poets is that of friendship, which is assimilated to a model of counsel to project an idealised social space in which friends meet to exchange ideas freely and to discuss contemporary issues affecting the health of the commonwealth. This space is dramatised in the exchange between Willy and Cuddy in the fifth eclogue of *The Shepheards Pipe* which is dedicated to Brooke. Its chosen theme, the relationship between poetry and counsel, moves a private discussion between friends into the realms of public debate. Browne is encouraging Brooke to set his *The Ghost of Richard the Third* before the public, and the eclogue reflects on what this might mean in 1614. Pastoral is combined with georgic to bring pastoral into the public domain. Like Spenser before him, Browne took a georgic view of poetry which sees it as a redemptive, cultivating labour akin to a humanist concept of counsel. Willy and Cuddy are portrayed as 'countrymen' whereby the shepherd–poet is translated into a citizen actively tending the political landscape of the commonwealth. The eclogue stages a debate about issues of freedom of speech that were also engaging Brooke in parliament. The idealised public sphere that would enable such a debate to take place is constituted dialectically through a structural opposition to a state of tyranny. Brooke, in his companion eclogue dedicated to Browne in the same volume, defended intellectual freedom within a context of political repression: 'Thought hath no prison and the minde is free / Under the greatest King and tyrannie.'[56] Willy's response to tyranny in the fifth eclogue is to enthusiastically insist on the ethical and political autonomy of the poet, boldly advising Cuddy that 'Thou canst give more to kings then kings to thee,'[57] and 'if ther's none deserves what thou canst doe, / Be then the Poet and the Patron too.'[58] The poet, released from the constraining structures of court culture, assumes an autonomy that qualifies him as a cultural spokesman.

Christopher Brooke is a particularly interesting figure. He was a professional lawyer who was the member for York in all of James's parliaments, and clearly saw his poetry as a counterpart to membership of parliament, in that it was a medium through which he actively participated in the political life of the commonwealth.[59] *The Ghost of Richard the Third* is a study of court tyranny. There is evidence that histories of Richard III were used against Robert Cecil, and it is possible that Brooke's poem may have once been intended as part of the defamation campaign that Croft has identified.[60] The history of Richard III provided a particular formulation of tyranny which related it to the failure of counsel, and the figure of Richard, especially in terms of his rise to power, took on the appearance of the evil counsellor. Brooke's Richard does have associations with the evil counsellor and he concentrates on his perversion of public language and his use of faction to overthrow a weak monarchical state. The evil counsellor had wider political implications and can also be read as symbolising the breakdown of the relationship between the king and conciliar institutions, such as parliament. The 1610 and 1614 parliaments have been characterised in terms of a communications breakdown between king and Commons. Much of the disagreement arose over impositions – whether they were part of the king's prerogative, or a form of taxation that should be legislated by parliament. Brooke put the case in the 1614 parliament that James was in danger of using his absolute prerogative against the liberty and property of the subject: 'If the King may impose by his absolute power, then no man can be certain what he has, for it shall be subject to the King's pleasure.'[61] *The Ghost of Richard the Third* moves beyond the figure of the evil counsellor to develop a definition of tyranny able to incorporate monarchical absolutism which is not thought to take place until the 1640s.[62]

Brooke was part of a working group in the 1610 and 1614 parliaments that included his friends John Hoskins, Richard Martin, William Hakewill, and Robert Phelips.[63] John Hoskins has become notorious for his speeches in the last days of the 1614 'Addled' parliament, and Brooke, Hakewill, and Phelips were probably amongst those members who had their papers on impositions burnt soon after its dissolution. The summoning of parliament intensified talk in 1614; it brought members of the political elite into London from the provinces and threw issues to do with counsel, and public language in general, into sharp relief. Chamberlain reported that the news of the impending dissolution of parliament had been greeted in the Commons with 'many bold and petulant speaches':

> The truth is yt shold seeme by theyre cariage, and by that I have heard from some of them, that there was never knowne a more disorderly house, and that yt was many times more like a cockpit then a grave counsaile, and many sat there that were more fit to have ben among roaring boyes then in that assemblie.[64]

It is important to note that Hoskins and his friends in parliament, Brooke, Hakewill, Martin, and Phelips, were also leading figures in the London tavern societies and Inns of Court circles that were responsible for much of the production and circulation of verse libels and satires in the period. It leaves us with the question, what was the relationship between counsel and this type of disorderly discourse described by Chamberlain, with its connections to oppositional politics and the world of roaring boys and the cockpit? One way of answering this question, as I have been suggesting in this essay, is in terms of a plurality of political languages that are located in and arise out of the practices of a number of different communities that are jostling for public space in the early seventeenth century.[65]

Notes

[1] George Wither, *The Shepherds Hunting: Being, Certain Eglogs written during the time of the Authors Imprisonment in the Marshalsey* (London, 1615), sig. B5v.

[2] Anne Lake Prescott, 'Evil Tongues at the Court of Saul: the Renaissance David as Slandered Courtier', *The Journal of Medieval and Renaissance Studies*, 21 (1991), 163–86 (pp. 166, 168).

[3] *Letters of John Chamberlain*, I, 499.

[4] David Lindley, 'Embarrassing Ben: The Masques for Frances Howard', *English Literary Review*, 16 (1986), 343–59 (p. 347).

[5] For a discussion of these verses, see David Lindley, *The Trials of Frances Howard: Fact and Fiction at the Court of King James* (London and New York: Routledge, 1993), pp. 115–17.

[6] Pauline Croft, 'The Reputation of Robert Cecil: Libels, Political Opinion and Popular Awareness in the Early Seventeenth Century', *Transactions of the Royal Historical Society*, 1 (1991), 43–69 (pp. 46–7); Cyndia Susan Clegg, *Press Censorship in Elizabethan England* (Cambridge: Cambridge University Press, 1997), pp. 202, 215.

[7] Croft, 'Reputation of Robert Cecil', p. 63.

[8] Alastair Bellany, '"Raylinge Rymes and Vaunting Verse": Libellous Politics in Early Stuart England, 1603–1628', in *Culture and Politics in Early Stuart England*, ed. by Kevin Sharpe and Peter Lake (Basingstoke and London: Macmillan, 1994), pp. 285–310 (pp. 290–1).

[9] A. R. Braunmuller, 'Robert Carr, Earl of Somerset, as Collector and Patron', in *The Mental World of the Jacobean Court*, ed. by Linda Levy Peck (Cambridge: Cambridge University Press, 1991), pp. 230–50 (pp. 242–3).

[10] George Chapman, *Andromeda Liberata. Or the nuptials of Perseus and Andromeda* (London, 1614), sig. ¶3r.

[11] For a discussion of Chapman's epithalamion, see Lindley, *Trials of Frances Howard*, pp. 131–2, 135–6, 139–41.

[12] Chapman, *Andromeda Liberata*, sig. ¶3r.

[13] Chapman, *Andromeda Liberata*, sig. ¶¶3v.

[14] Chapman, *Andromeda Liberata*, sig. ¶¶3v.

[15] George Chapman, *A Free and offenceles justification of a lately publisht and most maliciously misinterpreted Poeme: Entituled Andromeda Liberata* (London, 1614), in *The Poems of George Chapman*, ed. by Phyllis Brooks Bartlett (New York: Modern Language Association; London: Oxford University Press, 1941), p. 329.

[16] *Poems of George Chapman*, p. 328.

[17] *Poems of George Chapman*, p. 330.

[18] *Poems of George Chapman*, p. 330.

[19] University of Oxford, Bodleian Library, MS Don.c.54, fol. 24r. See also *The Poems of Sir John Davies*, ed. by Robert Krueger (Oxford: Clarendon Press, 1975), pp. 438–9; and Arthur Marotti, *Manuscript, Print, and the English Renaissance Lyric* (Ithaca and London: Cornell University Press, 1995), pp. 36–7, 327. Margaret Crum lists three other copies of this ballad (*First-Line Index of English Poetry 1500–1800 in Manuscripts of the Bodleian Library Oxford*, 2 vols (Oxford: Oxford University Press, 1969), II, 906. Roberts exchanged verses with other Inns of Court men and may have been on the margins of an Inns of Court circle gathered around John Hoskins, Richard Martin, John Donne, and Christopher Brooke,

(referred to later in this essay), which played a prominent role in the political culture of Jacobean London. The miscellany includes a rare copy of a Latin poem attributed to Hoskins, *Convivium Philosophicum*, which commemorates a meeting of this circle at the Mitre Tavern, and identifies a number of the participants in the margin (Bodleian, MS Don.c.54, fols 21ʳ–22ʳ).

[20] *The 'Conceited Newes' of Sir Thomas Overbury and his Friends*, ed. by James E. Savage (Gainesville, Florida: Scholars' Facsimiles and Reprints, 1968), pp. xv–xvi.

[21] Amongst the contributors, James Savage has identified Ben Jonson, John Donne, John Cooke (who contributed a commendatory verse to *Volpone*), Sir Thomas Roe (a friend of Donne), William Strachey, Benjamin Rudyerd, Anne Clifford, Lady Sackville, Sir Ralph Shelton, Lady Southwell (daughter of Charles Howard, Earl of Nottingham), Sir Henry Wotton, John Webster, and Thomas Dekker.

[22] 26 November 1612, *Letters of John Chamberlain*, I, 394; Linda Levy Peck, *Northampton: Patronage and Policy at the Court of James I* (London: George Allen and Unwin, 1982), pp. 81–2.

[23] 17 December 1612, *Letters of John Chamberlain*, I, 396.

[24] *The Life and Letters of Sir Henry Wotton*, ed. by Logan Pearsall Smith, 2 vols (Oxford: Clarendon Press, 1907), II, 22–23.

[25] 17 February 1614, *Letters of John Chamberlain*, I, 509.

[26] 5 January 1614, *Letters of John Chamberlain*, I, 499.

[27] 3 March 1614, *Letters of John Chamberlain*, I, 515.

[28] Allan Pritchard, '*Abuses Stript and Whipt* and Wither's Imprisonment', *Review of English Studies*, 14 (1963), 337–45 (pp. 340–1).

[29] David Norbrook, *Poetry and Politics in the English Renaissance* (London: Routledge & Kegan Paul, 1984), p. 10.

[30] *Records of the Stationers' Company, 1602 to 1640*, ed. by William A. Jackson (London: The Bibliographical Society, 1957), p. 73; William A. Jackson, 'Counterfeit Printing in Jacobean Times', *The Library*, 15 (1934–35), 364–76 (pp. 364–6).

[31] George Wither, *Abuses Stript, and Whipt* (London, 1615), p. 45.

[32] Pritchard, 'Wither's Imprisonment', p. 345.

[33] The warrant was signed by Northampton, the Duke of Lennox, Charles Howard, Earl of Nottingham, the Earl of Suffolk, Gilbert Talbot, Earl of Shrewsbury, Edward Somerset, Earl of Worcester, the Earl of Pembroke, Lord Knollys, Sir Henry Wotton, and Sir Thomas Egerton, Lord Ellesmere. *Acts of the Privy Council of England, 1613–1614* (London, 1921), XXXIII, 391.

[34] J. H. Baker, *An Introduction to English Legal History*, 3rd ed. (London: Butterworths, 1990), p. 538; Peck, p. 83.

[35] *Letters of John Chamberlain*, I, 396.

[36] 17 December 1612, *Letters of John Chamberlain*, I, 396; 7 May 1613, *Letters of Wotton*, II, 23; *Tacitus*, trans. by John Jackson, 5 vols (Cambridge, Mass.: Harvard University Press; London: William Heinemann, 1920), IV, 59–63.

[37] George Wither, *A Satyre: Dedicated to his Most Excellent Majestie* (London, 1614), A6ᵛ.

[38] John R. Knott, *Discourses of Martyrdom in English Literature, 1563–1694* (Cambridge: Cambridge University Press, 1993), p. 8.

[39] Quoted in Clegg, *Press Censorship*, p. 189.

[40] M. Lindsay Kaplan, *The Culture of Slander in Early Modern England* (Cambridge: Cambridge University Press, 1997), p. 16.

[41] This seems to be a characteristic of defences of satire against the charge of libel, see Clegg's discussion of the satires of the 1590s (*Press Censorship*, pp. 210–11). For further discussion of *A Satyre* and libel, see my *The 'Shepheards Nation' : Jacobean Spenserians and Early Stuart Political Culture* (Oxford: Clarendon Press, 2000) pp. 175–8.

[42] At his examination before the Privy Council in 1621 about a passage in his *Wither's Motto* where he said that he had witnessed the fall of his enemies, he replied that he meant 'the late Earle Northampton'. O'Callaghan, *Jacobean Spenserians*, pp. 185, 237.

[43] Croft, 'Reputation of Robert Cecil', p. 68; Thomas Cogswell, 'Underground Verse and the Transformation of Early Stuart Political Culture, in *Political Culture and Cultural Politics in Early Modern England*, ed. by Susan D. Amussen and Mark A. Kishlansky (Manchester and New York: Manchester University Press, 1995), pp. 277–300 (p. 287); Robert Darnton, *The Literary Underground of the Old Regime* (Cambridge, Mass. & London: Harvard University Press, 1982).

[44] Nancy Fraser, 'Rethinking the Public Sphere: A Contribution to the Critique of Actually Existing Democracy', in *Habermas and the Public Sphere*, ed. by Craig Calhoun (Cambridge, Mass, & London: M.I.T. Press, 1996), pp. 109–42 (p. 22).

[45] Wither, *Abuses Stript, and Whipt*, sig. B5[r].

[46] Richard Brathwaite, *A Strappado for the Divell. Epigrams and Satyres alluding to the time, with diuers measures of no lesse Delight* (London, 1615), sig. C3[v]–C4[r]. Another contributor to the volume, John Davies of Hereford, was also involved in a campaign against the imprisonment of his patron, Henry Percy, Earl of Northumberland. See Stephen Clucas, '"Noble virtue in extremes" : Henry Percy, ninth Earl of Northumberland, patronage and the politics of stoic consolation', *Renaissance Studies*, 9:3 (1995), 267-291 (pp. 273-80).

[47] Wither, *The Shepherds Hunting*, sig. C2[r].

[48] Lindley, 'Embarrassing Ben', pp. 348–9.

[49] William Browne, *The Shepheards Pipe* (London, 1614), sig. A2[r].

[50] Browne, *The Shepheards Pipe*, sig. D2[r].

[51] Powlet, along with Brooke and his fellow 'Sireniac' MPs, such as Robert Phelips, John Hoskyns, and Richard Martin, had placed verses before *Coryate's Crudities* (1611).

[52] Browne, *The Shepheards Pipe*, sig. D1[r].

[53] Kathleen Tillotson, 'Drayton, Browne, and Wither', *Times Literary Supplement*, 27 November 1937, p. 911; Clayton Roberts and Owen Duncan, 'The Parliamentary Undertaking of 1614', *English Historical Review*, 93 (1978), 481–98 (p. 489).

[54] Browne's Inn, the Inner Temple, had been closely associated with the Earl of Leicester under Elizabeth, while in the first half of James's reign, Gray's Inn was supported by the Bacon family and the Cecils (Norbrook, *Poetry and Politics*, p. 83; W. J. Loftie, *The Inns of Court and Chancery* (Southampton: Ashford Press, 1985), p. 71).

[55] Joan Grundy, *Spenserian Poets: A Study in Elizabethan and Jacobean Poetry* (London: Edward Arnold, 1969), p. 81. For further discussion of this print community, see my *The 'Shepheards Nation'*, pp. 35–41.

[56] Browne, *The Shepheards Pipe*, sig. F6[r].

[57] Browne, *The Shepheards Pipe*, sig. E3[v].

[58] Browne, *The Shepheards Pipe*, sig. E4[r].

[59] For further discussion of Brooke and his *Ghost of Richard the Third*, see my '"Talking Politics": Tyranny, Parliament, and Christopher Brooke's *The Ghost of Richard the Third* (1614)', *The Historical Journal*, 41 (1998), 97–120.

[60] Croft, 'Reputation of Robert Cecil', pp. 43–69; Margaret Hotine, '*Richard III* and *Macbeth* – Studies in Tudor Tyranny', *Notes and Queries*, 236 (1991), 480–86.

[61] *Proceedings, 1614*, p. 95.

[62] James Daly, 'The Idea of Absolute Monarchy in Seventeenth-Century England', *Historical Journal*, 21 (1978), 227–50 (p. 235); O'Callaghan, *Jacobean Spenserians*, pp. 78–81.

[63] Martin was not a member of the 1614 Parliament but he did appear in the House on behalf of the Virginia Company.

[64] 9 June 1614, *Letters of John Chamberlain*, I, 538.

[65] See also J. G. A Pocock, *Essays on Political Thought and History* (London: Methuen, 1972), pp. 16–20.

7

Purging Troubled Humours: Bacon, Northampton and the Anti-Duelling Campaign of 1613–1614

Alan Stewart

This paper was prompted by a passage in James's speech to both houses at the beginning of the Addled Parliament, on Tuesday 5 April 1614. Having pledged that he would be no merchant, James answers a complaint which has evidently been made against him:

> And whereas it is given out that my proclamations are instead of laws because of making my long proclamation against duels was not that they should be as laws but to express myself against fighting and massacring one another until such time as a statute could be made against it, which I conceived to be a godly action.[1]

An alternative version reads more vividly:

> I never mean by proclamation to assume the power of the law, but to all remedies where the mischief could not tarry for a law. In that of duels, I published it not as a law but I saw it a shame that for a lack of a law my people perished, and every shaghead fellow that came out of the Low Countries but with one sleeve was a lawmaker in this point what concerns reputation.[2]

James is defending one of two proclamations against duelling that he had issued within the past six months. These proclamations were in turn bolstered by other publications encouraging and justifying opposition to what was seen as a dangerous new vogue – indeed, Linda Levy Peck refers to 'a campaign against duelling'.[3] Why should a simple proclamation against duelling have caused the king to defend himself in the opening speech to the 1614 parliament? Trying to understand this, I found not so much a concerted campaign as a tale of conflict, both of institutions, and of personalities – namely, Henry Howard, Earl of Northampton, and Attorney General Sir Francis Bacon. While I do not venture a generalised argument based on what is, after all, a single issue debate, I believe it stands as a peculiarly suggestive example of the complexity of the issues facing the king and his advisers at the beginning of the Addled Parliament.

I start with the news of 9 September 1613, as forwarded from John Chamberlain in London to Sir Dudley Carleton:

> Though there be in shew a setled peace in these parts of the world yet the many private quarrells among the great ones prognosticat troubled humors which may breed daungerous diseases yf they be not purged and prevented. I doubt not but you have heard the successe of the combat betwixt Edward Sackvile and the Lord Bruse (or Kinlos) twixt Antwerp and Lille wherin they were both hurt, the Lord Bruse to the death so that Sackvile is driven to take Sanctuary, whence by corruption or connivence I heare he is escaped. Here is speach likewise that the Lord Norris and Sir Peregrin Willoughby are gon foorth for the same purpose, and that the Lord Chandos and the Lord Haye are upon the same termes. There was a quarrell kindling twixt the earles of Rutland and Montgomerie, but yt was quickly quenched by the King, beeing begun and ended in his presence. But there is more daunger twixt the earle of Rutland and the Lord Daves, though I heard yesterday yt was alredy, or upon the point of compounding. But that which most men listen after is what will fall out twixt the earl of Essex and Master Henry Howard, who is challeged and called to account by the earle for certain disgracefull speaches of him: they are both gotten over, the earle from Milford Haven, the other from Harwich, with ech of them two seconds [...].[4]

Chamberlain's letters are often studded with accounts of quarrels, some of them leading to duels, but what he diagnoses here is a more serious trend of 'troubled humors'. Commentators then and now have dealt with the duelling craze in various ways: as the natural outcome of a period of peace, 'a hot-blooded generation [growing] up on the stories of its gallant forefathers' exploits, and [pining] for chances to show its own mettle';[5] as the residue of a now outmoded sense of honour;[6] or as yet another unfortunate import from the overly temperamental French and Italians. Whatever the cause, it seems that the king was sincerely disturbed by the new national pastime, and determined to take steps to nip it in the bud.

The progression of the 'campaign' that bloomed from James's concern requires clarification. I shall be discussing five texts: a memorandum of advice from the Attorney General to the king; a proclamation dated October 1613; an account of a case heard in the Star Chamber in January 1613/14; a second proclamation dated February 1613/14; and a tract printed to accompany the second proclamation. These texts, which cross-reference each other, were evidently intended to form a single campaign, but it is the tacit discrepancies between them that interest me.

Probably in September 1613, either by commission or on his own initiative, the newly installed Attorney General, Sir Francis Bacon, presumably looking for an issue on which to make his mark, drew up a manuscript memorandum entitled 'A proposition for the repressing of singular combats and duels.'[7] He suggests that any ordinance that James might establish should 'not look back to any offence past, for that strikes before it warns.' He also wants it to 'be declared to be temporary, until a parliament; for that will be very acceptable to the parliament; and it is good to teach a parliament to work upon an edict or proclamation precedent.' The proclamation itself should be 'grave and severe [...] induced, by the overflow of the present mischief.' In suggesting due punishment, he points to the nature of the duellers: 'first, I consider that offence hath vogue only amongst noble persons, or persons of quality. I consider also that the greatest honour for subjects of quality in a lawful monarchy, is to have access and approach to their sovereign's sight and person, which is the fountain of honour; and though this be a comfort all persons of quality do not use; yet there is no good spirit but will think himself in darkness, if he be debarred of it.' He therefore advises that the offender 'be banished perpetually from approach to the courts of the King, Queen, or Prince.' Second, the offender should 'receive a strict prosecution by the King's attorney, *ore tenus*, in the Star-Chamber.' This prosecution should proceed 'without respect of persons, be the offender never so great'; the fine imposed should be 'irremissible'. Bacon spreads wide the proposed net of offenders: those taking part in any singular combat, even if death does not ensue; those 'pass[ing] beyond the seas' in order to fight a duel, even if the duel does not take place; anyone sending, accepting, carrying or delivering a challenge; anyone 'appoint[ing] the field, directly or indirectly, although it be not upon any cartel or challenge in writing'; and anyone agreeing to be a second.

The first proclamation, 'prohibiting the publishing of any reports or writings of Duels', was dated 15 October 1613.[8] There can be no doubt that Bacon's advice had been taken to heart, and in most cases implemented. However, a close reading points up some telling quibbles. Bacon advises strongly that the offender 'receive a strict prosecution by the King's attorney' – himself – '*ore tenus*, in the Star-Chamber', and explains that the *ore tenus* aspect was vital, 'for the fact being notorious, will always be confessed, and so made fit for an *ore tenus*.'[9] In the proclamation, the king would have offenders 'to bee brought *ore tenus*, or otherwise, as the case shall require in the Starrechamber', suggesting that there might be cases that would not be best heard *ore tenus*, and significantly omitting to mention the Attorney General.[10] Whereas Bacon suggests perpetual banishment from court and a fine, the proclamation mentions only the former and reduces the sentence: 'for the space of seven yeeres'.

In the last line, which reads very much as a last-minute addition, the proclamation states: 'And if any man should find himselfe grieved with any whisperings or rumours spread abroad, misreporting the cariage of any such matter, he may resort to our Commissioners Marshall, woh [*sic*] shall right him in his Reputation, if they finde he be wronged.'[11] This introduces for the first time what I suggest becomes an obstacle to Bacon's agenda – 'our Commissioners Marshall', the commissioners of the court of the Earl Marshal. The personality behind this addition, I suggest (for reasons which will become clear), was the Lord Privy Seal, Henry Howard, Earl of Northampton, who had a vested interest in advising potential duellers to 'resort to our Commissioners Marshall.' After James's accession, Northampton had been appointed as one of the Commissioners, and had subsequently come to dominate the Commission dealing with the workings of the Earl Marshalship and the office of arms.[12] He immersed himself in the literature on duelling, compiling information about the practice abroad from Sir John Finet, Sir Francis Cottington and Sir Henry Wotton, and commissioning discourses from Sir Edward Coke, Sir Robert Cotton, and various of the Society of Antiquaries concerning its English traditions.[13] He has even been credited with the authorship of a tract entitled 'Duello Foil'd', although scholars now believe it more likely that he merely read and commented on this.[14]

Bacon, who was not one of the Commissioners, clearly saw this as a threat, and realised that he had to move fast if he were to keep control of the prosecution of this issue. On the last day of the legal term in the Star Chamber, according to Chamberlain, Attorney General Bacon 'made a motion or rather gave intimation that all that challenged others, or went beyond seas to fight shold be censured in the starchamber, which is like to prove a better course to cut of duells than any that hath yet ben thought on.'[15] When the new legal term commenced, the first case brought in the Star Chamber, on 26 January, was Bacon's: a test case against William Priest, gentleman, and Richard Wright, esquire – Priest 'for writing and sending a Letter of challenge, together with a stick which should bee the length of the weapon'; and Wright (his second) 'for carrying and delivering the said letter and sticke unto the partie challenged', even though the challenge was not accepted.[16] The case was heard in the presence of many of the great and good of British society: Lord Chancellor Ellesmere, Archbishop of Canterbury George Abbot, Lord Privy Seal Northampton, Lord High Admiral Charles, Earl of Nottingham, Bishop of London John King, Lord Chief Justice Sir Edward Coke, Lord Chamberlain Thomas, Earl of Suffolk, Lord Chief Justice of the Common Pleas Sir Henry Hobart, Edward Lord Zouch, Treasurer of the Household William Lord Knolles, Comptroller Edward Lord Wotton, Vicechamberlain John Lord Stanhope, and Chancellor of the Exchequer Sir Julius Caesar.[17] Priest and Wright were found guilty: Priest was fined £500, Wright 500 marks, and both were sent to the Fleet Prison and ordered to make an admission of their guilt at the next Surrey assizes.[18] More importantly, the Court enjoined Attorney General Bacon:

> to have speciall care to the penning of this decree, for the setting forth in the same summarily the matters and reasons which have beene opened and delivered by the Court touching the same, and never-the-lesse also at some time convenient to publish the perticulers of his speeche and declaration, as very meete and worthy to bee remembred, and made known to the world, as these times are.[19]

This should not only be read at the Surrey assizes where Priest and Wright were to acknowledge their offences, but also be 'published and made knowne in all Shires of this Kingdome.'[20] The Assize judges were required 'to cause this decree to bee solemnly read and published in all the places and sittings of their severall Circuits, and in the greatest assembly, to the end that all his Majesties subjects may take knowledge and understand the opinion of this honorable Court in this case.'[21]

Bacon opens his speech by explaining that he brings the case 'to see if this Court can doe any good to tame and reclaime that evill which seemes unbrideled', namely 'private *Duells*'.[22] It was, in effect, a show trial, not only for the offence, but for the court in which it was being prosecuted, the Star Chamber. Bacon's choice of court was loaded. The Star Chamber was often used by the Crown's law officers to bring prosecutions without the inconvenience of a jury. During the sixteenth century the law of misdemeanours – covering criminal libel, forgery, perjury, subornation of perjury, conspiracy, and attempts to commit crime – had been, according to Professor Baker, 'largely the creation of the Star Chamber'.[23] It was to this area that the Attorney General would direct the matter of duels. The two men who stood before them are perhaps not of the quality he might have desired: 'I could have wished that I had met with some greater persons, as a subject for your censure, both because it had bin more worthy of this presence, and also the better to have shewed the resolution my selfe hath to proceed without respect of persons in this businesse.'[24] But this case is convenient:

> finding this cause on foote in my predecessors [Sir Henry Hobart's] time, and published and ready for hearing, I thought to loose no time, in a mischeefe that groweth every day; and besides it passeth not amisse some-times in government, that the greater sort be admonished by an example made in the meaner and the dogge to be beaten before the lyon. Nay I should thinke (my Lords) that men of birth and quality will leave the practise, when it begins to bee vilified and come so lowe as to Barber-surgeons and Butchers, and such base mechanicall persons.[25]

In his sketch of the heinousness of duelling, Bacon creates a link with James's previous proclamation: 'therefore the King, in his last Proclamation, doth most aptly and excellently call them, *bewitching Duells*. For, if one judge of it truely, it is noe better then a sorcery that enchanteth the spirits of young men, that beare great myndes.'[26]

Turning to the required remedies, Bacon isolates four 'as the most effectuall for the repressing of this depraved custome of perticuler Combats.' First, uncontroversially, 'that there doe appeare and bee declared a constant and settled resolution in the State to abolish it'.[27] In his second point, however, Bacon unexpectedly turns his attention to the Commissioners of the Earl Marshal:

> Secondly, care must be taken that this evill bee noe more cockered, nor the humor of it fed; wherein I humbly pray your Lordships that I may speake my mind freely, and yet be understood aright. The proceedings of the great and noble Commissioners Marshall, I honor and reverence much, and of them I speake not in any sort; But I say the compounding of quarrells, which is other-wise in use, by private noble men and gentlemen, it is so punctuall, and hath such reference and respect unto the receyved conceipts, whats before hand, and whats behindehand, and I cannot tel what, as without all question it doth, in a fashion, countenance and authorise this practice of *Duells*, as if it had in it some-what of right.[28]

Despite the careful disclaimers, distinguishing the attempts of the Commissioners Marshal from private gentlemen, the thrust of Bacon's argument is inescapable. Attempts to compound quarrels may be well-intentioned, but their effect is 'in a fashion, [to] countenance and authorise' the practice. By contrast, as his third point, Bacon has to 'acknowledge that I learned out of the Kings last proclamation the most prudent and best applied remedy for this offence (if it shall please his Majestie to use it) that the wit of man can devise.'[29] This 'most prudent and best applied remedy' turns out to be banishment from court which, we may recall, was in fact the suggestion of Bacon himself. Here, however, Bacon does concede that the offender should 'bee banished and excluded from his Court for certaine yeares', rather than perpetually, as he first suggested.[30]

In his final point, Bacon continues his slighting attack on other courts' dealing with the problem, when he comes to discuss the claim that English law 'provided no remedy for *lies* [charges of falsehood] and *filippes* [blows].'[31] 'The Civilians [civil lawyers],' he mocked, 'they dispute whether an action of *Injury* lie for it, and rather resolve the contrary.'[32] Once again, the Star Chamber rides to the rescue: 'if there be extraordinary circumstances of despight and contumely, as in cases of libells and bastanadoes [beatings with a stick], and the like, this Court taketh them in hand and punisheth them exemplarly.'[33] Although the Star Chamber lacks the power to prosecute capital offences, Bacon takes it 'to bee a ground infallible, *that wheresoeuer an offence is capital, or matter of fellony, if it be acted, there the combination, or practise, tending to that offence is punishable in this Court, as a high misdemenor.*' It follows that duelling 'is a case fit for the censure of this Court.' Presenting precedents to back his argument, Bacon declares, 'These things are well knowne, and therfore I needed not so much to have insisted uppon them, but that in this Case I would be thought not to innovate any thing of mine own head.'[34]

Listing the actions which would be counted as examples of this offence, Bacon asserts that 'If any man shall revive a quarrell by any scandalous bruites or writings contrary to a former Proclamation, published by his Majesty in that behalfe, that in all these cases his Majesties Atturney generall, in discharge of his duety by the favour and assistance of his Majesty and the Court, would bring the offenders of what state or degree soever to the justice of this Court, leaving the Lords Commissioners Marshall to the more exact remedies.'[35] Here the Attorney General is given considerable rein, at the expense of the Commissioner; again in summing up, Bacon requests of the Lord Chancellor a strengthening of his position as Attorney General, namely, 'that in case I be advertised of a purpose in any to goe beyond the sea to fight, I may have granted his Majesties writ of *Ne exeat regnum* [he may not leave the kingdom] to stoppe him.'[36]

We might think that this performance would have pre-empted any counter-bid by the Commissioners. However, Bacon's speech was only known immediately to those in Star Chamber, and despite the insistence of the court that he publish the proceedings for nationwide circulation, his printed account was not entered into the Stationers' Register until 5 March 1613/14.[37] In the meantime, on 4 February, a further proclamation was issued 'against private Challenges and Combats: With Articles annexed for the better directions to be used therein, and for the more judiciall proceeding against Offenders.'[38] This was accompanied by 'a more large discourse annexed', *A Publication of his Majesty's Edict and severe Censure against Private Combats and Combatants*.[39] Chamberlain noted on 17 February: 'This weeke here came foorth a long proclamation with a booke annexed of reasonable bulke, against challenges and duells, which seems a curious peece of worke, and though at first yt was commonly attributed to Sir Fra: Bacon, yet by the little I have read of both, I did quickly acquit him, and did easilie discern that yt came from some higher hand.'[40] Chamberlain's identification of the author as not-Bacon is, I believe, very telling. It suggests that an astute contemporary observer was well able to detect the differing nuances of argument emerging in what was meant to be a coherent campaign. The author of the tract – and judging by the style, of the second proclamation itself – was indeed 'some higher hand'. A more precise identification was made by the seventeenth-century owner of a copy now in the British Library's Grenville collection, who writes: 'The style hath a Character, and an Affectation peculiar to the E. of Northampton; and which runs thro all he wrote.'[41] Bacon had presumably known of Northampton's tract when he prosecuted Priest and Wright, which might explain his insistence on belittling the work of the Commissioners. In his speech, he declares, 'For the remedies I hope some great and noble person will put his hand to this plough, and I wish that my labours may be but fore-runners to the worke of a higher and better hand.'[42] Northampton's tract was indeed, in his own words, 'upon the anvil' in January; in fact, it had been ready for publication for some two or three months. On 18 November 1613, the earl had informed Sir Thomas Lake that he was waiting to publish it: 'The proclamation about Duels had been published before this, but that I was desirous to give time to the last that was done by the King himself, that the subjects which are most remote might have time to rivet and imprint [...] When this impression is fully settled, then will I bring my patch upon the stage.'[43]

The second proclamation proposes a 'speedie course for the stopping of a Vaine that bleeds both incessantly, and inwardly': James commands 'That after fortie dayes expired, which Wee prescribe to begin instantly from the publication of Our prohibition, no man shall presume in their wonted maner [...] either to send or accept of Challenges, or to seeke satisfaction by any other meanes then those, which are made good either by the Lawes of the Kingdome, or the Court of Honour.'[44] Significantly, the 'Court of Honour' makes an appearance, but nowhere in the proclamation is there any reference to the penalties proposed by Bacon, nor to the prosecution of offenders in the Star Chamber.[45]

In Northampton's 119-page supporting document, the Star Chamber is mentioned only once – and then simply because Northampton is quoting the October proclamation. All power in this tract is given to the Commissioners of the Earl Marshalship. They would remedy potential quarrels: either personally (the Lords in Commission were to deal with gentlemen in court, in the City of London and twenty miles around the City, and with all cases involving peers and nobles), or by a devolved authority (to the Lords Lieutenant and their deputies). James had 'commanded the Lords in Commission for the office of *Earle Marshall*, whom the wisdom of precedent times held fittest to judge matters of this kinde that touch honor to the quicke.'[46] All those in danger of entering into duels are urged to the Earl Marshal's court 'for the cleansing of all green wounds, as for the healing of old ulcers.' James, after consultation with the judges, has understood 'that though there can be no proceeding by *the Common Law*, against one *Subject* that hath slaine another by agreement upon *Challenge* to fight in forraine parts; yet by appeale, so often as it shall please Us to appoint a *Constabel* and *Marshall* of *England*, but for the present onely, both to heare and adjudge the cause, the partie thus offending may bee condemned in that *Court* to death.'[47]

It is clearly the 'Northampton' proclamation of February 1613/14 – and possibly its lengthy accompanying tract – to which James is referring in his parliamentary opening speech two months later. It would seem that Northampton's printed proposal to claim the jurisdiction of an entire swathe of public disorder to the lords of the Commission had not been popular. Significantly, Bacon's initial advice to James urged that the measures should be temporary and subject to endorsement by a parliament. Northampton, on the other hand, in the same month that he published his tract, fiercely opposed the calling of a new parliament. It may well be impossible to appreciate the importance of the anti-duelling campaign without taking into account the shadow cast by the forthcoming parliament.

But perhaps we should be wary of jumping to conclusions. This is after all a rather muffled debate buried in the minutiae of speeches, proclamations and tracts. It does not by itself amount to a pitched battle between the Star Chamber and the Court of the Earl Marshal, nor even to personal lobbying for power between the Lord Privy Seal and the Attorney General. It is more revealing about contemporary procedures of counsel, the drafting of speeches and proclamations, and the uses and effects of print. Like any political figure, James was to some extent dependent on his advisers. The words of the king, the words ascribed to the Crown, were based on the words of others. James's voice against duelling – heard as a single voice – spoke the words of at least two high-level advisers, and their words were not always compatible. So what of his speech to the newly-assembled Houses of Parliament? Again we need to be careful. James may have defended his February proclamation, but then his parliamentary speech drew heavily on a memorandum forwarded by Sir Francis Bacon. Might it be that in James's apparent defence we also hear Bacon's attack on the February proclamation and (implicitly) a return to his original proposals of the September 1613 memorandum?[48]

In 1982, Linda Levy Peck wrote, 'From 1613 on the Crown led a campaign against duelling enforced in Star Chamber and the court of Earl Marshal. Northampton was its author and most active propagandist until his death.'[49] I would argue that this needs to be qualified. Certainly there was a campaign against duelling, certainly it was led by the Crown, and certainly it involved both the Star Chamber and the court of Earl Marshal. But to see Northampton as its sole author suggests a coherence behind this campaign which did not exist. Like so many unanimously supported initiatives of the Jacobean era, the campaign against duelling provided an opportunity for other, more personal agendas to be pursued.

Notes

[1] James to the Houses of Parliament, 5 April 1614. University of Oxford, Bodleian Library, Carte MS 77, fols 145–46, printed in *Proceedings, 1614*, pp. 13–19 (p. 18).

[2] James to the Houses of Parliament, 5 April 1614. Hampshire Record Office, Herriard MS XX. 1, printed in *Proceedings, 1614*, pp. 473–6 (p. 476).

[3] Linda Levy Peck, *Northampton: Patronage and Policy at the Court of James I* (London: George Allen & Unwin, 1982), p. 161.

[4] John Chamberlain to Sir Dudley Carleton, 9 September 1613, London. Public Record Office, State Papers 14/74 art. 56; printed in *Letters of John Chamberlain*, I, 474–7 (pp. 474–5).

[5] V. G. Kiernan, *The Duel in European History: Honour and the Reign of Aristocracy* (Oxford: Oxford University Press, 1988), p. 81.

[6] Mervyn James, 'English Politics and the Concept of Honour, 1485–1642', in *Society, Politics and Culture: Studies in Early Modern England* (Cambridge: Cambridge University

Press, 1986), pp. 308–415.

[7] Francis Bacon, 'A proposition for the repressing of singular combats or duels' [1613]. First printed in David Dalrymple, *Memorials and Letters Relating to the History of Britain in the Reign of James the First* (Glasgow: Robert and Andrew Foulis, 1762), pp. 51–2; see also *The Letters and the Life of Francis Bacon* ed. by James Spedding, 7 vols (London: Longmans et al., 1861–1874), IV, 397.

[8] *A Proclamation Prohibiting the Publishing of any Reports or Writings of Duels* (London: Robert Barker, 1613) [Hinchinbrooke, 15 October 1613], printed in *Stuart Royal Proclamations*, vol 1, *Royal Proclamations of King James I, 1603–1625*, ed. by James F. Larkin and Paul L. Hughes (Oxford: Clarendon Press, 1973), pp. 295–7. This proclamation was described by Chamberlain as 'a proclamation penned by the Kings owne hand about the late quarrell betwixt the earle of Essex and Master H. Howard', Chamberlain to Carleton, 27 October 1613, London. Public Record Office, State Papers 14/74, art. 89; *Letters of John Chamberlain*, I, 481–4 (pp. 483–4). Essex had challenged Howard after Howard impugned his virility following Essex's divorce from Howard's kinswoman Lady Frances Howard. Although the pair went to Flanders to fight the duel, they were halted by the authorities there. However, the seconds in the case quickly circulated 'different writings' on the case, which forced the Privy Council to intervene. On 14 October, Chamberlain wrote to Carleton: 'The quarrell twixt the earle and Master Henry Howard is compounded and taken up by the King himself: but the matter is not altogether ended there, for the seconds on both sides do varie in relating the cariage of the whole cause, and have geven out different writings, wherupon they have been convented and called in question by the Lords and a writing conteyning the whole matter and most materiall circumstances tendered to subscribe, which beeing accordingly don by Master Devoreux and Captain Owseley, the earle disavowes yt and renounces them; and they to cover theyre oversight in subscribing to a thing they had not advised upon, nor as much as perused, but only heard read by Dudley Norton [clerk of the Council], lay the fault upon him, as supposting [substituting fraudulently] and foisting in a writing varieng in divers points from that which was read them, and upon this they stoode, offering to maintain yt by oath, sacrament or the sword: but the counsaile have thought best to have the matter husht and injoyned them (or Master Devoreux at least who only appeared), to recall all cartells and to prosecute this cause no farther neither by word nor writing.' Chamberlain to Carleton, 14 October 1613, London. PRO, SP 14/74, art. 86; *Letters of John Chamberlain*, I, 477–80 (pp. 478–9). This might well explain the focus of this first proclamation on the writing of reports of duels.

[9] Bacon, 'A proposition' [1613]; Spedding, *Letters and Life*, IV, 397.

[10] *Proclamation Prohibiting Publishing of Reports*; Larkin and Hughes, *Royal Proclamations*, p. 296.

[11] *Proclamation Prohibiting Publishing of Reports*; Larkin and Hughes, *Royal Proclamations*, p. 297.

[12] On 5 February 1604/5, the Commissioners were Thomas Sackvile, Earl of Dorset, Lord High Treasurer; Lewis Stuart, Duke of Lennox; Charles Howard, Earl of Nottingham; Thomas Howard, Earl of Suffolk; Edward Somerset, Earl of Worcester; Charles Blount, Earl of Devonshire; Henry Howard, Earl of Northampon. See G. D. Squibb, *The High Court of Chivalry: A Study of the Civil Law in England* (Oxford: Clarendon Press, 1959), p. 232.

[13] Peck, *Northampton*, pp. 156–7, 160.

[14] See University of Oxford, Bodleian Library, Ashmole MS 856; British Library, Cotton MSS, Titus C.i; Peck, *Northampton*, p. 247 n. 57.

[15] Chamberlain to Carleton, 9 December 1613, London. PRO, SP 14/75, art. 44; *Letters of John Chamberlain*, I, 490–92 (p. 491).

[16] All references are to *The Charge of Sir Francis Bacon Knight, his Majesties Attourney Generall, touching Duells, upon an information in the Star-chamber against Priest and Wright. With The Decree of the Star-chamber in the same cause* (London: Robert Wilson, 1614), here at sig. E3^{v}–E4^{r}. On this hearing see Daniel R. Coquillette, *Francis Bacon* (Stanford, CA: Stanford University Press, 1992), pp. 167–70.

[17] Bacon, *Charge*, sig. E3^{r-v}.

[18] Bacon, *Charge*, sig. H^{r-v}.

[19] Bacon, *Charge*, sig. H2^{r}.

[20] Bacon, *Charge*, sig. H2^{v}.

[21] Bacon, *Charge*, sig. H2^{v}. Sir Edward Coke was also enjoined to report in print his statements 'touching the law in this case of *Duells* [...] as hee hath formerly done divers other Cases, that, such as understand not the law in that behalfe, and all others may better direct themselves, and prevent the danger thereof hereafter' (Bacon, *Charge*, sig. H2^{v}–H3^{r}). However, Coke, perhaps showing signs of his future conduct, failed to obey this demand. His *A Booke of Entries* (London: Societie of Stationers, 1614), does not deal with duelling, and indeed his comments on duels only make it into print posthumously. See *The Third Part of the Institutes of the Laws of England*, 4th edn (London: A. Crooke et al., 1669), p. 158, where Coke largely adopts Bacon's analysis: 'And if any Subject by word, writing or message, challenge another to fight with him, this is also an offence before any combate be performed, and punishable by Law [...] Or such offenders may be punished in the Star-Chamber.' This discussion is not included in the earlier edition: *The Third Part of the Institutes of the Laws of England Concerning High Treason, and other Pleas of the Crown, and Criminall causes* (London: M. Flesher for W. Lee and D. Pakeman, 1644), Chapter 72, 'Of Monomachia, Single combate, Duell, Affrays, and Challenges, and of Private revenge', sig. Y^{r}–Y2^{r}.

[22] Bacon, *Charge*, sig. A3^{r-v}.

[23] J. H. Baker, *An Introduction to English Legal History*, 3rd edn. (London: Butterworths, 1990), p. 137.

[24] Bacon, *Charge*, sig. A3^{v}.

[25] Bacon, *Charge*, sig. A3^{v}.

[26] Bacon, *Charge*, sig. B2^{r-v}.

[27] Bacon, *Charge*, sig. B3^{v}.

[28] Bacon, *Charge*, sig. B4^{v}.

[29] Bacon, *Charge*, sig. B4^{v}–C^{r}.

[30] Bacon, *Charge*, sig. C^{r}.

[31] Bacon, *Charge*, sig. D^{v}. The *OED* defines 'fillip' as 1. 'A movement made by bending the last joint of a finger against the thumb and suddenly released it [...]: a smart strike or tap given by this means', and 2. 'In a wider sense: A smart blow (with the fist, etc.)' (V, 912).

[32] Bacon, *Charge*, sig. D^{v}–D2^{r}.

[33] Bacon, *Charge*, sig. D2^{v}.

[34] Bacon, *Charge*, sig. D3^{r}–D4^{r}.

[35] Bacon, *Charge*, sig. G^{r-v}. Significantly, this concession is recorded only in the account of the hearing, not in the preceding transcript of Bacon's speech (Bacon, *Charge*, sig. G^{r-v}, D4^{v}).

[36] Bacon, *Charge*, sig. E^{r}.

[37] *A Transcript of the Registers of the Company of Stationers of London: 1554–1640*, ed. by Edward Arber, 5 vols (London and Birmingham: privately printed, 1875–94), III, 248b.

[38] *A Proclamation against Private Challenges and Combats: With Articles annexed for the better directions to be used therein, and for the more judiciall proceeding against Offenders* (London: Robert Barker, 1613 [i.e. 1613/14]) [4 February 1613/14, Westminster], printed in Larkin and Hughes, *Royal Proclamations* pp. 302–8.

[39] *A Publication of his Majesties Edict, and Severe Censure against Private Combats and Combatants* (London: Robert Barker, 1613 [i.e. 1613/14]), STC 8498.

[40] Chamberlain to Carleton, 17 February 1613/14, London. PRO, SP 14/76, art. 27; *Letters of John Chamberlain*, I, 508–11 (p. 509).

[41] MS notes opposite titlepage of *A Publication of his Majesties Edict*, BL shelfmark G.2312. The book is not listed in Robin Alston, *Books with Manuscript: A Short-title Catalogue of Books with Manuscript Notes in the British Library* (London: The British Library, 1994).

[42] Bacon, *Charge*, sig. B3^{v}.

[43] Northampton to Sir Thomas Lake, 18 November 1613. PRO, SP 14/75, art. 13; quoted in Spedding, *Letters and Life*, IV, 398 n. 1.

[44] Larkin and Hughes, *Royal Proclamations*, pp. 303, 304.

[45] Earlier in the proclamation James asks 'to what purpose serve the Lawes of God, the provisionall instruments of men, and the course of ordinarie Justice in the Common wealth (whether Wee respect the Court of Chivalrie, or the Civill Courts).' Larkin and Hughes, *Royal Proclamations*, p. 303.

[46] Bacon, *Charge*, sig. C2^{r}.

[47] Bacon, *Charge*, sig. N4^{v}. There is also an interesting slippage in the text from the Court of the Earl Marshal to a comparison with a French 'Court of Chivalry'. The Court of the Lord High Constable and Earl Marshal of England had been prominent in the mid-fourteenth century as a court with jurisdiction over military matters such as treason, ransom, contracts with sutlers, and disputed coats of arms. By the mid-sixteenth century, however, the high office of Constable of England was abolished, and the court in abeyance. But, as J. H. Baker writes, 'the court has understandably been confused with that belonging to the earl marshal alone. This *Curia Marescalli*, or High Court of Chivalry, was revived by James I as a court of honour, which not only tried the right to distinctions of honour and coat armour but also redressed affronts to honour such as slander.' Indeed, this High Court of Chivalry is the only English court still to use the procedure of the Civil Law, although it has sat only once since 1737 – in the 1955 case of Manchester Corporation v Manchester Palace of Varieties Ltd, after the Palace Theatre displayed the Manchester Corporation's crest on a pelmet above the main curtain. Baker, *Introduction to English Legal History*, pp. 141–2 and 142 n. 26; Squibb, *High Court*, pp. 123–7.

[48] Dr John Cramsie suggests to me that James might have thought it strategically wise to sacrifice a proclamation to satisfy at least one parliamentary grievance: perhaps Bacon mischievously suggested Northampton's February proclamation?

[49] Peck, *Northampton*, p. 161.

PART III

TEXT AND TRADE

8

'The Language of the Public': Print, Politics, and the Book Trade in 1614

Joad Raymond

I cannot speak the language of the public; I understand nothing of the matter.
(Ranulph Crew, Speaker in the Commons, 1614)[1]

I condiscended against all thought and purpose on my part [...] not onely to coppie it out and put it in paper, for the private use of some; but to commit it to the Presse, for the more publike good of many, which were not present auditors: Every good thing being so much the better the more common it is; and writing being ordayned of GOD to be a meane of the teaching of his Church, as well as lively voyce.
(Thomas Wilson, preacher, 1614)[2]

While the London-based scribal culture of the year 1614 explored the contours and implications of the disagreement between king and commons with relative freedom and energy, the press was silent on the matter. This terseness of the print medium speaks both to revisionist and post-revisionist debate over the nature of the conflict in 1614, and to the constitution and status of the book trade, or the trade in inexpensive, topical books, in Jacobean England.[3] In the same letter to Alice Carleton that first mentioned the writs for what was to become known as the 'Addled Parliament', the newsletter-writer John Chamberlain mentions the disgrace of a woman, and a threat 'to publish her fowle faults in print to her further shame' (the letter is torn and so the identities and circumstances of his subjects are uncertain).[4] Writing to Dudley Carleton six weeks later, in the dog days of the parliament, Chamberlain describes the excitability of Sir Henry Wotton over news of court and parliament: 'having Master Pories discourse there with me, and making some mention of it by chaunce, he was with child till he had seen it [...] Touching the printing of it, you need not doubt, for there was never any such purpose but only spoken merely.'[5] The printing of John Pory's newsletter had itself become the subject of rumour, it seems; but for those who could not afford an expensive subscription to a manuscript newsletter service, or who did not move among those who could, this itch of news was unlikely to be scratched but only chafed with further rumour. Recent research has demonstrated the very lively culture of manuscript communication and exchange sustained in early modern England. Historians of the book have tended to reify the smudged boundary between manuscript and print, and to understate the capacity of manuscript circulation to reach beyond the coterie to a large and diverse audience.[6] Yet for Carleton and Thomas Wilton, in the preface to a published sermon, print had a special quality. It seemed, in theory if not in practice, to embrace an even larger audience than the warm voice or the 'private use' of hand copies, to promise 'further shame' than word of mouth, to carry further than that which was 'merely' spoken; to be, in Milton's phrase of 1644, 'more publick then preaching'.[7] The purpose of this paper is to consider how far these powers of publicity extended in the year 1614.

I

I will begin with a parachutist's-eye-view of the output of printing presses in the British Isles in the year 1614, based on a statistical analysis of publications; in the next section I will present a pig's-eye view of some particular truffles which suggest the way in which news, particularly of the Addled Parliament, could be filtered through printed books.[8] The complementary perspectives advise caution for longer-term accounts of the evolving relationship between print and politics.[9]

Figure 1 offers an overview of press output in the period 1588 to 1688. It shows at first glance that 1614 was not an exceptional year in terms of total press output: 444 items appeared, fewer than the 510 and 524 items in the surrounding years. The figure is 6% lower than the mean for the decade 1610–19, which was 471 items. These figures are subject to not unfamiliar provisos. First, title-counts pay no heed to size of edition, and thus it cannot be assumed that there was a proportionate number of books injected into society. An edition might run to 1500 copies, more in the case of Bibles, or be as few as 250. Secondly, title-counts do not designate the number of pages or words printed; among the titles to grace the bookseller's stall in 1614 was Walter Ralegh's *History of the World*, which makes the same impact upon figure 1 as a two-sheet pamphlet. Yet this fact can reveal another aspect of production: if we assume that the productive capacity of London presses, and the supply of raw materials, were relatively inelastic, then years in which a high number of titles were produced were likely to see a decrease in average length of works. Thirdly, figures rely to some extent on the accuracy of imprints and colophons, which may create anomalies. The year of publication stated upon the title page is accepted in most cases (the year commencing on Lady Day), though some booksellers or printers may have endeavoured to increase the shelf-life of their product by post-dating their title pages. Such enterprising practices probably have a minimal effect on overall figures. Fourthly, the figures are subject to the vagaries of survival rates; a significant number of all titles from this period have disappeared entirely. Perhaps no more than two-thirds of all works have survived.

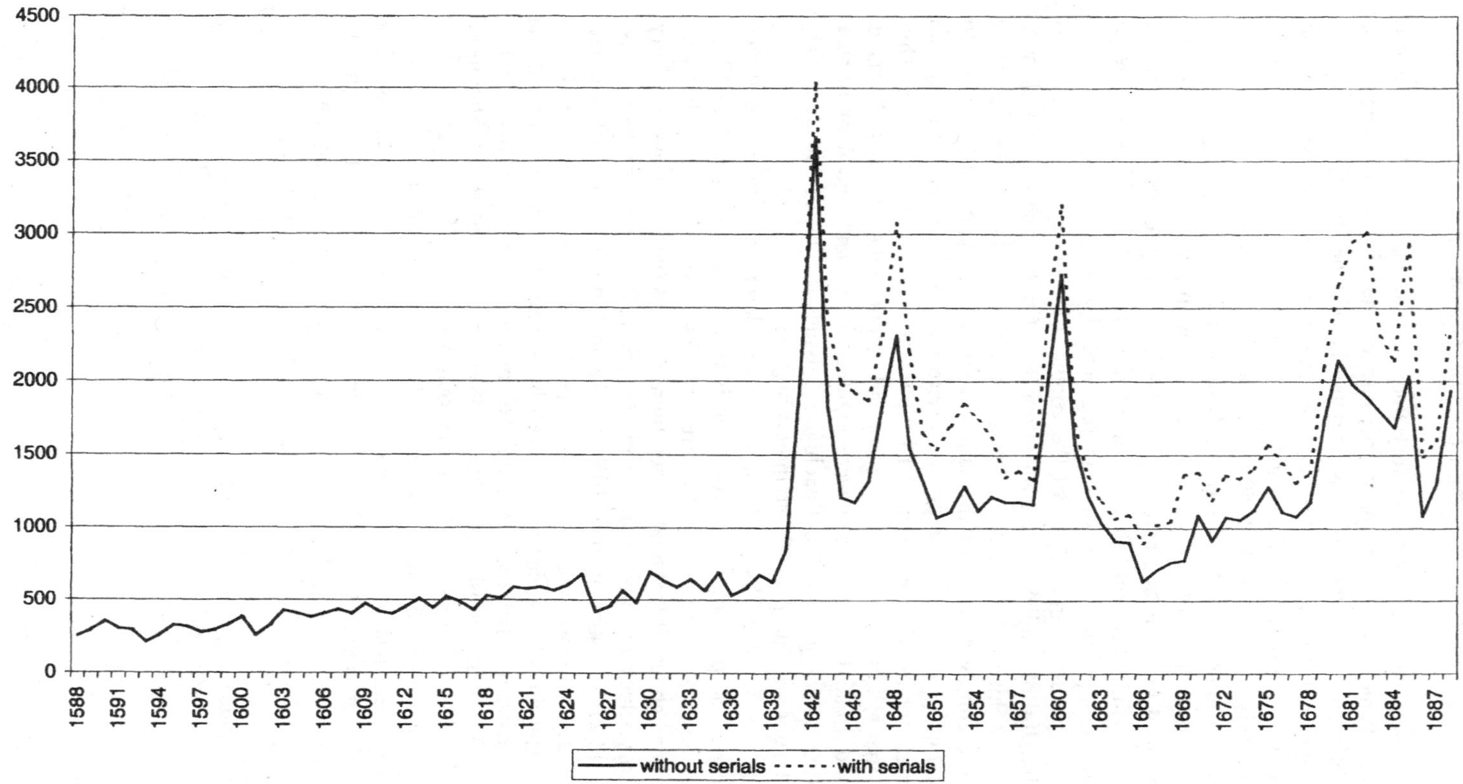

Figure 1: Press output (annual publications with and without serials) 1588–1688

Survival rates, moreover, may be very uneven: I suspect that they increase through the seventeenth century, partly because of the efforts of a handful of assiduous collectors, and that the increase is quite sharp in the 1640s.[10]

From Figure 1 it is clear that in the later seventeenth century years of political turmoil or crisis are marked by a dramatic increase in the number of publications. Most significantly 1641–2, 1648, 1659–60, 1679–80 and 1685 all saw significant peaks in activity; even 1653, the year of the dissolution of the Long Parliament, the introduction and dissolution of the Nominated Assembly, and the inauguration of the Instrument of Government, reveals a modest hike. Despite the appearance of continuous growth, a different pattern obtains before 1641–2. Either there were no real crisis years, or political crises were not registered by the press.

For the purposes of an analysis of the content of printed books I have discounted a handful of English books printed overseas (in St Omer – concerns were expressed about this in parliament), and multiple issues or editions (because many of these were simply reissues of the same sheets in a variant state, and would distort a picture of the role of the press). Where there are multiple editions with extra materials, or in different formats, I have included them in my survey. Thus the figures that follow pertain to the content and output of the presses in England, Scotland and Ireland (where there were eighteen items and one item printed, respectively), including reprints but excluding reissues, a total of 354 items. The first set of results are extrapolated into three tables.

Table 1 shows these 354 publications broken down into broad categories. Almost 40% of the press output of 1614 consisted of religious materials (Bibles, sermons, theological tracts); works of current affairs (news pamphlets, almanacs) only constituted about 10% of total output; literary works (ballads, classics, poetry, drama, history, plus a few miscellaneous pieces), about 20%; practical works (law, medicine, didactic), about another 10%; works in Latin 9% and official publications about 8%. Most books appeared in quarto or octavo format: the 10% of books appearing in folio format was boosted by a high incidence of slim official publications; more than half the duodecimo volumes were theological in content.

Of these 354 items considered, 169, or 48% were entered in the Stationers' Register; whereas 185 items, or 52% of the total, were not. These figures include not only new entries (and transfer of rights), but items for which rights to copy appear to have remained in a stationer's hands. The figures are significant. Don McKenzie demonstrated the declining frequency of entering books in the Stationers' Register through the seventeenth century; in 1644 about 20% of all books and pamphlets were entered in the Stationers' Register; in 1668 this had declined to about 17.5%; in 1688, only 7%.[11] The figures for 1614 tell a different story. If we include all published items, we arrive at a figure of 48% of items being registered. But if official items and books printed for the Stationers' Company are discounted, we arrive at a figure of 59%. Most printing outside London was

Table 1: Categories of publications

Category	items
Almanacs	15
Ballads	2
Bibles	19
Classics (in trans.)	3
Didactic	26
Drama	9
History	13
Latin	32
Law	8
Medicine	2
Miscellaneous	13
Moral	6
News	18
Official	28
Petitions	3
Poetry	38
Politics	2
Sermons	45
Theology	72

Table 2: Format of publications

Format	items	% of total
Folio	36	10.17%
S.sh.fol	10	2.80%
Quarto	168	47.46%
Octavo	112	31.64%
12mo	21	5.90%
16mo	4	1.13%
24mo	1	0.28%
32mo	1	0.28%
64mo	1	0.28%

Table 3: Place of publication

Place	items	% of total
London	308	87.00%
[London]	5	1.40%
Edinburgh	17	4.80%
Cambridge	5	1.40%
Oxford	18	5.08%
Dublin	1	0.28%

unregistered because it was protected by Royal patent, and if we discount these items, and Bibles (printed under Royal patent by Robert Barker or the Stationers' Company), we arrive at a figure of about 69% of books being registered (or at least appearing to be printed under the rights of an earlier entry in the Register).[12] Hence we can conclude that over two-thirds of publications subject to registration were in fact entered in the Register. Entrance rates are divided by format in Table 4. The entry rate for quartos, perhaps the most demotic of publishing formats, is high; that for folios conspicuously low (though if we discount official items and Stationers' Company publications we arrive at a figure of 53%). This must qualify suggestions that the practices of the book trade went largely unregulated. Maureen Bell, examining the periods 1594–6, 1614–16 and 1634–6, records a rate of entrance (or the reassignment of existing entries) of about 60%, 58% and 50% respectively; taking official printing and works covered by patents into account she finds that on average 75% of publications observed the customary legal procedure and thus can be said to have been published in an 'orderly manner'.[13]

Table 4: Entrance by format

Format	Items	entered	%
Folio	36	10	27.70%[14]
Quarto	168	97	57.74%
Octavo	112	58	51.79%
Duodecimo	21	11	52.38%

There is little evidence, except in registration rates, of government intervention in the press. Two items which caused public scandal, Ralegh's *History of the World* and George Chapman's *Andromeda Liberata* were both entered (as was Wither's *Abuses*, first published in 1613 and reprinted in 1614, which may have been a cause of his imprisonment).[15] Edward Allde, Thomas Snodham and John Trundle were each fined £5 by the Court of the Stationers' Company for printing an anonymous news book on the wars in Germany, 'because the said booke was never entred'.[16] Passages of Tobias Gentleman's *Englands way to win wealth, and to employ ships and marriners* appear to have been deemed censurable; though it was hardly malicious or surreptitious as it was both registered and presented to the king.[17] This may suggest that the institutions responsible for the government of the press – the Privy Council, parliament, Stationers' Company, the episcopate, and the court – were satisfied with the degree of their control. The state papers for 1614 are strikingly silent on matters of the printing press, in contrast with the girning and carping audible right through the 1640s.

In 1614 authorial anonymity was uncommon. About 8% of publications were anonymous. In practice the figure may have been higher, as it does not include those works the authors of which were identified only by initials, though this sometimes worked as an effective guise, or as a means of revealing the author's identity only to a restricted audience. Anonymity became increasingly frequent through the seventeenth century. In the years around 1600 only a handful of publications were anonymous; by the second half of the century a rate around 60% was common. These later figures exclude news periodicals (technically anonymous, though the identity of their editors was often known to their readers), and so under-represent anonymity in book production as a whole.[18] As authorial anonymity became more common it generally ceased to be malicious: it developed into a convention of writing, an acceptable mode of self-presentation, especially in cheap or polemical print. Anonymity which was eloquent at the turn of the century, and was perhaps still so in the 1640s, had become commonplace by the end of the century. Yet there was little that was minatory about the anonymous publications of 1614, which were mainly news items and literary works (suggesting the two main causes or motives of anonymity), plus a few didactic texts.

Neither were the handful of books (eighteen items, or 5.1%) which appeared without an imprint particularly significant. Later in the century publisher and printer anonymity occurred at rates similar to authorial anonymity (though perhaps augmented by author publication, as marked by the imprint 'Printed in the Year').[19] Five of these eighteen books were anyway entered in the Stationers' Register, three were petitions, two official texts published in Oxford, leaving only a handful of books that look remotely surreptitious. The most significant among these were two works that typify the exceptional nature of underground publication: the Catholic conversion text, *A Treatise written by Mr. Doctour Carier*, and *Catechesis ecclesiarum quæ in reno Poloniæ*, appearing with a false '1609' Racovian imprint.[20]

Not all the items published in 1614 dropped fresh from their authors' pens. About 30% of publications were reprints (by which I mean reprinted within Britain, not British reprints of overseas works). This is once again a minimum figure that counts only whole volumes, not parts of volumes, or volumes collecting previously published texts. Some reprints, however, were tuned to fit the times, or emphasised the continuity in errors and abuses.[21] Reprints were sometimes carefully timed interventions, works which conveyed new meanings not because of emendations or additions, but because circumstances had given them a new poignancy.[22] Reprints played a significant part in the political debate of the Allegiance controversy of 1688–9.[23] I suspect that the number of reprints (as an absolute figure rather than as a percentage) increased in peak years of book production. Also likely to carry new meanings in new contexts were translations, which constituted a significant part of the market (more than 12%, excluding Bibles). These included not only translations of literary works and classics, but foreign news items and works in most of the categories. The Addled Parliament was summoned while James VI and I was negotiating a possible French match for Prince Charles, which was a counter-bid against prospects of a Spanish marriage. The pro-Spain faction and the hotter sort of Protestants in parliament were thus invited to consider offering supply as an alternative to a dowry that would fund the Jacobean court and government. Meanwhile there was also thought to be a serious possibility of war breaking out in Cleves-Julich, into which England would be drawn.[24] There was plenty of opportunity to touch the pulse of the body politics through deliberatively allusive translation. The most notorious, inflammatory words of the Addled Parliament referred to fourteenth-century Sicilian history; they were interpreted to be an allusion to Anglo-Scottish relations in the 1610s.[25]

Table 5 breaks down aspects of publication according to content. It reveals a high incidence of reprinting in the areas of history and didactic works, and an incidence of 20–30% elsewhere, except in news publications, where there are signally few. Other significant traits by subject are indicated in this table. News items and plays were most likely to be anonymous; theology, didactic works and history most likely to be entered into the Stationers' Register. Tendencies in the choice of format for different kinds of book also emerge: news and plays were published in quarto; didactic works were most likely to appear in quarto, then in octavo. Sermons appeared in the ratio of about two quartos to one octavo, a ratio that would decline through the century. *All the Sermons of Samuel Hieron* may have been the first collection of sermons to appear in folio format (two years, incidentally, before Jonson's self-proclaiming *Workes*). Bibles appeared in the greatest spread of formats. Poetry, history and theology show a lesser diversity.

Table 5: Statistics by category

	Total	Folio	Quarto	Octavo	Other	Entered *incl.*	Anon	Reprints
Sermons	45	1	29 (64.4%)	15 (33.3%)		28 (62%)	0	12 (26.67%)
News	18		18 (100%)			11 (61%)	6 (33.3%)	1
Poetry	38	3 (7.9%)	19 (50%)	14 (36.84%)	1 x s.sh.fol 1 x 64mo	21 (55.26%)	4 (10.53%)	8 (21.05%)
Theology	72	4 (5.56%)	25 (34.7%)	31 (43%)	11 x 12mo 1 x 16mo	53 (73.6%)	2 (2.8%)	27 (37.5%)
Didactic	26		20 (76.9%)	6 (23.1%)		18 (69%)	2 (7.7%)	12 (46%)
Drama	9		9 (100%)			4 (44%)	3 (33.3%)	3 (33.3%)
Bibles	19	1	6 (31.6%)	7 (36.8%)	1 x 12mo 2 x 16mo 1 x 24mo 1 x 32mo			
History	13	6 (46%)	5 (38.5%)	1	1 x 12mo	9 (69%)	1 (7.7%)	7 (54%)

II

I have suggested that 1614 appears not to be a critical year in the output of the book trade; it is perhaps slightly more exceptional in the substance of the books published. Among the more interesting works are: masques by Thomas Campion and George Chapman; Chapman's *Odyssey* (1614?); *The Shepheards Pipe* by William Browne and others; Christopher Brooke's splendid *Ghost of Richard III*; works by George Wither and John Taylor; Sir Arthur Gorges' translation of Lucan; Sir Thomas Overbury's *Wife* (the late Overbury was mentioned once in the parliamentary proceedings, on 5 May);[26] Ralegh's *History of the World*; John Selden's *Titles of honor*; substantial publications by Sir Edward Coke; Tristram White's interesting and neglected *The martyrdome of saint George of Cappadocia*; and John Napier's invention of logarithms.

What the press did not offer, however, was any kind of sustained commentary, political or journalistic on the parliament or other political events of the year 1614. Liberty of speech within its doors was asserted as a principal liberty of parliament, and liberty of speaking was endangered by exposure outdoors. In particular, in a debate on 27 May the dangers of the king being informed and misinformed were raised, in fear of a sudden dissolution. The Journal of the Commons tersely records Sir Walter Chute's view of news hermeneutics: 'That misinformation certain'.[27] After the end of the session, and the imprisonment of four members, the Privy Council ordered the search of the papers of several members, some of which were disposed of by conflagration. But MPs expressed a more general concern that their actions and speeches were being carried abroad. Sir Richard Williamson, on 11 April, regretted that the 'actions of this House' were 'carried abroad though unjustly and disorderly.' The following day Sir Edwin Sandys observed that 'Great wrong [was] done the last parliament by the misreporting the speeches of many members of this House.' Four days later Sir Walter Cope found reason to describe 'rumour and report' as 'two bastards begotten by the people'. On 17 May Richard Martin, not a member of parliament but permitted to speak as a representative of the Council of Virginia, digressed from his proper subject to tax the House of Commons and 'some particular men, iterating their own speeches which formerly they had made.'[28] The anxieties expressed in Lords and Commons about their status, and the potentially deleterious effects of public representation, were presumably not focused on printed materials. They certainly would be in 1641, when the press invaded the privileges of parliament, though the effect was rather to enhance the status of parliament than to degrade it.[29]

Those pamphlets I have classified as 'news' contain either foreign news or wonder stories, for example: *A horrible creuel and bloudy murther; True and wonderfull. A discourse relating a strange and monstrous serpent, or dragon, lately discouered ... in Sussex; The miracle, of miracles ... which lately happened at Dichet in Sommersetshire; Deeds against nature, and monsters by kinde.*[30] Correspondence during the spring was rich with discussion of the parliament. In March John Chamberlain referred to the 'parlement busines' as 'the greatest entertainment we have'; and on 1 June he wrote: 'If it were not for the parlement we shold be utterly barren and have nothing to write.'[31] Chamberlain's letters suggest the prevalence of rumour among a broader public, a 'generall voyce', 'flieng bruites' and open ears.[32] Printed works also testify to the itch of news: *Mercurius Gallo-Belgicus* claims to be 'A discourse full of delight'; Bretnor's almanac for 1615 sighs 'We gape for Gudgions, listen after newes'; Campion's masque features Error, Rumour, Curiosity and Credulity; in *Andromeda Liberata* Chapman complains that the vulgar 'Blaze their opinions, which cannot be good [...] nor would heare | Of any newes, but what seditious were.'[33] Such appetites would have been ill-satisfied by printed reading-matter.

Nevertheless news could be filtered through non-news genres, official publications, sermons and poetry, creating a haphazard variety of topical discourse. Official publications, including royal proclamations and edicts, performed a news-function in themselves; much the same can be said of Attorney-General Bacon's judgement to Star Chamber concerning duels, published with the decree of Star Chamber against them.[34] While the parliament may never have completed its confirmation of the foundation of the hospital in Charter House, an anonymous account of this foundation was published at some point in 1614, indirectly commenting on parliamentary proceedings. Similarly a printed petition from the Stationers' Company outlined the proposed parliamentary act against the importation of books to protect domestic book production.[35]

The parliament of Paris shimmered in the British press. The *parlement* passed on 26 June 1614 an act against a work of resistance theory by the Jesuit Francisco Suárez (a book known to Sir Ralph Winwood),[36] an act which was duly translated and published in London, and which was discussed in the translated volume of

Mercurius Gallo-Belgicus.[37] The reporting of this foreign news may have been intended to reflect upon domestic contexts. Moreover the Addled Parliament concerned itself, inconclusively, with means of preventing the import of 'popish books'.[38] The spate of attacks on resistance theory in 1614 sermons and parallel anxieties expressed in the English parliament exploited the eirenic effects of attacking Jesuits.[39]

There were intersections between moments of parliamentary debate and printed texts, expressing shared interests, sometimes in similar language. Mr Middleton's concerns, raised just before the recess, about the import of tobacco – causing even divines to reek of its fumes – have their counterpart in a diabolical proclamation against tobacco in John Taylor's *Nipping or snipping of abuses*; in William Barclay's odd encomium *Nepenthes, or, The vertues of tabacco*; in Barnaby Rich's *Honestie of this Age*; and in the anonymous *Maske of flowers*.[40] As in parliament, Sunday sports were a contested topic in the press in 1614; the more topical sermons remonstrated against the Sabbath being 'impiously profained, by publike pyping, by open and lacivious dancing'. These competed with a reprint of a manual on good hunting and hawking.[41] The issue of the succession and the religious doctrine and discipline in the dominions of the Elector Palatine, which James had raised as a central theme of the parliament, was broached in numerous publications.[42]

On 13 April Christopher Brooke introduced a bill concerning apparel, troubled that 'women carry manors and thousand of oak trees about their necks', and that men and women wore gold and silver lace; his proposal was that the latter be immediately seized, and those who wore it 'should be accounted a vain idle fellow, etc., a fool by act of parliament.' William Worship, in an artful and dynamic sermon, entitled *Earth raining upon Heaven*, complained that 'The *Gallant* must have his *fleece* of *Vanitie*, at least, one *Locke* effeminately twisted', and that women were guilty of 'crisping, curling, building Towers on their heads: changing the colour with liquors, powders: borrowing, and buying, of the living, of the dead. Nay, they counterfait the *great Seale of Nature*, and walke with artificiall Complexions'.[43] *The Parliament of vertues royal*, a translation from Jean Bertaut by Joshua Sylvester, passes an act 'against profuse Prodigality', another reminder of the topical possibilities of translation and reprinting.[44] Others complained of prodigality in fashion and all things.[45] Correspondences with a speech by Secretary Winwood against recusants and idle clergy on 9 May, and the bishops' response to his accusations, can be found in printed elaborations of the problems of lazy preachers and of labelling men Puritans or Brownists.[46] Tensions in several printed sermons suggest the growing conflict between the proto-Arminianism of Lancelot Andrewes and Calvinist reactions against it, particularly as reflected in attitudes to preaching. Andrewes himself preached a sermon which emphasised the knee and the tongue; a number of other preachers rattled on about open ears and hearing.[47] Among these was a sermon by Leonard Wright originally preached and printed in 1589 – perhaps with a nod at the Marprelate Controversy – and reprinted in 1614, which complained both of 'certaine seditious preachers [...] every one having a Church-plot, or common wealth in his head' and of 'a sort of fickleheaded people: who having their eares itching for novelties, are apt and readie, upon every light occasion, to cast off the yoke of their obedience, and give heed to those spirits of error.'[48] William Harrison apologised for his collection of sermons: 'As therfore I was at first enduced to preach these sermons, so was I afterward perswaded to penne them, that by them the simpler sorte (for whose sake onely doe I now publish them) might have some plain direction how to heare for their profit.'[49] In this context Thomas Wilson's insistence, quoted above, on the virtues of the press as well as the voice might have been distinctly exhortatory. Richard Stock regretted: 'it is but the errour of great men to thinke they have a priviledge to be lesse reverent and regardfull in hearing, then the meanest'.[50] Most epigrammatic was William Worship: 'The Gospell for the eare, the eare for the Gospell, and both for the *Conscience*.'[51] Sir William Walter's complaint, on 27 May, of Bishop Neile, had distinct resonances in printed contemporary conflict: 'Divers dare sweare he preaches not twice a day.'[52] Perhaps also Christopher Neville's Ciceronian speech in the Commons on 3 June, in which he complained of those who, like the Bishop of Lincoln, were 'their masters' spaniels but their country's wolves', a common enough image for irresponsible pastors perhaps, which we find echoed in sermons.[53] The translation (apparently in late May) of Sigismund of Brandenburg's attempt to suppress contention raised by sermons, in his proclamation *Prohibiting all maner of Scandalls and Calumniations to be used by the Clergie, in the Pulpit or else-where*, was perhaps a wry reflection on this context.

These publications were not necessarily responding to parliamentary debate (some were definitely not); but the prevalence of analogies between parliament and the press suggests there was at least an element of sensitivity in the public press to speech within doors. The press offered little in the way of narrative, but it was firmly topical.

It was sermons and literary texts which performed the widest, if unsystematic, news function, by reporting and commenting on topical affairs. The masques performed to celebrate the marriage of Frances Howard and Sir Robert Carr, Countess and Earl of Somerset in December 1613 were the abstracts and brief chronicles of their time. Samuel Daniel's pastoral for the occasion was not printed; a shame really, as Chamberlain commented of it: 'The pastorall made by Samuel Daniell was solemne and dull, but perhaps better to be read than presented.'[54] But Campion's masque (which was, also according to Chamberlain, little commended),[55] and the Grays Inn *Maske of Flowers*, were, with Chapman's *Andromeda Liberata*, the most public commentaries on the event, notwithstanding the attentions of manuscript satirists.[56] Chapman's *Andromeda*, which opened with scornful comments on the appetite of the vulgar and prophane who hearkened for seditious news, subsequently became news itself, when it was subjected to unsympathetic interpretation.[57]

In the pastoral genre had coalesced a voice of anti-city and anti-court feelings. *The Shepheards Pipe*, a collection of pastoral verse by William Browne, George Wither, the MP Christopher Brooke and John Davies, which was entered in the Stationers' Register on 15 May, while Parliament was sitting, discussed Wither's imprisonment in the Marshalsea (also alluded to in Taylor's *Nipping or snipping of abuses*). Both *The Shepheards Pipe*, and Brooke's *Ghost of Richard III* (registered on 14 May), can be read as highly indirect commentaries on matters of royal prerogative then in debate. Pastoral imagery in sermons and poetry invites consideration as a means of reflecting upon the wider political circumstances of the country, and may have included a range of specific references to events evident to contemporaries though now requiring careful reconstruction.[58] Overt criticisms of courtly behaviour, however, were not far to seek, though always carefully qualified. Barnaby Rich wrote of those 'that do labour their owne advancements by base and servile practices, by lying, by slandering, by backbiting, by flattering, by dissembling [...] A princes Court is like a pleasant Garden, where the *Bee* may gather *Honny*, and the *Spider* sucke poyson: for as it is a Schoole of vertue to such as can bridle their mines with discretion, so it is a Nursery of vice, to such as doe measure their willes with witlesse vanity.' Richard Stock praised his subject, John, Lord Harrington: 'he did not misse ordinarily twice a day to heare the word publikely: no not when he was a Courtier'. In his sermon on the second anniversary of Prince Henry's death Daniel Price praised the prince for his imperviousness to 'the *Cankers* or *vipers* of a Courtly life, *Lust, Pride, Ambition, Irreligion*'.[59] The sentiments probably do not constitute a serious seam of anti-court sentiment amongst preachers, but they do share a set of premises with Spenserian poets genuinely sceptical of the court, and their prevalence at a time when rumours of 'undertaking' threatened to sink the parliament from the first, and dogged it for its short duration, cannot be attributed to mere rhetorical formula.

III

With a very different tenor to Thomas Wilson, the Wiltshire minister John Andrewes recognised the power of print to extend the reach of the voice. He expressed his anxiety in some verses appended to a theological work, printed in quarto:

> My Author did the impression buy
> And from the presse he did me take
> That none should sell me certainly
> But he himselfe which did me make.
>   Except it be his neerest friend
>   Which may me sell, both give and lend.[60]

A coterie readership such as Wilson intended may have understood his baffling – and unacknowledged – Shakespearean borrowing:

> [...] of the infinite and unspeakable mercy of God towards us most miserable sinners. The quantity [*sic*] of mercy is not strange, it droppeth as the gentle dew from heaven upon the place beneath, it is twise blest, it blesseth him that gives, & him that takes, it is mightiest in the mightiest, it becomes the *throne of Monarchie* better then his crowne; his Scepter shewes the force of temporall power, the attribute to awe & majestie, wherein doth sit the dread & feare of kings, but mercy is above the Scepters sway, it is inthroned in the hearts of kings, it is an attribute to God himselfe, and earthly powers do then show most like to Gods, when mercy teacheth justice.

> Thus may wee speake in some part and measure of mercy that should somewhat lodge in the heartes of men authorised: But not deliver a full and cleere discourse of the infinite, ineffable, and incomprehensible, compassionate, and provident God towardes us most miserable, and wretched sinners.[61]

In Andrewes's imagination, as in a Shakespearean history, rumour and news betokened instability, in authority and in interpretation. It was apparent to several authors that print might offer a means of creating and influencing publicity and opinion. While print may have been perceived in 1614 as the most public form of communication, it offered little of the apparent discursive or narrative powers of the manuscript culture of the day. The public to which Chamberlain ascribed a 'generall voyce' was probably a very small one. The print culture – and the phrase has a proleptic edge – did find means to broach news in an oblique and semi-informative fashion. Yet it was not until later in the century that the marketplace or print witnessed a division of labour between news and other forms of publication, that enabled the development of sophisticated modes of reportage, and of a pamphleteering press that registered the tremors of political crisis.

Notes

1 *Proceedings, 1614*, p. 22.

2 Thomas Wilson, *Christs farewell to Jerusalem, and last prophesie* (London, 1614; STC 25790), sig. A2^v.

3 For critiques of early-Stuart revisionism that engage with print culture, see David Cressy, *Travesties and Transgressions in Tudor and Stuart England* (Oxford: Oxford University Press, 2000), chapters 1–2; Adam Peter Fox, 'Rumour, News and Popular Political Opinion in Elizabethan and Early Stuart England', *Historical Journal*, 40 (1997), 597–620; Richard Cust, 'News and Politics in Early Seventeenth-Century England', *Past & Present*, 112 (1986), 60–90; Pauline Croft, 'The Reputation of Robert Cecil: Libels, Political Opinion and Popular Awareness in the Early Seventeenth Century', *Transactions of the Royal Historical Society*, 6th ser., 1 (1991), 43–69; Alastair Bellany, '"Rayling Rymes and Vaunting Verse": Libellous Politics in Early Stuart England, 1603–1628,' in *Culture and Politics in Early Stuart England*, ed. by Kevin Sharpe and Peter Lake (London: Macmillan, 1994), pp. 284–310; Thomas Cogswell, 'Underground Verse and the Transformation of Early Stuart Political Culture,' in *Political Culture and Cultural Politics in Early Modern Europe*, ed. by Susan Amussen and Mark Kishlansky (Manchester: Manchester University Press, 1995), pp. 277–300.

4 *Letters of John Chamberlain*, I, 514.

5 *Letters of John Chamberlain*, I, 529.

6 Ian Atherton, *Ambition and Failure in Stuart England: The Career of John, First Viscount Scudamore* (Manchester: Manchester University Press, 1999), pp. 153–6, and idem, '"The Itch Grown a Disease": Manuscript Transmission of News in the Seventeenth Century', in *News, Newspapers, and Society in Early Modern Britain*, ed. by Joad Raymond (London: Frank Cass, 1999), pp. 39–65; Harold Love, *Scribal Publication in Seventeenth-Century England* (Oxford: Clarendon Press, 1993), pp. 9–22 and *passim*; William S. Powell,

John Pory 1572–1636: The Life and Letters of a Man of Many Parts (Chapel Hill, NC: University of North Carolina Press, 1977).

[7] *Complete Prose Works of John Milton*, general ed. Don M. Wolfe, 8 vols (New Haven and London: Yale University Press, 1953–82), II, 548.

[8] These statistics are based on a database of publications in print in England, Scotland and Ireland, extracted from A. W. Pollard and G. R. Redgrave, *A Short-Title Catalogue of Books Printed in England, Scotland and Ireland: And of English Books Printed Abroad 1475–1640*, revised edn, 3 vols (London: Bibliographical Society, 1976–1991). Output figures are supplemented by Maureen Bell and John Barnard, 'Provisional Count of *STC* Titles 1475–1640', *Publishing History*, 31 (1992), 48–64; Bell and Barnard, 'Provisional Count of *Wing* Titles 1641–1700', *Publishing History*, 55 (1998), 89–97. Similar analyses, from which I will draw comparisons, are undertaken in: Judith Simmons, 'Publications of 1623', *The Library*, 5th ser., 21 (1966), 207–22; D. F. McKenzie, 'The London Book Trade in 1644', in *Bibliographia: Lectures 1975–1988 by recipients of The Marc Fitch Prize for Bibliography*, ed. by John Horden (Oxford: Leopard's Head Press, 1992), pp. 131–52; D. F. McKenzie, 'The London Book Trade in 1668', *Words*, 4 (1974), 75–92; and D. F. McKenzie, 'The Economies of Print, 1550–1750: Scales of production and Conditions of Constraint' in *Produzione e commercio della cara e del libro secc. XIII–XVIII*, Ser. II, Atti delle 'Settimane di Studi' e altri Convegni, 23 (Prato: Istituto Internazionale di Storia Economica 'F. Datini' Prato, 1992), pp. 389–425. Also useful is Mark Goldie, 'The Revolution of 1689 and the Structure of Political Argument: An Essay and an Annotated Bibliography of Pamphlets on the Allegiance Controversy', *Bulletin of Research in the Humanities*, 83 (1980), 473–564.

[9] For one such account see my *Pamphlets and Pamphleteering in Early Modern Britain* (Cambridge: Cambridge University Press, 2003).

[10] In Douglas C. Collins, *A Handlist of News Pamphlets 1590–1610* (London: South West Essex Technical College, 1943), pp. 102–21. Collins appends to his list of 271 news pamphlets published between 1590 and 1610 a further 93 pamphlets and 96 ballads entered in the Stationers' Register, which do not appear to have survived. The print-runs for each of these would have been between 250 and 1000 copies; this suggests a very high loss rate. Folke Dahl estimates a survival rate of about 0.013% for individual copies of English corantos published between 1624 and 1632; *A Bibliography of English Corantos and Periodical Newsbooks 1620–1642* (London: Bibliographical Society, 1952), p. 22. The figure of two-thirds is suggested in D. F. McKenzie's unpublished Lyell lectures, and a figure of between 60% and 70% is suggested in McKenzie's 'The London Book Trade in 1644', p. 134. See also Maureen Bell, 'Entrance in the Stationers' Register', *The Library*, 6th ser., 16 (1994), 50–4 (p. 54); and John Barnard, 'The Stationers' Stock 1663/4 to 1705/6: Psalms, Psalters, Primers and ABCs', *The Library*, 6th ser., 21 (1999), 369–75.

[11] D. F. McKenzie, 'The London Book Trade in 1644', p. 137; 'The London Book Trade in 1668', pp. 79, 85. If McKenzie's figures for entries excludes serials that entry rate is 16.9%.

[12] For a useful account of printing patents see Arnold Hunt, 'Book Trade Patents, 1603–1640', in *The Book Trade and its Customers 1450–1900: Historical Essays for Robin Myers*, ed. by Arnold Hunt, Giles Mandelbrote and Alison Shell (Winchester: St Paul's Bibliographies, 1997), pp. 27–54.

[13] Bell, 'Entrance in the Stationers' Register', p. 54.

[14] This figure is low in part because of the number of official publications in this format.

[15] David Norbrook, *Poetry and Politics in the English Renaissance* (London: Routledge, 1984), p. 209–13.

[16] Anonymous, *The wars in Germany, with the taking of townes by the marquesse Spynola* (STC 11796); see Stationers' Hall, Court Book C, 14 October 1614.

[17] Undated item, 'Extracts of censurable passages from a pamphlet lately published, and presented to His Majesty, entitled "The Trades Increase," on the importance of increasing English shipping', attributable to the year 1614 in *Calendar of State Papers Domestic, 1611–1618* (London: H. M. S. O., 1858), p. 263.

[18] Figures for anonymity appear in McKenzie, 'The London Book Trade in 1644', p. 136, and Goldie, 'The Revolution of 1689', *passim*; for a fuller discussion of the extent, nature, and significance of anonymity, see my *Pamphlets and Pamphleteering*.

[19] McKenzie, 'The London Book Trade in 1668', pp. 81, 84; see also W. W. Greg, *Some Aspects and Problems of London Publishing Between 1550 and 1650* (Oxford: Clarendon Press, 1956), pp. 82–9; M. A. Shaaber, 'The Meaning of the Imprint in Early Printed Books', *The Library*, 4th ser., 24 (1943–4), 120–41; Peter W. M. Blayney, 'The Publication of Playbooks', in *A New History of Early English Drama*, ed. by John D. Cox and David Scott Kastan (New York: Columbia University Press, 1997), pp. 383–422 (p. 390).

[20] STC 4623.5; STC 20083.3.

[21] Robert Tailor, *The Hogge hath lost his Pearle. A Comedy* (London, 1614; STC 23658), sig. A3^r; Leonard Wright, *A Display of dutie, dect with sage sayings, pythie sentences, and proper similies: Pleasant to reade, delightfull to heare, and profitable to practice* (London, 1614; STC 26027).

[22] Such is the case with Marchamont Nedham's *The excellencie of a free state: or, the right constitution of a Commonwealth ... With some errors of government, and rules of policie. Published by a well-wisher to posterity* (London, 1656), for example, a reprint of republican editorials from *Mercurius Politicus* from the years 1651–2, which could be read as a critique of Cromwell; or with Milton's publications in 1658. See J. G. A. Pocock, 'James Harrington and the Good Old Cause: A Study of the Ideological Context of his Writings', *Journal of British Studies*, 10 (1970), 38–9; *Political Works of James Harrington*, ed. by J. G. A. Pocock (Cambridge: Cambridge University Press, 1977), pp. 13–14, 34–40; Martin Dzelzainis, 'Milton and the Protectorate in 1658', in *Milton and Republicanism*, ed. by David Armitage, Quentin Skinner, and Armand Himy (Cambridge: Cambridge University Press, 1995), 181–205.

[23] Goldie, 'The Revolution of 1689', pp. 522–3. On reprinting see Joseph Laurence Black, 'Pamphlet Wars: The Marprelate Tracts and "Martinism," 1588–1688' (University of Toronto, Ph.D. thesis, 1996), ch. 5; Joseph Marshall, 'Reading and Mis-reading King James 1622–1642: Responses to the *Letter and Directions Touching Preaching and Preachers*', in *Royal Subjects: Essays on the Writings of James VI and I*, ed. by Daniel Fishlin and Mark Fortier (Detroit: Wayne State University Press, forthcoming). I am also indebted to an unpublished paper by Marshall, entitled 'Recycling and Originality in British Pamphlets, 1640–48', delivered at Cambridge University Library, 25 February 2000; see also my *Pamphlets and Pamphleteering*.

[24] *Limits of Revision*, pp. 11, 14; cf. *Proceedings, 1614*, p. 141.

[25] *Proceedings, 1614*, pp. 423, 428, 433.

[26] *Proceeding, 1614*, p. 160.

[27] *Proceedings, 1614*, pp. 368–9.

[28] *Proceedings, 1614*, pp. 54, 68, 90, 279.

[29] See A. D. T. Cromartie, 'The Printing of Parliamentary Speeches in November 1640–July 1642', *Historical Journal*, 33 (1990), 23–44; Joad Raymond, *The Invention of the Newspaper: English Newsbooks, 1641–1649* (Oxford: Clarendon Press, 1996), chapter 2.

[30] STC 12630; STC 20569; STC 14068; STC 809. On wonder pamphlets of this kind, see Alexandra Walsham, *Providence in Early Modern England* (Oxford: Oxford University Press, 1999); Cressy, *Travesties and Transgressions*; Peter Lake, 'Deeds against Nature: Cheap Print, Protestantism and Murder in Early Seventeenth-Century England', in *Culture and Politics*, ed. by Sharpe and Lake, pp. 257–83; idem, 'Popular Form, Puritan Content? Two Puritan Appropriations of the Murder Pamphlet from Mid-Seventeenth-Century London', in *Religion, Culture and Society in Early Modern Britain: Essays in Honour of Patrick Collinson*, ed. by Anthony Fletcher and Peter Roberts (Cambridge: Cambridge University Press, 1994), pp. 313–34.

[31] *Letters of John Chamberlain*, I, 519, 535.

[32] *Letters of John Chamberlain*, I, 502, 504, 515, 523, 550.

[33] Robert Booth, *A Relation of all matters passed, especially in the Low-Countries, touching the causes of the warre now in Cleveland. Together with such occurrences of note as have happened in Spain, Italie, England, Germany, Hungarie and Transylvania since March last to this present, 1614. Translated according to the originall of Mercurius Gallo-Belgicus* (London, 1614), p. 1; Thomas Bretnor, *A new almanacke and prognostication* (London, 1615, i.e. 1614; STC 420.8); Thomas Campion, *The Description of a Maske: presented in the Banqueting Roome at Whitehall ... at the Mariage of the ... Earle of Somerset and ... the Lady Frances Howard. Whereunto are annexed divers choyse Ayres composed for this Maske that may be sung with a single voyce to the Lute or Base-Viall* (London, 1614; STC 4539); George Chapman, *Andromeda Liberata. Or the nuptials of Perseus and Andromeda* (London, 1614; STC 4964), sigs. ¶4^v, B^r. See also Wright, *Display*, fol. 7^v; William Lithgow, *A most delectable, and true discourse, of an admired and painefull peregrination from Scotland to the most famous Kingdomes in Europe, Asia, and Affricke* (London, 1614; STC 15710); John King, *Vitis Palatina. A sermon appointed to be preached at Whitehall upon the Tuesday after the mariage of the Ladie Elizabeth her Grace* (London, 1614; STC 14989.5); Daniel Price, *Prince Henry, his second anniversary* (Oxford, 1614; STC 20300), p. 13.

[34] Francis Bacon, *The charge of sir Francis Bacon, His Majesties Attourney generall, touching duells* (London, 1614; STC 1125); cf. *Letters of John Chamberlain*, I, 509.

[35] *A briefe of the bill concerning printers, bookesellers and bookbinders* (London, 1614; STC 16786.2); *Proceedings, 1614*, pp. 118, 126, 293.

[36] *Proceedings, 1614*, p. xiv and n. 3.

[37] John Barnes, *An act or decree of the Court of Parliament of Paris, made the 26. and executed the 27. of Iune. 1614. Against a booke ... intituled Francisci Suares ... Defensio fidei Catholicæ & apostilicæ, adversus Anglicanæ sectæ errores: containing diuers principles and propositions repugnant to the soueraigne power of kings ... translated out of the French copie, etc.* (London, 1614; STC 19201).

[38] *Proceedings, 1614*, p. 185.

[39] Alexander Lumisden, *A heavenly portion* (London, 1614; STC 16924); King, *Vitis Palatina*; *Proceedings, 1614*, pp. 6, 14, 26, 74, 185, 421.

[40] *Proceedings, 1614*, p. 113.

[41] William Harrison, *The Difference of Hearers. Or, an Exposition of the parable of the sower. Deliuered in certaine sermons at Hyton in Lancashire* (London, 1614), sig. A7^v; Robert Horne, *Gods gentle remembrance* (London, 1614; STC 13821) sig. C^r; Juliana Berners, *A Jewell for Gentrie. Being an exact Dictionary, or true Method, to make any Man understand all the Art, Secrets ... belonging to Hawking, Hunting, Fowling and Fishing ... now newly published, and beautified* (London, 1614; STC 21520); *Proceedings, 1614*, *passim*.

[42] Henricus Alting, *A votive oration for the auspicial government of Fredericke the V. Palatine of Rhene* (London, 1614; STC 538.9); *A full declaration of the faith and ceremonies professed in the dominions of ... Fredericke, 5. prince elector palatine ... Translated into English by Iohn Rolte* (London, 1614; STC 19130); Alexander Julius, *Ob secundum et felicem eventum conjugij ... Frederici 5. electoralis palatinatus principis ... et ... Elizabethæ filiæ ... regis magnæ Britanniæ ... Carmen* (London, 1614; STC 14853); King, *Vitis Palatina*.

[43] *Proceedings, 1614*, p. 75; William Worship, *Earth raining upon Heaven, A sermon preached at the Assises at Nottingham, August 5, 1614* (London, 1614; STC 25994), p. 21.

[44] Joshua Sylvester, *The Parliament of vertues royal* (London, [1614?]; STC 23581), p. 59; Cambridge University Library copy, Syn. 8.61.96, has a MS date 1615.

[45] William Walker, *A sermon preached at the funerals of the right honourable, William, Lord Russell, Baron of Thorbaugh ... the 16 of September 1613.* (London, 1614; STC 24964), p. 49; Barnaby Rich, *The Honestie of this Age. Prooving by good circumstance that the world was never honest till now* (London, 1614; STC 20986), p. 23.

[46] *Proceedings, 1614*, pp. 185–6; Thomas L. Moir, *The Addled Parliament of 1614* (Oxford, 1958), p. 110; *Letters of John Chamberlain*, I, 528, 530; John Taylor, *The Nipping or Snipping of Abuses: or the woolgathering of Witte. With The Muses Taylor, brought from Parnassus by land, with a paire of Oares* (London, 1614; STC 23779); Lumisden, *A heavenly portion*; William Est, *Two sermons* London, 1614; STC 10539); Chapman *Andromeda Liberata*, sig. B^r; Nicholas Breton, *I Would, and would not* (London, 1614; STC 3664), stanzas 108–9; and, perhaps to prove their point, Barnaby Rich, *The honestie of this age* (London, 1614; STC 20986).

[47] Lancelot Andrewes, *A Sermon preached before His Maiestie, at Whitehall on Easter day last, 1614* (London, 1614; STC 622); Samuel Smith, *Davids Repentance, or, a plaine and familiar Exposition of the 51. Psalme* (London, 1614; STC 22841.7), pp 508–11; Peter E. McCullough, *Sermons at Court: Politics and Religion in Elizabethan and Jacobean Preaching* (Cambridge: Cambridge University Press, 1998), p. 122.

[48] Leonard Wright, *A Display of Duty* (1589; London, 1614; STC 26027), fol. 7^v.

[49] William Harrison, *The difference of hearers; or An exposition of the parable of the sower* (London, 1614; STC 12870), sig. A5^r.

[50] Richard Stock, *The Churches Lamentation for the loss of the Godly ... delivered in a Sermon at the funeral of John Lord Harington* (London, 1614; STC 23273), p. 86.

[51] Worship, *Earth raining upon Heaven*, pp. 2–3.

[52] *Proceedings, 1614*, p. 365.

[53] *Proceedings, 1614*, pp. 420 and 415, incl. n. 13; S. R. Gardiner, *History of England From the Accession of James I to the Outbreak of the Civil War 1603–1642*, 10 vols (London: Longman, Green & Co., 1883–4), II, 246. This was followed a few weeks later by a topical sermon entitled *Ephesus backsliding considered and applyed to these times, in a sermon* (London, 1614; STC 20352) by John Prideaux of Exeter College, who confessed to there being 'some *wolves* among the pastors' (p. 36).

[54] *Letters of John Chamberlain*, I, 507; cf. I, 504.

[55] *Letters of John Chamberlain*, I, 496. See also I, 499.

[56] Arthur F. Marotti, *Manuscript, Print, and the English Renaissance Lyric* (Ithaca and London: Cornell University Press, 1995), pp. 94–109; Alastair Bellany, '"Mistress Turner's Deadly Sins": Sartorial Transgression, Court Scandal, and Politics in Early Stuart England,' *Huntington Library Quarterly*, 58 (1996), 179–210; David Lindley, *The Trials of Frances Howard: Fact and Fiction at the court of King James* (London & New York: Routledge, 1993); and Anne Baynes Coiro, 'Milton and class identity: the publication of *Areopagitica* and the 1645 *Poems*', *Journal of Medieval and Renaissance Studies*, 22 (1992), 269–75.

[57] George Chapman, *A Free and Offenceles Justification: Of a lately published and most maliciously misinterpreted Poeme; Entituled Andromeda Liberata* (London, 1614; STC 4977).

[58] Norbrook, *Poetry and Politics in the English Renaissance*; Michelle O'Callaghan, '"Talking Politics": Tyranny, Parliament, and Christopher Brooke's *The Ghost of Richard the Third* (1614)', *Historical Journal*, 41 (1998), 97–120, and idem, 'Literary Commonwealths: A 1614 Print Community, *The Shepheards Pipe* and *The Shepherds Hunting*', *The Seventeenth Century*, 13 (1998), 103–23.

[59] Rich, *Honestie of this age*, pp. 11–12; Stock, *The Churches lamentation*, p. 84; Daniel Price, *Prince Henry his second anniversary*, p. 11.

[60] John Andrewes, *Christ his crosse* (London, 1614; STC 594), sig. L2^{v}.

[61] Andrewes, *Christ his crosse*, p. 34.

9

Intervention in the Cloth Trade: Richard Hakluyt, the New Draperies and the Cockayne Project of 1614

Rosalind Davies

This paper is concerned with the rivalry between the Clothworkers' Company and the Merchant Adventurers' Company leading to the collapse of the Merchant Adventurers' Company in 1614.[1] Between these two City companies lies the clash between the interests of an exporter and those of an employer: the Adventurers dealt with the export of cloth chiefly to Northwest Europe, whereas the Clothworkers represented clothiers, clothworkers and dyers – people whose livelihoods depended on the manufacture of cloth. They acted as a lobbying group, a kind of union. The Adventurers, on the other hand, are better described as a professional body, which did not trade as a company, but their members traded individually. The Merchant Adventurers dominated not only the English merchant community at the turn of the seventeenth century, but the economy of the Low Countries and Germany.[2] Robert Brenner's study of commercial change in England in the century between 1550 and 1650, *Merchants and Revolution*, is framed by what he calls the 'unquestioned leadership' of the Adventurers from page one onwards.[3] Indeed, commentary on merchant groups in the City frequently defines new trades or traders in relation to the old, established Merchant Adventurers.

The story of the evolution of the new trades and trade routes at the turn of the seventeenth century is, in many accounts, virtually the story of the Merchant Adventurers' failure to take the initiative in originating new trades; to move away from the existing markets of Northern Europe to exploit the potential of the eastern Mediterranean, Turkey or Russia. As Baumann's recent study of the Adventurers' trade confirms, the company located its markets according to the cloth finishing trade, hence the preeminence of Antwerp throughout the sixteenth century, as well as alternative sites in the Netherlands and the Hanseatic towns.[4] It was in these places that the processing of the unfinished cloth exported by the Adventurers was a primary trade. The unfinished state in which their cloths were exported divided the Merchant Adventurers from the newer trading companies, and from the alliance of traders headed by the Clothworkers' Company. Clearly, it was in the Clothworkers' interest to get the highest levels of employment for clothworkers, clothiers and dyers by only transporting cloth which was fully manufactured, that is, dressed and dyed cloth. However, the Merchant Adventurers were allowed by law to transport most of it undressed and undyed, and their markets got cheaper English cloth as a consequence, and kept their own workforce busy by dyeing it themselves.

The polarisation of interests between these City companies confirmed the Merchant Adventurers as exporters who sought to retain their monopoly on the short range cloth trade to Germany and the Netherlands, and the Clothworkers as a body whose members were best served by the transportation of finished cloth to more distant markets. The events of 1614, and the drive to increase royal revenue in which the cloth companies were implicated, have been closely studied by historians. Alderman William Cockayne's proposal, that a patent should be granted for a new company which would finish and dye all cloth before export, penalised the Merchant Adventurers for their trade in undressed cloth, which it was said, was a 'disadvantageous course of tradinge' in respect to His Majesties customs.[5]

I

The approach of most historians has been, rightly, to set the historical events of the 1614 parliament and the Cockayne Project in the context of the long-standing rivalry between the companies of the Merchant Adventurers and the Clothworkers. G. D. Ramsay, in his two classic articles, 'Clothworkers and Merchants Adventurers in Conflict' and 'Clothworkers, Merchants Adventurers and Richard Hakluyt', traces the conflict back to the middle part of the sixteenth century, as does Astrid Friis in the fullest account of the political machinations of 1614, *Alderman Cockayne's Project and the Cloth Trade*.[6] In this broader, more complex view, the affiliations of Richard Hakluyt in the merchant community have taken their place. It is no coincidence that an economic historian like Ramsay developed his thesis on industrial discontent to include Richard Hakluyt, and that Thomas Girtin, author of the only narrative history of the Clothworkers' Company, should also be the author of an essay entitled 'Mr Hakluyt, Scholar at Oxford.'[7] These scholarly trajectories are initiated by Hakluyt's status as a pensioner of both the Clothworkers and the Skinners' Company, together with the economic rationale of the *Principal Navigations*, compiled and edited by Hakluyt in four volumes, 1589, and 1598–1600 (although such a bald summary hardly does justice to the breadth of documents it contains). This essay will explore how the dynamics of the sponsorship and publication of the *Principal Navigations*, its mercantilist logic and its compound of territorial, religious and economic expansion, alerts us to other political, personal and institutional histories which are appended to the conflict between the Merchant Adventurers and the Clothworkers, and the events of 1614.

There is scope to investigate the relationship between Hakluyt as editor of the *Principal Navigations*, and the contested cargos, markets and profits of the cloth trade, in terms which go beyond Ramsay's statement that the promotion of longer-range trades and highly finished exports in the *Principal Navigations* must have been a 'welcome message' at Clothworkers Hall.[8] In the case of the Clothworkers' Company, much of interest about the patronage of Richard Hakluyt is documented, but it has not produced concepts or conclusions pertinent to the political contexts of Hakluyt's situation as a company pensioner. The assertion that the Company benefited from Hakluyt's scholarship, and that for the Company, 'learning' had a 'political edge' is, or has become, a commonplace which does little to advance the institutional and intellectual history of concern here.[9] Apart from the description of the arrangements of his pension, paid between 1577 and 1586, there has been no systematic study of Hakluyt's links to the merchant community. One specific area, his collection of documents, many of which must have come from company archive sources, is particularly ripe for analysis.

The main thrust of the discussion concerning Hakluyt's pension from the Clothworkers' Company, has been to stress the weakness of Hakluyt's position and the exceptional nature of the payments. For Ramsay, the payment of the pension, and certainly the number of years which Hakluyt's name remained in the Company's Court books, is 'astonishing'. Similarly, Thomas Girtin's account is punctuated by remarks about what 'normally' would have happened in the case of exhibitions and pensions, and what was uniquely arranged for Hakluyt.[10] In August 1577, Hakluyt 'beinge a Scoller in Christechurch in Oxforde who as he saith is alredie proceded maister of Arte and is entred into the studie of dyvinitie', was awarded the annual sum of £6 13s.[11] The continuance of the study of divinity was a condition of the pension, and in 1580 Hakluyt was appointed a tutor in divinity to another Company pensioner at Oxford, Gabriell Bowman.[12] This ecclesiastic emphasis was also expressed at this time in Hakluyt's preaching of sermons for the Clothworkers' Company. The persistence with which the pension was organised around Hakluyt's religious studies – in 1581 it was agreed that Hakluyt should be loaned the Company's copy of St Augustine's works for the furtherance of his study – is the first in a line of perceived anomalies which have been made the focus of the narratives of the Company's patronage.[13] However, it is the survival of the financial arrangement at the time at which Hakluyt was appointed to the position of Chaplain and Secretary to Sir Edward Stafford, resident ambassador in France, and the intervention of the Lord Treasurer Burghley in the payments for the remaining years of the pension, that has produced most disquiet, and the clearest picture of the protection Hakluyt must have received from the government and from powerful figures in the Company.

In August 1583, at Burghley's request and 'signified by his lettres', it was agreed that during his abode in France, Hakluyt would have his Company pension paid to him as before.[14] For Hakluyt, this was an emphatic move away from what he termed the 'duty' of his religious study and tutelage at Oxford, and towards his geographical interests, his 'intended course'.[15] The appointment also confirmed his usefulness to the English government in the activities of European intelligence gathering, positioned as he was in the Paris embassy, with access to European news, libraries, and the circulation of documents, maps and personal accounts. With the publication of *Divers Voyages* behind him, Hakluyt offered to accompany the voyage to Virginia in 1584 which was sponsored by Sir Walter Ralegh, and employ 'all his simple observations and reading' for its success.[16] It was also in connection with this expedition that Hakluyt wrote *The Discourse of Western Planting* (1584), and presented the book to Francis Walsingham.[17] Hakluyt's own compartmentalisation of knowledge – duty versus intellectual ambition – and the subsequent readings of Hakluyt's career and the history of the Clothworkers' Company by Ramsay and Girtin, exclude the possibility that the patronage relationship influenced the type, direction and credibility of his intellectual pursuit. In fact, the expectation of just the opposite, that Hakluyt's employments in the embassy should bring to an end his pension, precludes any acknowledgement that the Clothworkers' Company was acting as an intermediary between Hakluyt and his government patron. In this way, the effect of state endorsement, and the control of access to the means of promoting new trades, was as significant for the Company as it was for Hakluyt. The collection, editing and translation of documents for the *Principal Navigations* which occupied Hakluyt over the next decade, was an expression of mercantilist thought, the resources for which were, in part, controlled by the intervention and legitimation of the Privy Council. With respect to the Clothworkers' Company, account must be taken not just of the 'welcome message' of Hakluyt's activities, but of the Company's resulting proximity to the authority invested in the rationale and procedures of the *Principal Navigations*. Hakluyt's appointment to the embassy in Paris in 1583, and the continuation of his pension, brought the legitimising power of the state, and the promotion of new draperies, trades and trade routes into sharper focus for the Company.

Richard Staper, Quarter Warden of the Clothworkers' Company from 1576 (later to become Master in 1590), and Edward Dier, Master in 1576, were two influential figures in the establishment and perpetuation of Hakluyt's pension. Hakluyt wrote in the dedication of *Principal Navigations*:

> In respect of a generall incouragement in this laborious travaile, it were grosse ingratitude in mee to forget, and wilfull maliciousness not to confesse that man, whose onely name doth carrie with it sufficient estimation and love, and that is Master *Edward Dier*, of whom I will speake thus much in few words, that both my selfe and my intentions herein by his friendly meanes have been made knowne to those, who in sundrie particulars have much steeded me. More specially in my first part, Master *Richard Staper* Marchant of London, hath furnished me with divers thinges touching the trade of Turkie, and other places in the East.[18]

Staper was involved alike in the Levant Company from 1581 and the Barbary Company from 1585, and was well placed to assemble materials for Hakluyt's use. The main bulk of the Levant and Barbary materials, dating from 1579 to 1585, were probably derived from Staper, as well as perhaps a discrete group of documents on Brazil dating 1578 to 1580.[19] The work of David Beers Quinn in his edition of the *Principal Navigations* and later in *The Hakluyt Handbook*, provides useful detail on the provenance of Hakluyt's documents, revealing that a large number of them were obtained through contacts in the merchant community.[20] The finest body of materials in the *Principal Navigations* is that relating to the Muscovy Company. Of the 180 documents written after 1550 and printed in the 1589 volume, almost half relate to the Muscovy Company, or come from their archives. In the titles and subtitles to the printed documents, Hakluyt acknowledged the help he received from two important members of the Company, William Borough and

Anthony Jenkinson. Even if we discount the papers which Borough or Jenkinson may have had in their personal possession, a substantial number remain unallocated, and this suggests that Hakluyt had access to a company archive source.[21] Hand in hand with Burghley and Francis Walsingham, who as Secretary of State was Hakluyt's employer, and by whose warrant the *Principal Navigations* was entered in the Stationers' Register, these collaborations point to the marriage between the administrative machinery of government, the corporate librarianship of City trading companies, and the economic geography of mercantilist theories.

II

The division between the Merchant Adventurers and the newer trading companies in terms of markets and manufacture, is a division clarified in the statistical analysis of English cloth exports at the end of the sixteenth century. By the end of the 1590s, 71% of all cloth exports were exported through the hands of the Merchant Adventurers. Newer companies like the Muscovy Company took only 1.5%, the Barbary Company 2% and the Levant Company 6%.[22] In 1606 Germany and the Netherlands took 95,000 cloths, whereas the Levant and Italy took just over 8,000, Russia approximately 2,000 and the Barbary Coast less than that.[23] In 1614, before the intervention of the Cockayne Project, of the cloths exported to the traditional markets of the Netherlands and Germany, 57,000 were undressed and a meagre eleven were transported dressed. It is because of the Merchant Adventurers' monopoly that new traders like the Turkey Company, later to become the Levant Company, appealed for government backing for the export of dressed and finished cloth. Interest in establishing trade with Turkey within the Elizabethan privy council indicates that the advantages of regular trade routes into the eastern Mediterranean were well thought of for English commerce and shipping. Burghley kept an account of the course and time of sailing to the Levant, and a proposal put to him by Turkey merchants in 1582 asked for his assistance and favour specifically for the 'vent of [...] cloth and kersies of all sorts died and thorowlie dressed.'[24] The royal charter to the Russia Company sanctioned in 1566 included a clause which decreed that the Company was prohibited from exporting any manner of cloths unless 'they shall be all dressed, and for the most part dyed within this realme.'[25] This policy effectively left the Merchant Adventurers' monopoly on undressed cloth intact, and preserved their relationship with the Netherlands and the Hanseatic traders who had built a large industry around dyeing imported English cloth. The conjunction between the new trades and the export of finished cloth was sealed in the vision of the patents and privileges granted to the new companies, which directed them away from the strongholds of the Adventurers' trade in unmanufactured cloth.

That exports should consist of highly finished articles, towards the price of which the cost of labour contributed a maximum proportion, was a central part not only of the economic theory of the *Principal Navigations*, but of intermittent legislation from the reign of Henry VII onwards, designed to protect the workforce. Arguments in favour of securing new markets and confining imports to necessities as opposed to luxuries, aimed as E.G.R. Taylor has said, to foster 'an expanding cloth industry, necessitating an alert and progressive manufacturing and merchant class.'[26] Instructions given to Morgan Hubblethorne, a dyer, who travelled to Persia in 1579, and recorded in the *Principal Navigations*, declared that:

> the clothes of the Realme have no good vent, if good dying be not added: therefore it is much to be wished, that the dying of forren Countreies were seene, to the end that the arte of dying may be brought into the Realme in greatest excellencie: [...] and of the vent of clothes, will follow the setting of our poore on worke, in all degrees of labour in clothing and dying.[27]

The *Discourse of Western Planting* presented to Queen Elizabeth by Hakluyt in 1584 to gain her support for the Virginia ventures, stated that existing English trade routes were 'growen beggarly or dangerous' because of harassment by Spanish shipping, therefore English trade needed to expand its horizons. For the benefit of the unemployed, Hakluyt argued that English cloth was to pass out of the country 'full wroughte by our naturall subjectes in all degrees of labour.'[28] In some notes on the Levant trade, the English factor in Constantinople was instructed not to carry any white cloth on his return to Turkey but only dyed, 'so that the subjects of the realme may take as much benefit as is possible.'[29]

The relevance of the organisation of trading companies to the development of mercantilist thought and trade policies, is the subject of an essay by F. J. Fisher, and is all the more valuable for its interest in forms of corporate organisation, an aspect which histories of individual companies have ignored.[30] Fisher argues that in the early years of the seventeenth century, the old forms of corporate organisation, defined by the static regulation of economic activity, gave way to the view that industry was 'dynamic, something demanding not merely regulation, but encouragement, development, creation.'[31] As the Clothworkers' Company shook off its municipal status and moved into politics at the end of the sixteenth century, the trades with which its members were involved took on increasing economic benefits. Pauline Croft has shown how English commerce with Spain and Portugal in dyed and finished cloths, established a trading pattern which heightened the economic importance of the textile industry.[32] The rise in imports which went with the vigorous trade in new draperies was, Croft says, crucial to the development of the cloth industry itself, as olive oil, used in the preparation of raw wool and dyes, was among the Iberian imports.[33] These associated markets increased the value of England's cloth trade by resourcing the employment and skills of dyers and clothmakers, and driving up the level of exports. Set against the promotion and creation of the trades in new draperies in earlier decades is the arbitrary regulation which was attempted by the Cockayne Project.

Historical accounts of the 1614 parliament have implicated the Merchant Adventurers Company in James's drive to increase the royal income. William Cockayne, alderman of the City, proposed to the Privy Council that a patent should be granted for a new company which would 'finish' or dye all cloth before export. This meant changing the way that the most numerous and powerful cloth exporters had worked for centuries by exporting unfinished cloth. Cockayne and his co-promoters claimed that finishing the cloth before export would secure the king £20,000 a year, or an extra five shillings on every cloth.[34] In the lead-up to the 1614 parliament Sir Julius Caesar, Chancellor of the Exchequer, gathered details on 'projects' likely to be profitable to the king. In June 1613 he compiled a memorial for other commissioners employed on the same business, which listed projects likely to be successful and projects likely to fail. As well as plans to sell off old houses, castles and defective titles, the 'Cockayne project' was on the 'successful' list, described as the 'forbidding of transportation of clothes undrest and undied.'[35]

III

Until the king and his government threw their weight behind the opponents of the Merchant Adventurers in 1612, the Adventurers had the best of the debates about the type of cloth that should be exported, providing more answers than the Clothworkers had objections. The Clothworkers, on the other hand, were successful agitators and brought several petitions to parliament. In 1586 the Privy Council intervened in a controversy between clothiers and Merchant Adventurers. In fact the late 1580s saw a flurry of complaints from clothworkers and clothiers, and in 1587 the governor of the Adventurers, Richard Saltonstall, wrote to Francis Walsingham to object to the constraints placed upon his company, which as he saw it, was at the mercy of every 'light complaint' brought by their opponents.[36] Both sides repeatedly invoked the statutes laid down by several kings and queens which had not been properly enforced. In 1487 Henry VII had ordered that no cloth was to be carried out of the country until it had been barbed, rowed or shorn, in an attempt to ensure a supply of work to poor artisans. In 1512 Henry VIII re-enacted this statute, and in 1566 it was supplemented and modified again. The two main obstacles to the successful prosecution of these laws was, as the Adventurers argued, that there was no market for finished cloth in the Netherlands, where the cloth trade had its own finishing industry. Secondly, because of the importance and longevity of the cloth trade between England and Northwest Europe, there was a history of lax administration of these statutes.[37]

Another sequence of petitions and replies begins in 1590, at which time the Clothworkers' Company put forward 'an opinion' that no woollen cloths should be transported until they had been fully manufactured.[38] In their counterattack the Adventurers claimed that this would be an adverse move for the profitability of the whole trade, for if the whole trade were to fall into decay, everybody dependent upon the cloth trade, including the clothworkers and dyers would lose their livings. The Adventurers cleverly exploited the range of trade routes and markets which the new English trades were developing, inferring that the Clothworkers had an expanding and promiscuous market for coloured cloth in eastern Europe, the East and West Indies and the Barbary Coast.[39]

In May 1599 the Clothworkers were again putting articles before parliament, objecting to the Merchant Adventurers' privilege and to the 'decaie and overthrowe of manie hundred thousande of Clothworkers.'[40] Specifically they complained that by the licence granted to them after the statute of 1566, the Adventurers were supposed to reserve cloths under the price of £6 a piece for dressing and dyeing. According to the Clothworkers, the Adventurers were only shipping cloths worth ten, twelve, or fourteen pounds a piece so as to avoid having to export manufactured cloth. The cloth that was allowed to be dressed was of such poor quality that it would not withstand workmanship.[41] The first landmark for the opponents of the Merchant Adventurers came in 1604 when the Clothworkers' Bill against the transportation of undressed cloth began its journey through the House of Commons, and was passed in March 1606.[42]

Customs books gave early, decisive evidence against the Merchant Adventurers. A memorial in the State Papers observed that 'His Majestie is very much prejudiced in his Customes' by about £150,000 a year by the export of undressed white cloth.[43] What the Clothworkers had been saying for years now got the seal of royal agreement. 'His hignes Subjectes are much distressed by want of the great imployment and benefit, which they should receave by the full manufacture [of cloth].' The writer of the memo suggested that the Adventurers should be penalised for their 'disadvantageous course of tradinge', and a sum of money be demanded from them. In March 1613 all interested parties, the Clothworkers, the Adventurers, the office of customs and members of the Privy Council were invited to express their opinions on a 'project' brought to the king which asked for the enforcement of the statutes relating to the dyeing and dressing of cloth in England. In return, the petitioners would allow King James, his heirs and successors 'five shillings stirling upon every cloath so dressed, died and transported, which is like to amount to the yearely sume of twenty thousand pounds at the least.' At least one disgruntled member of the Merchant Adventurers knew who to blame for the fresh impetus behind the Clothworkers' complaints. The anonymous merchant wrote:

> Itt pleased Mr Allderman Cockaine to charge the marchaunt adventurors to be very Idell and unskillful marchauntes in their bussynes, as though they knewe nothing but to buy a white cloth [on] Thursdays, and to shipp it [on] Munday, and brought into the Land unproffitable Commodetyes, as Silkes, Velluettes, and such toyes.[44]

Cockayne's project is largely infamous as one of 'the classic cases of ill-conceived government intervention in the economy.'[45] Whether or not James failed to realise the motives of Cockayne and his promoters, the breaking of the monopoly of the Merchant Adventurers in 1614 coincided with the attempt to increase royal income. William Cockayne was an Eastland Company merchant trading to the Baltic, and his company provided the Governor, Deputy, Treasurer and seven assistants for the new company that was formed after the demise of the Adventurers. The Levant and Italy Companies provided another five members.[46] Following the royal proclamation of July 1614 in which the Merchant Adventurers' Company was dissolved, Cockayne announced the birth of a company to be known as the New Merchant Adventurers formed, allegedly, for the purpose of dressing and dyeing cloth at home for lucrative returns.[47] However, it soon became clear that Cockayne's company was more interested in itself selling unfinished cloth to the old markets than establishing a finishing industry. The Cockayne project was in essence an attempt to capture a portion of the profitable trade in white, undressed cloths to Germany and the Low Countries, while maintaining the trade in dressed cloth at its pre-existing levels. So as one commentator has expressed it, the initial promise to finish all textile exports actually was the means to prise open the rich trade in undressed cloths, and to force the old Merchant Adventurers to participate in a new division of the traditional trade.[48]

The dénouement to this drama is the reinstatement of the old Merchant Adventurers' Company in December 1616 after English cloth exports had dropped by a third. The transition from the old Adventurers to the new had upset the equilibrium in the European markets: the Dutch reaction to the potential threat to their dyeing industry was a prohibition on the import of dyed cloth. Whereas the old Adventurers had the capital to buy cloth from clothiers once a week, the new company bought large quantities in a short period and intended to sell it gradually. This had two side-effects. Firstly, it kept the new Company's funds tied up, which it could not afford, and secondly, it lead to another round of vociferous complaints from clothiers who found there was no regular demand for their product. In the summer of 1616 the government ordered cloth merchants to buy their cloth weekly in an attempt to remedy the deadness of the trade.[49] By late 1616 cloth exports from London were down one third on the peak of the trade in 1614. Two years later in 1618 the trade had recovered enough only to reach the levels of 1603.

The promotion of new markets, new trade routes and new manufactured commodities, is a compound of old debates and new expediency. William Cockayne rode to prominence on the back of long-standing grievances among clothworkers, but his new company left the manufacturing classes as isolated as before. King James himself merged the two temporalities when he declared the end of the Merchant Adventurers' Company in 1614, and recalled a history of manufacture and employment protection, which in 1614 he claimed to be renewing. His proclamation against the exportation of undressed cloth read:

> It was the work of one of Our Noble Progenitours, King Edward 3. to convert the wools of this kingdom, formerly vented Raw, into Cloth, thereby to procure unto Our loving Subjects the profite arising, aswel upon the Manufacture, as upon the Materiall, and to let Our owne people on worke for their better sustentation and comfort.[50]

Intervention in England's cloth trade in the sixteenth and seventeenth centuries has a history more complex than either statute regulations or profit motives. The temptation in summarising this history is to offset the quantification of the cloth trade revenue produced by government ministers and William Cockayne in 1614 in search of an answer to the financial embarrassments of the Stuart regime, against a less specific climate of opinion arranged around the potential national asset of long-range trades and the maximisation of highly finished exports. The patronage offered to Richard Hakluyt, in its layering of government legitimation and corporate sponsorship, raises another dimension to the cloth trade's presence in the political arena. The Clothworkers' advance against the monopoly on undressed cloth held by the Merchant Adventurers through petition and legislation, was underwritten by their access to the resources, political and literary, for the expansion of manufacture and export, and the claiming of new trades through textual labour.

Notes

[1] I am grateful to Conrad Russell and Pauline Croft for their helpful comments on an earlier draft of this essay.

[2] See Wolf-Rüdiger Baumann, *The Merchants Adventurers and the Continental Cloth-trade (1560s–1620s)* (Berlin and New York: Walter de Gruyter, 1990).

[3] Robert Brenner, *Merchants and Revolution. Commercial Change, Political Conflict, and London's Overseas Traders, 1550–1653* (New Jersey: Princeton University Press, 1993).

[4] Baumann, *Merchants Adventurers,* especially Chapter one, 'Motives of the Merchants Adventurers for Shifting Their Marts, and Their Criteria of Site Selection', pp. 7–18.

[5] Public Record Office, State Papers 14/71, no. 105.

[6] G. D. Ramsay, 'Industrial Discontent in Early Elizabethan London: Clothworkers and Merchants Adventurers in Conflict', *The London Journal,* 1:2 (1975), 227–39, and idem, 'Clothworkers, Merchants Adventurers and Richard Hakluyt', *English Historical Review*, 92 (1977), 504–21. Astrid Friis, *Alderman Cockayne's Project and the Cloth Trade* (Copenhagen: Levin & Munksgaard & London: Oxford University Press, 1927).

[7] Thomas Girtin, *The Golden Ram: A Narrative History of the Clothworkers Company 1528–1958,* 2nd edn (Aylesbury: The Worshipful Company of Clothworkers, 1958); and idem, 'Mr Hakluyt, Scholar at Oxford', *Geographical Journal*, 119 (1953), 208–12.

[8] Ramsay, 'Clothworkers, Merchants Adventurers and Richard Hakluyt', p. 521.

[9] See Ramsay, 'Clothworkers, Merchants Adventurers and Richard Hakluyt', p. 514. For interpretations of the effects of patronage on the organisation of intellectual activity which have informed my arguments, see *Patronage and Institutions. Science, Technology, and Medicine at the European Court 1500–1750*, ed. by Bruce T. Moran (Woodbridge: The Boydell Press, 1991).

[10] See Ramsay, 'Clothworkers, Merchants Adventurers and Richard Hakluyt', p. 520; and Girtin, 'Mr Hakluyt, Scholar at Oxford', pp. 208, 210.

[11] The Clothworkers' Company, *Orders of the Courts 1558–1581*, fol. 210. The figure which Hakluyt received from the Skinners' Company in the year 1573–4, was significantly less than his Clothworkers' Company pension, a total of 26s. 8d. See *Records of the Skinners of London, Edward I to James I*, ed. by John James Lambert (London: Sir Joseph Clauston & Sons, 1933), p. 373.

[12] *Orders of the Courts 1558–1581*, fol. 240^{v}.

[13] *Orders of Courts 1581--1605*, fol. 2^{v}. Ramsay goes as far as to suggest that the presentation of the works of Augustine could have been a 'polite reminder' of the conditions of Hakluyt's pension at a time when he must have been working on the *Divers Voyages touching the Discoverie of America* (London: Thomas Woodcocke, 1582).

[14] *Orders of Courts 1581–1605*, fol. 28.

[15] These are the descriptions Hakluyt gave to his career before the appointment as chaplain. *The Principal Navigations, Voiages and Discoveries of the English Nation*, ed. by Richard Hakluyt (London: George Bishop & Ralph Newberie, 1589), epistle dedicatory, sig. *2.

[16] *Calendar of State Papers Domestic, 1581–90*, pp. 150, 169.

[17] *CSPD, 1581–90*, p. 377.

[18] *Principal Navigations* (1589), fol. 4^{v}.

[19] *Principal Navigations*, ed. by D. B. Quinn and R. A. Skelton, 2 vols (Cambridge: Cambridge University Press, 1965), I, xli.

[20] *Principal Navigations*, ed. by Quinn and Skelton, I, xiv–xli and *The Hakluyt Handbook*, ed. by D. B. Quinn, 2 vols (London: The Hakluyt Society, 1974), I, *passim*.

[21] *Principal Navigations*, ed. by Quinn and Skelton, I, xxxix.

[22] Lawrence Stone, 'Elizabethan Overseas Trade', *Economic History Review*, 2nd series, 2 (1949–50), 30–58 (p. 50).

[23] Barry E. Supple, *Commercial Crisis and Change in England 1600–1642* (Cambridge: Cambridge University Press, 1959), p. 258.

[24] British Library, Lansdowne MS 34, fol. 177.

[25] Printed in *Principal Navigations* (1589), p. 396.

[26] *The Original Writings and Correspondence of the Two Richard Hakluyts*, ed. by E. G. R. Taylor, 2 vols (London: The Hakluyt Society, 1935), II, 238 (hereafter *Writings and Correspondence*).

[27] 'Certaine directions given by Master Richard Hackluyt of the Middle Temple, to Master Morgan Hubblethorne, Dyer, sent into Persia 1579', in *Principal Navigations* (1589), p. 454.

[28] Richard Hakluyt, *The Discourse of Western Planting* (1584), in *Writings and Correspondence*, II, 238.

[29] 'A briefe remembrance of things to bee indeavoured at Constantinope, and at other places in Turkie, touching our Clothing and Dying [...]written by M. Richard Hakluyt of the Middle Temple, Anno 1582', in *The Principal Navigations, Voiages, Traffiques and Discoveries of the English Nation*, 3 vols (London: George Bishop, Ralph Newberie & Robert Barker, 1598–1600), II, 160.

[30] F. J. Fisher, 'Some Experiments in Company Organisation in the Early Seventeenth Century', in *London and the English Economy, 1500–1700*, ed. by P. J. Corfield and N. B. Harte (London & Ronceverte: The Hambledon Press, 1990), pp. 43–60.

[31] Fisher, 'Experiments', p. 51.

[32] Pauline Croft, 'English Commerce with Spain and the Armada War, 1558–1603', in *England, Spain and the Gran Armada: Essays from the Anglo–Spanish conferences, London and Madrid 1988*, ed. by M. J. Rodriguez Salgado and Simon Adams (Edinburgh: John Donald Publishers, 1991), pp. 236–63.

[33] See Croft, 'English Commerce with Spain', pp. 247–9.

[34] 'Considerations touching the Clothworkers and Dyers suite', PRO, SP 14/72, no. 69 (1 March 1613).

[35] BL, Lansdowne MS 165, fol. 225^{v}.

[36] PRO, SP 12/198, no. 35 (February 1587).

[37] The only concession to the Clothworkers was the modification in the 1566 legislation, which said that for every nine undressed cloths exported, one dressed cloth should also be

exported. Further, that all cloths which came from Kent and Suffolk should be reserved for dressing and dyeing before export. PRO, SP 12/224, no. 105 [1593], and PRO, SP 12/271, no. 3 (6 June 1599).

38 This is gathered from the Merchant Adventurers' reply in PRO, SP 12/235, no. 93 [1590], 'Against an opinion that it shalbe convenient to permitt no woollen clothes to be transported until they have receaved their whole workemanship, and colour in this Realme.' This was followed in 1592 by a petition delivered by the 'poor handycraftes men of Clothworkers' against the Adventurers' bill, and a reply by the Adventurers in the same year. See Hatfield House Library, Cecil Papers, vol. 139, fols 299 and 307 respectively.

39 PRO, SP 12/244, no. 105 [1593].

40 PRO, SP 12/270, no. 128 (May 1599).

41 The Adventurers argued the other side of the case. In June 1599 they repeated earlier claims that the cloths that were dressed were 'so badlye handled that the merchants will not by any meanes buy them.' PRO, SP 12/271, no. 3 (6 June 1599).

42 *Journal of the House of Commons*, 64 vols (London: HMSO.), I, 291.

43 PRO, SP 14/71, no. 105 [1612].

44 PRO, SP 14/72, no. 69 [1 March 1613].

45 Derek Hirst, *Authority and Conflict: England 1603–1658* (London: Edward Arnold, 1986), p. 118.

46 Supple, *Commercial Crisis*, p. 36.

47 For the printed text of the proclamation see PRO, SP 14/187, no. 29.

48 Supple, *Commercial Crisis*, p. 36.

49 See PRO, SP 14/88, nos 40, 50 and 51 (August 1616).

50 'A Proclamation against the exportation of Clothes, undyed and undressed contrary to law.' PRO, SP 14/187, no. 29.

PART IV

TEXTS AND CONTEXTS

10

Sir Walter Ralegh's *Dialogue betweene a Counsellor of State and a Justice of Peace*

Anna Beer

Sir Walter Ralegh's *Dialogue betweene a Counsellor of State and a Justice of Peace* (1615) is an important response to the perceived failure of the 'Addled Parliament' of 1614. Although the work can be understood in terms of Ralegh's personal political ambitions, marking his return to manuscript advice and supplication to the king after the suppression of *The History of the World*, Ralegh's intervention into parliamentary politics is not merely a further indication of his personal frustrations within the patronage system.[1] I want to argue that the formation and circulation of the work can tell us much about the scribal communities that characterised the formation of a parliamentary identity. Ralegh's political analyses also deserve attention, not least because they would become so influential in the following decade. Here, however, I will outline the nature of Ralegh's response to the debates of 1614, a response that sheds further light on early Stuart thinking about the thorny issues of absolutism, royal prerogative, taxation and common law, but which develops into a passionate defence of the need for a public sphere characterised by freedom of speech.

Three or four years before the writing of the *Dialogue*, Ralegh wrote *A Dialogue between a Jesuit and a Recusant*, a work designed to show that English recusants are loyal to their Oath of Allegiance, despite the best efforts of the Jesuits who have infiltrated the court.[2] Rather surprisingly, considering the content of the rest of the work, the Jesuit and Recusant end up discussing impositions, which the former argues have been laid by James 'upon his people, contrary to the Laws and Customs of the Land, as hath been directly proved in the last Parliament.'[3] The Recusant, however, rejects the notion that the law binds the king because 'either for his honour or safety, or for the defence of his Allies' he can act outside the law.[4] He has already suggested: 'What if Currans were never brought into the Land, were the Commonwealth any whit the worse? Let those that have sweet tongues pay for their palat', which leads seamlessly into an attack on noblemen who used to 'live in their Countries and kept Hospitality, they fed the poor, and were beloved and followed.'[5] The Jesuit has more to say, however, about James's problems: 'what can a Prince do that is poor, and hath not the love of his people?' He receives the following answer: 'for the love of the people, if he want it, he may again recover it in a week.'[6]

These issues, of impositions, the king's poverty, and the love of the people (or the lack of it), all figure prominently in the later *Dialogue*. In the earlier work, however, Ralegh appears unclear as to exactly how James can recover the love of the people. During the following few years, the passing attack on the failure of the nobility to fulfil their traditional responsibilities would develop into a full scale assault on the 'great ones' who were destroying the kingdom and who could and should be delivered up to the new political force, the 'people', and their representatives, the Commons. Whilst in the *Jesuit* dialogue, the issues are tacked on to the end of a work dominated by subjects which characterise Ralegh's previous work, such as foreign policy, the art of war, and the Roman Catholic/Spanish threat, in the later *Dialogue* he focuses exclusively on internal politics, national history and secular arguments. One reason for the new focus may have been the presence in the Tower of London of John Hoskins, whose political thinking will be discussed later. First, however, I want to argue that Hoskins is significant because of his active role within what has been variously described as 'textual communities', a 'community of exchange' or 'active transcriptional cultures' predicated on scribal publication, and having their genesis in the Inns of Court, the environment in which Ralegh met Hoskins as early as 1597–8 when they performed together in the Christmas season.[7] This active transcriptional culture continued to thrive during the early years of James's reign, and would become important to the circulation of parliamentary news: William Hakewill described much later how the parliamentary collections he 'imparted many years since to some of my friends' were 'by the length of time multiplied into very many copies.'[8] More important still, it continued despite and indeed because of imprisonment, which says something about its durability, and perhaps about the Jacobean state's unwillingness or inability to regulate scribal publication.[9] It also suggests that the Tower prisoners lived in conditions of relative freedom with easy access to friends on the outside.[10] In Hoskins's case, there is ample evidence that he got letters out via visitors and, perhaps more significant, that Latin supplicatory works to the king asking for release were translated into English and prepared for a much larger circulation.[11] This active transcriptional culture was closely connected with the formation of a parliamentary identity, not least because 'records, treatises, documents, and archives were collected and studied: the business of Parliament, especially its rights and precedents, was examined critically. Almost all of this activity relied on manuscript sources.'[12]

In this context, the fact that the *Dialogue* was a scribal publication becomes more than an indication of the failure of the print publication of *The History of the World*, and far more of a significant act in itself. As Love argues, 'printed text was, with a few high risk exceptions, a censored and controlled text; the scribal text, a free one', thus the scribal text was often 'a vehicle for ideological debate within the governing class', and a way of evading censorship.[13] The following description, by H. R. Woudhuysen, of the kind of author who chose manuscript publication mirrors Ralegh's situation remarkably closely: 'The author whose work failed to attract a publisher; the author who wanted to 'target' a patron or a group of patrons; the author who, for one reason or another, eschewed print; the author who wanted the immediate dissemination of his writings – all found that manuscript production favoured their work.'[14]

Although it is hard to establish the extent to which Ralegh controlled the circulation of his work, critics who have considered the circulation of the *Dialogue* all agree that it was intended for a wider audience than the king.[15] It would make sense that Ralegh tapped into the transcriptional networks known and used by Hoskins. Some of his surviving manuscripts were circulated at the time of writing (British Library Stowe MS 177 uses the word 'nowe' in its heading), whilst others were perhaps copied later in the aftermath of Ralegh's execution, taking their places alongside the letters and speech from the scaffold that would form Ralegh's political identity in the following years.[16] Roger Twysden's copy, dated 1622, is headed 'the lady Ralegh did assure me this was her husbands doeing' indicating Bess Ralegh's active involvement in this transcriptional culture.[17]

What is hard to fathom is why a work clearly written in the early part of 1615 was probably only presented to the king in the autumn of that year, the date suggested by its position in the State Papers. It is more obvious why Ralegh presented and circulated both a full and an abridged version.[18] The abridged version is headed 'Out of [...]' and makes no attempt to maintain the narrative flow. What it does do is cut most of the historical narration and focus attention on the topical issues: assignations, farming, the sale and management of Crown lands, the accountability of the king's ministers, impositions, evil counsel and counsellors, free speech, the king's prerogative, and imprisonment. There are also a few personal anecdotes and a scattering of political axioms. Despite these cuts, Queen Elizabeth still appears three times. The abridged version indicates that the use of history and dialogue, ostensibly neutral modes, is a blind: the work is both topical and partisan, not to mention contentiously nostalgic for the 'late Queene'.

But if – as Conrad Russell and Kevin Sharpe have argued – there was a desire for consensus and certainty in the face of disharmony and confusion, then Ralegh's dialogue, in both its abridged and full form, seems to offer much reassurance to its readers.[19] Not only does Ralegh work towards the clarity sought by James in his discussions of the dissemination of the Oath of Allegiance (just as Philalethes, a participant in a dialogue of 1615, *God and the King*,[20] asks for the long oath to be reduced so that he can remember it, Ralegh will conveniently reduce his *Dialogue* to bite-size portions), but his Justice says, as he takes over the narrating of parliamentary history, 'My good Lord, *To avoyde confusion*, I will make a short repetition of them all [...].'[21] The appeal to history as dialectic is of course specious: as Thomas Sloane has shown the art of dialogue is 'actually more deeply intertwined with rhetoric than with dialectic, not simply in the dialogue's literary dimension, its eloquence, but in its overt efforts to please and move as well as to teach an audience outside the dialogue.'[22] Thus, in Ralegh's *Dialogue*, there is no final conversion scene but rather an impassioned assertion of the Justice's moral integrity, designed to validate his arguments.[23]

Ralegh's Justice may avoid confusion, but he does not avoid some hard-hitting political analyses. Two sources of danger haunt the *Dialogue*. For the Counsellor 'these parliaments are daungerous for a king',[24] an understandable viewpoint since he has just been hearing about the depositions of Richard II and Edward II 'those kings deposed by parliaments.' For the Justice, representing Ralegh's views, however, 'it is a thing most daungerous for a king to be without Treasure,'[25] because this makes him vulnerable to rebellious subjects and necessity.[26] Since James is in desperate financial trouble, since the people are armed and at the height of their power,[27] a solution is needed, and fast. Even in the face of this kind of dire warning, the Counsellor, out of moral cowardice, will not change his stance: 'Well Sir, All this notwithstanding we dare not advise the king to call a parliament.'[28]

The Counsellor dares not advise the calling of a parliament because the *Dialogue*'s political analyses are predicated on a simple formula. Parliaments give kings money when 'generallye hated' evil counsellors are removed.[29] Moreover, kings who deliver up their favourites show that they are reasonable, rather than governed by passion. The Justice lists the political, financial and moral benefits accrued by Richard II when he eventually delivered up the Earl of Suffolk:

> the king had both his fyne, his Thousand pound lande, and a Subsidy to boote: and thoughe for the present it pleased the king to fancye a man, whome, all the worlde hated (the kings passyon overcomming his judgement), yet cann it not be called a dishonor for the king to believe the generall Counsell of the kingdome and to preserve it before his particular affecion, especially when Suffolk was prooved false, even unto the king himself: for were it otherwise love and affecion might be called frenzy and madness, for it is the nature of humane passions that the love bred by fidellity doth chaunge itself into hatred, when the fidellity is first chaunged into falshoode.[30]

Richard's ensuing problems are clear with the hindsight of history: 'had King Richard 2. delivered upp to Justice but 3. or 4. he had still helde the love of his people and thereby his crowne, lief, and estate.'[31]

History modulates to prediction. King James will find that 'the buylding of your owne fortunes and factions hath bene your dilligent studdyes' and then 'perchaunce cast himself uppon the generall love of the people' and 'leave as many of your Lordshipps as have pilfered from the crowne to their examinacion.'[32] Recent events add urgency to the case. The Justice and Counsellor debate whether, if any 'tumult' had followed the Benevolence of 1614, certain great ones would indeed have been 'delivered' over to 'the people.' The Justice while claiming ignorance nevertheless gives examples of Henry VIII doing it, and Machiavelli advising it.[33] As the Counsellor points out, the Justice is avoiding his question and merely giving examples, so the Justice spells out the full political implications:

> My good Lord, the people have not stayed for the kings delivery neither in England nor in France: your Lordship knowes how the Chauncellor, Treasurer and Chief Justice with many other att severall tymes have bene used by the Rebells: And the Marshalls, Constables, Treasurers, and Bishopps in Fraunce have been cutt in peeces in Charles the 6th tyme.[34]

Of course, there is not much evidence that a 'tumult' did follow the collection of the Benevolence. There was some opposition, especially in Devon, Somerset, and Warwickshire and Josias Nicholls caused trouble in Kent. The main problem, as Thomas Cogswell has shown in his study of Leicestershire, was that whilst the 'local gentleman had promised £1000' only £400 was in fact collected.[35] But it has allowed Ralegh to describe Chancellors, Treasurers, and Chief Justices being cut into pieces.[36]

Alongside this insistence on the delivering up of great ones and the gleeful rehearsal of their demises, the Justice also supports a number of practical initiatives. He recommends the introduction of assignations which would allow James to consult a summary of incomings and outgoings in 'a little Rolle' which 'might quiett his hart.'[37] He recommends, along with almost every other political commentator, better management of the Crown lands, offering a fairly detailed financial breakdown of the amounts that could be raised thereby, and arguing that although the king has given away lots of land since he came to England he could and should claim it back.[38]

This practical advice extends to the discussion of impositions, which Ralegh is happy to defend on the grounds of expediency. The nature of Ralegh's defence deserves attention, not least to provide further evidence for Linda Levy Peck's argument that 'many of the concerns of the 1620s were directly foreshadowed in the interlocking of financial, legal and political issues over the introduction of impositions.'[39] It is the ways in which Ralegh 'interlocks' ideas, rather than the coherent theoretical analysis of, for example, the legality of impositions that is significant. The *Dialogue* is a corrective to interpretations of early Stuart political culture which privilege the search for legal clarity or consensus, and supports Johann Somerville's critique of the tacit assumption that everyone believed in the 'rule of law' and that 'the monarch's prerogative was governed by law.'[40]

The Justice begins by arguing that impositions encourage greed and corruption in great ones and 'grudging and all complaynt' in the people. The latter could be averted if the impositions 'which were laide by the Advise of a few', should 'be in parliament laide by the generall Counsell of the kingdome.'[41] The same point will be made later about the Benevolence of 1614: James's 'loving Subjects in generall are willing to supply him, if it please him to call a parliament, for that was that common aunsweare to all the Sheriffs of England, when the late Benevolence was demaunded.'[42]

This for the Counsellor is a curtailment of the king's 'absolute power'.[43] The Justice quickly counters:

> And by what power is it donne in parliament, but by the kings absolute power? mistake it not (my good Lord) for the *three Estates* doe but advise as the privye Counsell doth, which advise (if the king imbrace) becomes the kings Act in the one, and the kings Lawe in the other, for without the kings acceptacion, both the private and publique advise are but emptye egg shells.[44]

Parliament, seen as general council, does not infringe James's absolute power but reinforces it.

The point seems clear, but confusion lies ahead. On the one hand, the Justice argues somewhat slyly that impositions are not in fact legal unless authorised by parliament: 'when Imposicions are layde by parliament, they are gathered by the authority of the law, which (as aforesaid) rejecteth all complaints, and stopps every mutinous mouth.'[45] On the other hand, the Justice also argues that 'there is nothing in the *Great Charter* against Imposicions, and besides that, necessity hath perswaded them.'[46] This confusion over the legality of impositions is characteristic of debate at the time. In the parliaments of 1606 and 1610 members such as Hedley, Hakewill and Hoskins had argued that they were in breach of common law and not in the remit of the king's prerogative. Bate's Case had proved that the king could levy taxes without consent, and that the law could be breached in the name of *salus populi*, or in a 'case of necessity' by the king's 'absolute power', and that matters of state should be ruled by the rules of policy, as opposed to those of law.[47] Yet, at the same time, Robert Cecil could argue in response to the Petition of 7 July 1610 which argued that impositions should be abolished, that the 'King hath the law to justify him and precedents to speak for him.'[48]

What the Justice seeks to demonstrate is the irrelevance of these kinds of legal debates to the reality of political life. He, for example, defends the law-breaking rebels in Richard II's time but is also quite happy, conversely, to defend the fact that Richard II 'did not proceede legally with Gloucester and others', especially since 'this was not the first tyme that the kings of England have donne things without the Counsell of the law, yea and contrary to the law.'[49] The Justice asks the Counsellor to 'remember the surgald proverbe, *That Necessity hath noe Lawe*' and states 'the *Rule, That the immortall pollicy of a State* cannot permitt of any law or priviledge whatsoever, but in some particular or other the same is necessarily broken.'[50] It is the king's prerogative to 'practise many things without the Advise of the lawe.'[51]

Ralegh, predictably, is concerned to demonstrate and condemn the fact that the Lords abuse the law and to defend the king's prerogative powers:

> It's you my Lords that, when the Subject hath some tyme neede of the kings prerogative, doe then use the strength of the lawe; And when they requyre the lawe, you afflict them with the prerogative, and treade the great *Charter* (which hath bene confirmed by Sixteene Acts of parliament) under your feete, as a torne parchment, or wast paper.[52]

The prerogative (significantly of a 'Religious Prince') is thus better than the law: 'Nay I wilbe bould to say it, that except the lawes were better observed, the prerogative of the *Religious Prince* hath manifould lesse perills then the letter of the law hath.'[53] As he argues in his Preface to James:

> all binding of a king by Law, uppon the advantage of his necessity, makes the breach itself lawfull in the king, his charters and all other Instruments being noe other than the surviving wittnesses of an unconstrained will: *Princeps non subjicitur legi nisi sola voluntate sua. Scilicet libera, Mirus motus et certa scientia*, necessary words in all the kings grants, wittnessing that the same grants were given willingly freelie and knowingly.[54]

Ralegh maintains, therefore, that, since the law cannot and should not be used to bind kings (in part, at least, because 'necessity hath no law'); that since discussions of the legality or illegality of impositions or the opposition to the Benevolence are irrelevant to the condition of England (since these debates do not get money for the king); and that since the law does not, in any case, serve the people of England because it is abused by the Lords, appeals to law are therefore pointless, and thus theorising about legality and justice is a waste of time. This point is made right at the start of the *Dialogue* when the Justice considers the case of Oliver St John. The latter had joined Ralegh in the Tower in the early months of 1615 as he awaited his hearing for dissuading the Benevolence of 1614, his case based in part on an appeal to history.[55] Convicted in April, he was released in June 1615. Both St John's appeal to Magna Carta and 'the lawes of the land', and the significance of the Benevolence are adjudged irrelevant and dismissed in one short sentence: 'what's that to the kings debts?'.[56] This, of course, returns us to our starting point, that it 'is a thing most daungerous for a king to be without Treasure.'[57]

All of this advice is framed within the traditional political discourses of love and the health of the body politic: for example, the Justice argues that a failed parliament is like a dangerous disease,[58] and the body politic is being damaged by the sale of the king's lands: its heart, eyes, and soul are 'heavy unto death' that 'soe many other goodly Mannors have passed from his Majestie.'[59] These are James's own models for the relationship between the king and subject.[60] In his opening speeches to the 1614 parliament, he rejects a language of trade ('I told you I would not deal with you like a merchant'), and proposes, indeed insists upon, a 'parliament of love': 'whosoever would not assure me of the love of the people I should think he were no good subject.'[61] The problem is that Ralegh does not assure James of the 'love of the people': at best he suggests it is precariously held. Even at his most eloquent on the subject, there is a certain tactlessness in his suggestion that James might need Ralegh's prayers in the matter:

> It is therefore Love (most Renowned Soveraigne) that must prepare the way for your Majesties following desires: It is Love which obeyes, which suffers, which gives, which sticks att nothing: which Love, as well of your Majesties people, as the Love of God, that your Majestie may always houlde, shalbe the contynuall prayer of
>
> Your Majesties most
humble vassall
W: Rawleigh.[62]

James's appeal to a 'parliament of love' was thrown back in his face by John Hoskins, in his speech of 3 June 1614 when he argued that 'This a parliament of love. All the arguments now used, arguments of fear.'[63] This was followed by the reference to the Sicilian Vespers, which most diarists were keen to point out they did not understand, which precipitated the dissolution of the parliament and Hoskins's imprisonment.[64] It is these 'arguments of fear' that engage Ralegh, rather than the other elements of the Sicilian Vespers speech. He is strangely silent on 'riot and dissoluteness' and shows a remarkable lack of anti-Scottish sentiment, unlike Hoskins who demanded that all 'strangers' should be sent back to their own countries. The Sicilian Vespers reference is thus not significant for its content, but for the way it exposes what is sayable and unsayable, and in the reporting on the speech, what is understandable and what it is best not to understand.

To conclude, therefore, I want to return to the implications of scribal publication, and the *Dialogue*'s imagination of a polity which permits freedom of speech. Ralegh's very first words in his Preface to James are that 'Those that are supprest and hopelesse, are commonly silent.'[65] Ralegh, of course, never content with the common, will not be silent, and instead develops a powerful discussion of the place of free speech within an absolute monarchy. As I have argued elsewhere, Ralegh presents a vision of parliament as a public space in which a form of freedom of speech can take place: the *Dialogue* is his 'most sustained attempt to write about the people as a political entity and to make claims for a public space in which opinions can be voiced in safety.'[66]

James would not have appreciated this. For a start, the 1614 parliament had been granted, on paper at least, the privileges Ralegh is demanding. The three petitions for access to his Majesty, freedom of speech, and freedom from arrest, traditionally requested by the Speaker, were granted by the king in a speech customarily delivered by the Lord Chancellor.[67] Moreover, the king had argued in the parliament of 1610 that it was 'sedition in Subjects, to dispute what a King may do in the height of his power', and had asserted 'I would not have you judge in general of my prerogative.' Later he would tell his judges that 'As for the absolute Prerogative of the Crowne, that is no Subject for the tongue of a Lawyer, nor is lawfull to be disputed.'[68] No matter that Ralegh appears to support the tactical use of the royal prerogative: his very discussion of the matter is iniquitous.

It is no surprise, therefore, that the *Dialogue* echoes with the Justice's requests to be given 'leave to speake freely', a request justified by biblical precedents, ironically using the same biblical wisdom literature that James used to justify his demands for 'discretion and moderation' in his subjects and that 'no man' could or should 'search the heart of a king' (Proverbs, 25:3).[69] Whilst Ralegh stops short of searching James's heart, he does offer a challenging model of the interlocking of political freedoms. The king's will is, of course, free and his word must be given freely. Money should be given by parliament freely (the phrase is used five times):

> A constrayned assent is the Assent of a captive and not of a king, and therefore there was nothing then donne either legally or Royally: For if it be not propperly a parliament, where the subject is not free, certeynely it can be none, where the king is bounde.[70]

In this context, one would expect that the first objection to a parliament considered by Ralegh should be unanswerable. It is 'the supposition that your Majesties subjects will give nothing, but with the Adjunction of their owne Interest, interlacing in one and the same Act or Lawe, your Majesties Relief and their owne Liberties.'[71]

The Justice is quick to point out that any anxieties are 'but frivilous', since the 'bonds of Subjects to their kings having beene alwayes wrought out of iron, the Bonds of kings to their subjects woven but of cobwebb':[72] it appears that Adjunction and interlacing bear no relation to bonds or being bound. He claims that his review of history will prove this point, but his examples do precisely the opposite.[73]

The Justice offers numerous examples of this 'trafficke of assurances' but none are very comforting. Henry III in his '9th year he had the 15th penny of all goods given him, uppon condicion to confirme the Great Charter: for by reason of the warres in Fraunce, and the losse of Rochell, he was then forced to consent to the Lords in all they demaunded',[74] whilst Edward I in his:

> 33th year [...] confirmed the Charter out of his owne Royall disposicion: And the States (to shew their thankfulness gave the king for one year the 15th parte of all their revenues of the land, and of the Cittizens the sixth penny of their goodes: And in the same year the king used the Inquisicion called *Trayle Baston*, by which all Justices and other Magistrates were greevously fyned that had used extorcion or bribery, or otherwise misdemeaned themselves, to the great contentment of his people.[75]

These are just two examples which link royal revenue with the confirmation of Magna Carta and the reform of government. Similarly, although the Justice states explicitly that 'kings are bounde by their piety only, and by noe other obligacions', his analysis of history suggests otherwise.[76] Only a few lines after this statement of theory, the Justice recounts that 'in the parliament of London, in 38th year, he had given him the tenth parte of all the Revenues of the Churche for three yeares, and 3 marks of every knights fee throughout England, uppon his promise and oath for the observing of *Magna Charta*.'[77] Thus when the Justice complains that:

> there are of your Lordships that (contrarie to the direct letter of the Charter) imprison the kings Subjects, and deny them the benefitt of the lawe to the kings disproffitt, and what doe you otherwise thereby (if the Imposicions be in any sorte greevous) but *renovare dolores*, and withall digg out of the dust the long buryed memorye of the Subjects former contentions with their kings.[78]

he is being somewhat ingenuous. What else is Ralegh doing other than digging contentions out of the dust? The purpose of his digging is clear. Historical precedent (couched here in telling parentheses), is used to validate his happy prediction that James will yield to parliament's demands. Since James will 'never of himself question' the situation, parliament will offer a humble petition, an honest suit, to which the king will yield, and thus be furnished and supplied: 'the like having bene donne in soe many kings tymes heretofore.'[79]

Ralegh is coming very close to Hoskins's crime of 'alledginge impertinent histories', but his appeal to a common history ('our history') and to a body of public knowledge (for example 'the Commission which your Lordshipp may reade att large in the booke of Statutes') seeks to legitimate his claims.[80] Moreover, he positions his use of potentially impertinent history within a vision of an ideal polity in which the subject is free in parliament, within which he has freedom of speech guaranteed. This is justified by the claim that the king is a king of free men and not of slaves, thus the king's and the subject's freedoms are interlaced, at least rhetorically. This appeal to a public space within which 'generall Counsell' can be formulated and received is complemented by a condemnation of advice that remains merely private and therefore 'partiall'.[81] The condemnation of private advice (quite literally, privy counsel), is implicit in the form of the dialogue itself which involves a private man, the Justice/Ralegh, going public with his advice, whatever the personal and political cost may be. As the Counsellor attempts to silence the Justice with threats, Ralegh subverts dialogue's claim to be 'the generic embodiment of civility', and its usual pretence to 'thrash the matter out without the blatant suppression of the dissenting voice', by enacting the suppression of the truth-telling voice.[82]

The Counsellor may dismiss the Justice's arguments by appealing to a political world dominated by personal access in which 'It's all one, your papers cann neither aunsweare nor Reply; but we cann', but the Justice counters by promoting the idea of a public, written debate.[83] Those who oppose the calling of a parliament should:

> sett downe your Reasons in wrighting, why you either mislike it or feare it, and such as wishe and advise it, to sett downe Aunsweares to your objecions: And soe shall the king prevent you laying the calling or not calling on his Majestie, as some of you great Counsellors have donne in many other thing, shrinking upp their shoulders and saying, *The king will have it soe*.[84]

Just as the *Dialogue* is digging contentions out of the dust, it is also enacting the very debate it recommends.

It is therefore no surprise that, in answer to the explicit question as to what would be required of the king if a new parliament was called, the Justice answers:

> The first thing that would be requyred, would be the same that was requyred by the Commons in the 13th year of Henry 8th (to witt) That if a man of the commons house should speake more lardgely then of duty he ought to doe, all such offences should be pardonned and that to be of *Recorde*.[85]

As David Colclough has shown, early-modern rhetorical handbooks attempted 'with varying degrees of success, to delineate a sphere where the reader will be able to exercise his or her civic abilities. Finding a convincing equivalent to the assembly or forum, though, was more than most English writers could (or dared to) manage, and many of the greatest anxieties surrounding rhetoric and free speech in this period centre on its proper place.'[86] What Ralegh's *Dialogue* does is both to imagine and create in a material sense a 'space' or 'place' for free speech.

This was Ralegh's final completed work in prison. A few months after the *Dialogue* found its way in to the State Papers, Ralegh achieved his own personal freedom (of sorts), probably through the intercession of George Villiers. To return to the model of patronage relationships with which I began, it is just possible that the *Dialogue* might have been an attempt to curry favour with the rising Villiers faction who would instigate investigations into the Overbury affair in October 1615. The result would be the delivering up of Robert Carr, who would find himself occupying the same Tower rooms recently vacated by Ralegh. This has a certain narrative neatness to it, but blunts the political significance of the *Dialogue*. This work, precipitated by the imprisonment of Hoskins, one which celebrates parliament's role as general counsel, which promotes impeachment with vicious energy, which suggests that a threatening 'tumult' is probable rather than possible, and above all, which defines and enacts the role of public debate, would have far more important consequences for English political culture than it would have for Ralegh himself.

Notes

1 Linda Levy Peck, *Court Patronage and Corruption in Early Stuart England* (London: Routledge, 1993), p. 74 and Anna R. Beer, *Sir Walter Ralegh and His Readers in the Seventeenth Century: Speaking to the People* (London: Macmillan, 1997), Chapter 3.

2 Ralegh's authorship of this work is not certain. The one manuscript copy (Cambridge University Library MS Add. 27, fols 29^r–62^v) is incomplete and dates from the mid-seventeenth century. There is however a direct quotation from a work by Ralegh, *The Art of War by Sea*. Page references are to the edition in *An Abridgement of Sir Walter Ralegh's History of the World. To which is added, his Premonition to Princes. With some genuine remains, published by P. Ralegh* (London: P. Ralegh, 1698).

3 *Abridgement*, p. 63.

4 *Abridgement*, p. 69.

5 *Abridgement*, p. 63.

6 *Abridgement*, p. 67.

7 See David Colclough, '"Of the alleadging of authors": The Construction and Reception of Textual Authority in English Prose' (unpublished doctoral thesis, University of Oxford, 1996), pp. 105–6; Baird Whitlock, *John Hoskyns, Serjeant-at-Law* (Washington DC: University Press of America, 1982), p. 476; Harold Love, *Scribal Publication in Seventeenth-Century England* (Oxford: Clarendon Press, 1993), p. 219; and H. R. Woudhuysen, *Sir Philip Sidney and the Circulation of Manuscripts 1558–1640* (Oxford: Clarendon Press, 1996), pp. 164–9, n. 5.

8 *Proceedings, 1610*, I, xliii, n. 6, cit. Woudhuysen, *Sir Philip Sidney*, p. 183.

9 See Peter Beal, *In Praise of Scribes: Manuscripts and their Makers in Seventeenth-Century England* (Oxford: Clarendon Press, 1998), on Thomas Wilson, p. 89.

[10] Ralegh's circle of 'friends' during his imprisonment (to use John Racin's term in *Sir Walter Ralegh as Historian: An Analysis of The History of the World*, Salzburg Studies in English Literature, 2 (Salzburg: Institut fur Englische Sprache und Literatur, 1974), p. 5), is well documented, and includes Ben Jonson, Thomas Harriot, Robert Burhill, and John Hoskins. See Whitlock, *John Hoskyns*, pp. 474–76. Oswald and John Hoskins petitioned the Privy Council for 'accesse' and 'leave to repaire unto' their brother, 'at fytt and convenyent tymes, so that it be in your presence, or in the presence or hearing of such as you shall appoint', p. 477.

[11] See Whitlock, *John Hoskyns*, p. 478. The Latin poem his wife presented to the king in acknowledgement of New Year's Day was translated into English for a wider public.

[12] Woudhuysen, *Sir Philip Sidney*, p. 389.

[13] See Love, *Scribal Publication*, p. 184 and p. 191 and Woudhuysen, *Sir Philip Sidney*, p. 388.

[14] Woudhuysen, *Sir Philip Sidney*, pp. 387–8. For an alternative view of print licensing and the importance of legitimisation, see Anthony Milton, 'Licensing, Censorship, and Religious Orthodoxy in Early Stuart England', *The Historical Journal*, 41 (1998), 625–51.

[15] Richard Cust's assertion that the work was suppressed and his claim that Ralegh 'argued firmly against' impositions (*The Forced Loan and English Politics, 1626–1628* (Oxford: Clarendon Press, 1987), pp. 155, 156) need to be treated with caution. See Beer, *Sir Walter Ralegh*, p. 64. Pierre Lefranc confuses the manuscript and print versions, arguing that the title of the 1628 print edition, *The Prerogative of Parliaments*, was offensive to the king: *Sir Walter Ralegh, ecrivain, l'oeuvre et les idees* (Paris: Librarie Armand Colin, 1968), p. 206.

[16] 'On New Year's Day 1619 John Holles instructed his son in London "I would have yow gather up as many of Sir W. Rawlies verses, and letters as yow can, ex unguibus leonem".' Quoted in Woudhuysen, *Sir Philip Sidney*, p. 158. There is proof of a manuscript tradition stretching through to the late seventeenth century: see Beer, *Sir Walter Ralegh*, p. 182.

[17] See Beer, *Sir Walter Ralegh*, Chapters 5 and 6, for evidence of the *Dialogue*'s continued political relevance through the seventeenth century, in manuscript and print form.

[18] If the survival rate is a good indicator, the abridged version was not so prevalent. See British Library, Lansdowne MS 806 for an example.

[19] See for example Conrad Russell, *The Crisis of Parliaments: English History 1509–1660* (Oxford: Oxford University Press, 1974); p. 282 on the 'exceptionally confused House' of 1614. Kevin Sharpe, *Politics and Ideas in Early Stuart England: Essays and Studies* (London: Pinter, 1989), p. 180.

[20] Richard Mocket, *God and the King: Or, a Dialogue showing that our Soveraigne Lord King James, being immediate under God within his Dominions, Doth rightfully claime whatsoever is required by the Oath of Allegeance* (London, 1615).

[21] Walter Ralegh, 'Dialogue betweene a Counsellor of State and a Justice of Peace', Public Record Office, State Papers, 14/85, fol. 6[r], my emphasis.

[22] Thomas O. Sloane, *On the Contrary: The Protocol of Traditional Rhetoric* (Washington D.C.: The Catholic University of America Press, 1997), p. 90. Cf. p. 88: 'Dialectic begins in uncertainty and proceeds through inquiry toward more certainty, at least among experts. [...] Rhetoric, however, begins in controversy and proceeds through inquiry

to find the means whereby this or that audience – whether expert or not – may be attracted to a certain resolution of the controversy.'

[23] Roger Deakins in his study of early-modern dialogues argues that a conversion scene is the norm, 'The Tudor Prose Dialogue: Genre and Anti-Genre', *Studies in English Literature*, 20 (1980), 1–23, (p. 21).

[24] PRO, SP 14/85, fol. 12r.

[25] PRO, SP 14/85, fol. 30v.

[26] PRO, SP 14/85, fol. 15r. The personal and highly specific anecdotes, such as the Justice's reminiscences of his Elizabethan parliamentary days (see fol. 16v), clinch the issue.

[27] PRO, SP 14/85, fol. 15r.

[28] PRO, SP 14/85, fol. 30r.

[29] PRO, SP 14/85, fol. 16r.

[30] PRO, SP 14/85, fol. 17r.

[31] PRO, SP 14/85, fol. 14r–v.

[32] PRO, SP 14/85, fol. 24r.

[33] PRO, SP 14/85, fols 25v–26r.

[34] PRO, SP 14/85, fol. 26r.

[35] Thomas Cogswell, *Home Divisions: Aristocracy, the State and Provincial Conflict* (Manchester: Manchester University Press, 1998), p. 15. Cust, *Forced Loan*, pp. 153–4, argues for 'considerable opposition' and points to the historical arguments of the Somerset JPs. For Nicholls, see Peter Clark, 'Josias Nicholls and Religious Radicalism 1553–1639', *Journal of Ecclesiastical History*, 28 (1977), 133–50.

[36] Sir Arthur Ingram, the 'well paid middleman' (Peck, *Court Patronage and Corruption*, p. 156), through whom Thomas Howard, Earl of Suffolk farmed currants, had been sworn as cofferer of the king's household in February 1615, but had subsequently lost his position. The Counsellor uses him as a scapegoat for the 1614 Benevolence (fol. 26r).

[37] PRO, SP 14/85, fol. 19v. Ralegh's historical precedent is the appointment of the Lords Appelant in the time of Richard II (see fol. 17v).

[38] PRO, SP 14/85, fols 12v, 19v, 23v and elsewhere.

[39] Peck, *Court Patronage and Corruption*, p. 539.

[40] Johann P. Sommerville, 'English and European Political Ideas in the Early Seventeenth Century: Revisionism and the Case of Absolutism', *Journal of British Studies*, 35 (1996), 168–94, (p. 170). Alan Cromartie, for example, argues that 'Coke's ideas were dangerous to kings, because the omnicompetence of law supplied him with a never-failing standard by which to judge monarchical behaviour', whilst Kevin Sharpe argues, in his analysis of the parliamentary debate on impositions in 1610 that the certainty of law was sought as a remedy for political confusion. Alan Cromartie, 'The Constitutionalist Revolution: the Transformation of Political Culture in Early Stuart England', *Past & Present*, 163 (1999), 76–120 (p. 100). Sharpe, *Politics and Ideas*, p. 180.

[41] PRO, SP 14/85, fol. 28r.

[42] PRO, SP 14/85, fol. 30v.

[43] PRO, SP 14/85, fol. 28r.

[44] PRO, SP 14/85, fol. 28r.

[45] PRO, SP 14/85, fol. 28v.

[46] PRO, SP 14/85, fol. 29r.

[47] Sharpe, *Politics and Ideas*, p. 191; Cromartie, 'Constitutionalist Revolution', p. 94.

[48] Pauline Croft, 'Fresh Light on Bate's Case', *The Historical Journal*, 30 (1987), 523–39, (p. 524).

[49] PRO, SP 14/85, fol. 21^{r-v}. The rebels 'all loved the king (for they did him no harme having him in their power)', (fol. 18^{v}). The 'taking of Armes cannot be excused in respect of the lawe, But this may be said for the Lords[...].' (fol. 19^{r}).

[50] PRO, SP 14/85, fol. 21^{v}.

[51] PRO, SP 14/85, fol. 29^{r}.

[52] PRO, SP 14/85, fol. 29^{r}.

[53] PRO, SP 14/85, fol. 30^{r}.

[54] PRO, SP 14/85, fol. 1^{v}.

[55] He cites for example: '25 Edward I cap. 5 that none such be drawne into custome and cap. 6 that henceforth be taken as such under taxes free graunts or impositions but by the assent of the realm, and for the good of the same', BL, Sloane MS 1856.

[56] PRO, SP 14/85, fol. 3^{r}.

[57] PRO, SP 14/85, fol. 30^{v}.

[58] PRO, SP 14/85, fol. 2^{r-v}.

[59] PRO, SP 14/85, fol. 13^{r}.

[60] So, for example, James equates excessive nose-blowing with the prerogative: 'For he that overmuch strains and blows his nose will cause blood. So, if a prince should stretch his prerogative, it would cause his people to bleed': 5 April 1614, *Proceedings, 1614*, p. 17.

[61] Speeches on 9 and 15 April, *Proceedings, 1614*, pp. 17, 19 and 44.

[62] PRO, SP 14/85, fol. 2^{v}.

[63] *Proceedings, 1614*, 3 June 1614, p. 417.

[64] On 3 June, Hoskins asked 'that there may be better care taken for the sales of his lands,' and went on: 'That we have nothing but ill examples of all riot and dissoluteness. To send all strangers home to their countries (and upon that he used the phrase of the Sicilian Vespers, which I understood not)[...].' (*Proceedings, 1614*, pp. 422–3).

[65] PRO, SP 14/85, fol. 1^{r}.

[66] Beer, *Sir Walter Ralegh*, p. 68.

[67] *Proceedings, 1614*, p. 17, n. 37.

[68] Speeches of 21 March and 21 May 1610. Quoted in Somerville, 'Revisionism and the Case of Absolutism', p. 183, n. 48.

[69] Ralegh cites Ecclesiastes, 'keepe not back Councell [...] when it may doe good', (fol. 3^{v}); Solomon, 'Will your Lordshipp pardon me if I speake freelye? for I speake out of Love, which (saith Salomon) covereth all trespasses', (fol. 12^{v}); and Proverbs,'Yes my Lord, for it's saide in the proverbs, where many Counsellers are there is health', (fol. 20^{v}). For a typical use of the same wisdom literature to argue the opposite, that 'where the word of a king is there is power, and who may say unto him what dost thou?', see *God and the King* (1615), 'imprinted by his Majesties speciall priviledge and command', p. 29. For James's speech to parliament on 5 April 1614, see *Proceedings, 1614*, p. 18. For a fascinating analysis of the practice and significance of this kind of 'parrhesiastic justification' see David Colclough, '*Parrhesia*: The Rhetoric of Free Speech in Early Modern England', *Rhetorica*, 17 (1999), 177–212, especially p. 202, which mentions the use of Job, another of Ralegh's biblical authorisers.

[70] PRO, SP 14/85, fol. 9^{r}.

[71] PRO, SP 14/85, fol. 1^{r-v}.

[72] PRO, SP 14/85, fol. 1^{v}.

[73] As does his famous use of the body politic metaphor. Ralegh argues that the king, the head, should yield to the feet, the people, since the king's and the subject's freedoms are intertwined and the head suffers 'by participation' in the pain of the feet, fol. 2^{r}.

[74] PRO, SP 14/85, fol. 6^{r}.

[75] PRO, SP 14/85, fol. 10^{v}.

[76] PRO, SP 14/85, fols 7^{v}–8^{r}.

[77] PRO, SP 14/85, fol. 8^{v}.

[78] PRO, SP 14/85, fol. 29^{r}.

[79] PRO, SP 14/85, fol. 23^{v}.

[80] PRO, SP 14/85, fol. 17^{v}. See Whitlock, *John Hoskyns*, p. 488. See also the Justice on the availability of Elizabethan legal papers, fol. 27.

[81] PRO, SP 14/85, fol. 18^{r}.

[82] Patricia Coughlan, *Spenser and Ireland: An Interdisciplinary Perspective* (Cork: Cork University Press, 1989), pp. 59–60.

[83] PRO, SP 14/85, fol. 31^{v}.

[84] PRO, SP 14/85, fol. 30^{v}.

[85] PRO, SP 14/85, fol. 27^{r}.

[86] Colclough, '*Parrhesia*', p. 188.

Crack Kisses Not Staves: Sexual Politics and Court Masques in 1613–1614

James Knowles

The relation of the magnificence of my lord Somerset's marriage is too large to be here inserted.
(John More to William Trumbull, 7 January 1614)

There was never the like bravery and vanity seen as hath been the most part of all these unholy days.
(Sir John Throckmorton to William Trumbull, 11 January 1614)[1]

The ambivalence expressed by the diplomat William Trumbull's correspondents about the marriage of the royal favourite Robert Carr, Earl of Somerset and Frances Howard, Countess of Essex and its celebrations has persisted. Over seven days between 26 December 1613 and 6 January 1614 Campion's *Somerset Masque,* Jonson's *Challenge at Tilt, At a Marriage*, and his *Irish Masque at Court,* the anonymous *Masque of Flowers,* sponsored by Francis Bacon (perhaps part-written by Thomas Bushell) and Middleton's (lost) *Masque of Cupids* were all performed. The specific political and cultural tensions caused by the Carr–Howard nuptials have, however, been overshadowed by later events – notably the sensational trial in 1615 of the Earl and Countess of Somerset for the murder of Sir Thomas Overbury, which confirmed contemporary rumours that their relationship had been adulterous.

Many of the confusions around the Carr–Howard match and the associated, lurid propaganda about the degeneracy of Jacobean court culture have been dispelled by David Lindley's meticulous studies of events 1612–16. In 'Embarrassing Ben' Lindley explores the 'uncomfortable disparity' between panegyric and intractable political reality in *The Challenge at Tilt* and *The Irish Masque at Court* as Jonson attempted to square the masque's idealised images with his previous involvement in celebration of Frances Howard's first marriage.[2] Lindley teases out the 'layers of embarrassment' for Jonson, illustrating how *The Challenge at Tilt* exploits hopes that this marriage might prove fertile and encourage factional rapprochement, in order to praise the match, a move which echoes many discussions of the Carr–Howard union in 1613–14. These arguments, developed in *The Trials of Frances Howard,* consider Frances Howard as exemplifying the subordinate position of women under early modern patriarchy and the collusion of many modern historians and literary critics with the misogynistic propaganda of earlier centuries.

Although Lindley provides a welcome re-assessment of one of the most overblown 'scandals' of the Jacobean period, his studies perhaps underestimate the significance of both Carr's position as favourite and his marriage as political issues. Whereas Lindley stresses the 'complacency' of *The Irish Masque* and its subordination of urgent Irish parliamentary issues to the marriage celebrations, contemporaries regarded the marriage as an intensely political event heralding a major factional realignment. The Earl of Northampton's description of Frances as a 'dainty pot of glue' uncomfortably suggests how the marriage cemented the bonding between two key individuals, Thomas Howard, Earl of Suffolk and Carr.[3] These political calculations were central to many contemporary commentators. For example, Roger Wilbraham baldly listed the Howard gains as Suffolk became:

> Lord Treasurer; his son-in-law, the Earl of Somerset, Lord High Chamberlain and the most potent favourite in my time [...] the Chancellor of Exchequer and many other officers placed by his means and his son in law Somerset's, that great favourite.[4]

Amidst these power politics Frances Howard *was* little more than adhesive. This essay locates Carr at the centre of the masquing sequence, arguing that the embarrassments felt by Jonson stemmed not just from his role in celebrating the earlier Essex–Howard match and political and national union project it symbolised but more from the origins of Carr's preferment. Carr's increasingly political role in the power vacuum created by the deaths of the Earl of Salisbury and Prince Henry allowed for an unprecedented degree of influence, redefining the concept of the favourite. In particular, the origins of this power in royal favour were most problematic and the 'open secret' which the Somerset match threatened to articulate was the interconnection of male power relations and sodomitical relations: Carr's very position embodied this issue.[5] In this sense, McClung and Simard's discussion of the critical vilification of Donne's Somerset epithalamium – which argues that the anxieties expressed by critics about the Carr–Howard match reflect displaced unease over the potentially sexual nature of the relations between Carr and James – can also be traced in the wedding masques.[6]

This chapter suggests that some of the tensions in these nuptial masques register widely expressed sensitivities over the bridegroom and the means of his ascendancy and that the invocations of fertility which characterise these texts stem less from epithalamic convention than the urgent need to contain Carr's potentially disruptive desires. Indeed, rather than the effacement – literal and political – which Lindley traces in texts such as the *Irish Masque*, the 1613–14 masques deployed a strategy of facing down criticism of the marriage. Thus these masques not only translate the highly sexualised language about Carr from the libels circulating contemporaneously into the licensed discourses of the masque, they also reiterate the boundaries of acceptable discourse through an intense concern with decorum and civility, especially in Jonson's *Irish Masque* which depicts opponents of the

Carr–Howard match as disloyal savages. Strikingly, these masques and the final pendant text, Daniel's *Hymen's Triumph*, debate sexual mores through differing representations of Hymen and Cupid, but also in the forms of the masque in which the King's 'newborn creatures' are contrasted with the female recreations of the Queen's court.[7]

'The most potent favourite of my time': Carr and the Jacobean favourite[8]

> You know the *primum mobile* of our court, by whose motion all other spheres must move, or stand still; the bright sun of our firmament, at whose splendour or glooming all our marigolds of the court open or shut. In his conjunction all other stars are prosperous, and in his opposition mal-ominous. There are higher spheres as great as he, but none so glorious.[9]

As his contemporaries recognised, Carr's marriage marked an important new step not only in the earl's fortunes but also in the role and significance of the favourite.[10] In the aftermath of Cecil's death, James I seems to have decided to re-assert his own power, using Carr as the broker between the two dominant court factions, moving decisively away from the combined forces of minister and Privy Council to the bedchamber favourite.[11] This decision, combined with the increased distribution of royal bounty, gave Carr a new power and significantly altered the meaning of the role of the favourite. As Bacon noted in 1616 'it is no new thing for Kings and Princes to have their privados', but Carr emerges as a very new thing in English terms, 'a politico'.[12] Indeed, Linda Levy Peck has argued that both James and Carr may have imitated Spanish models notably the dominant political and cultural position of the Duke of Lerma. Thus while James drew upon the centralised bounty of the Spanish court, Carr adapted Lerma's policy of aristocratic display and collecting. Carr has, in recent studies, emerged as a key figure in the collecting of Italian, especially Venetian, art and sculpture in England, a cultural trend which was not only 'avant-garde' but associated in some contemporary minds with the ideal of 'magnificence'.[13]

Carr transgressed the boundaries of the English court. He was a Scot raised to the English peerage, he moved from the bedchamber to the bureaucracy, and most in his role as Lord Chamberlain he broke the English rule separating the inner and outer chamber heads in the court structure.[14] This dual position, which granted him unrivalled control over patronage and access to the king, was recognised and the Venetian ambassador reported that 'he [Carr] is to dispose of everything' and that James made all policy decisions with him, confiding in Carr 'above all others'.[15] James I wrote to Carr in similar terms asking 'do not all court graces and place come through your office as Chamberlain [...].' and pointing out Carr's 'infinite privacy' with him.[16]

Carr depended on a highly ambiguous intimacy with James. A letter from the Earl of Suffolk describes the complex overlapping of personal and political connection in Carr's rise, commenting 'Carr is now most likely to win the Prince's affection and doth it wondrously in a little time.' Suffolk progresses rapidly from how James 'leans on his arm, pinches his cheek, smoothes his ruffled garment' to political realities: 'where it endedth, I cannot guess, but honours are talked of speedily for him.'[17] Indeed, this intimacy, especially its consequent transgression of the normative boundaries of the court, rendered Carr vulnerable. Offices, like the secretaryship, which supplied Carr's influence, were frequently sites for the accusation of unnatural sexual practices.[18] In particular, his close implication in a series of relations with other men, most notably Sir Thomas Overbury, Northampton and the king, laid Carr open to accusations of sodomy. Carr's relations with Overbury seem to have occasioned most comment and Roger Wilbraham described Overbury as 'Somersett's bedfellow, mynion and inward councellor', while Francis Bacon commented on their 'excess [...] of friendship' claiming that Overbury had made Carr his 'idol'.[19] The confusion of different roles (bedfellow, minion, councillor) encapsulates many of the anxieties which attended inter-male relations in this period. The suggestion of 'excess' resonates as the figure of the friend, one of the cornerstones of Renaissance homosocial relations, which threatened to overlap with the reprobate category of the sodomite. This dangerous duality informed both personal connections and the fundamental power relations in patronage and clientage.[20]

Certainly, both the annulment and Carr's rise increased awareness of male sexuality. Jacobean culture was characterised by a broad sexualisation of culture, not only in the eroticised languages of power and alliance, but in the interconnection of political and bodily metaphors, an element accentuated by the explicit sexual languages of contemporaneous political poetry often heightened at crisis points such as the Carr–Howard match. Whereas Lindley reads this versiferous explosion as an expression of misogynist anxieties about female sexuality it seems that *male* sexuality is equally implicated, especially in a society where manliness, the idealised male body and male bonds underpinned political discourses and structures.

The divorce case, for instance, raised the issue of who was responsible for the failure of marital relations. One contemporary poem suggests how, although Frances Howard's body was the centre of the examinations for sexual capacity, the issue also reflected upon Essex:

> This Dame was inspected but Fraudė interjected
> A maide of more perfection
> Whome the midwyffes did handle
> whilst the Knight held the candle
> O there was a cleare inspectione
> Nowe all forraigne wrytters,
> crye out on those myters
> That allowe this for virginitye
> And talke of Ejection and want of Erection
> O there is a sound dyvinitie.[21]

'Talke of Ejection and want of Erection' was widespread and Archbishop Abott noted that 'since that time much sport had been made at the Court and in London' about the titillating sexual details.[22] Members of the Howard faction referred to Essex as 'my Lord the Gelding' while Northampton teased Carr claiming that to decipher his handwriting caused less pain than 'that which a man takes in crackinge a swete nutte to tast the kirnell or but lyke the payne which my La. Fraunces shall feele when the sweete streame followes.'[23] Northampton even urged Carr: 'If my lord would draw his sword in defence of a good prick it were worth his pains.'[24]

Carr's position made him the frequent target of politico-sexual innuendo. One poem depicts Carr as a bubble:

When Carr in court at first a page beganne
He sweld and sweld into a Gentleman
And from a gentleman and bravely dight
he sweld and sweld till he became a knight
At last forgetting what he was at first
He sweld into an Earle and then he burst.[25]

Obviously, the 'swelling' here can be read as sexual as much as titular, and the poem continues that sense of 'excess', in power, wealth, dress and manners, which surrounded Carr. The 'burst[ing]' here may be an ironic image of the very detumescence with which the Howards taunted Essex. Indeed, such sexual punning informs many of the poems about James and Carr, and these often deal in sexual innuendo about the exact means of the favourite's rise to power:

Let any poor lad, that is handsome and young,
With *Parle vous France*, and a voice for a song,
But once get a horse, and seek out good James,
He'll soon find the house, 'tis great near the Thames.
It was built by a priest, a butcher by calling,
But neither priesthood nor trade, cou'd keep him from falling
As soon as you ken the pitiful loon,
Fall down from your nag, as if in a swoon:
If he doth nothing more, he'll open his Purse,
If he likes you, ('tis known he's a very good Nurse)
Your Fortune is made, he'll dress you in Sattin,
And, if you're unlearn'd, he'll teach you dog Latin.
On good pious *James* Male Beauty prevaileth
And other Men's fortunes on such he in-taileth.[26]

This parodic 'Advice to the sons of men' connects sexual and religious deviance (Wolsey's palace) and concludes with an obscene pun which meshes Carr's new found fortune with sodomy: sexual 'in-tailing' leads to financial entailing.

Even the apparently heteroerotic Carr–Howard match reflected upon manliness and the male body. The sexual and political impotence represented by the failure of the original Devereux–Howard match, which had inaugurated the Jacobean union, compounded the shadowy sense of national prowess under threat. These *male* implications were only strengthened by the links between Carr's advancement and James's preference for 'Male Beauty'. So, paradoxically, the solution for a 'crisis' in personal and national politico-sexual potency lay in the marriage of the Scots male favourite of the king, whose very position threatened to expose the overlapping discourses of patronage, friendship and sodomy in the Jacobean bedchamber. In these circumstances the insistent invocations of fertility throughout the 1613–14 masques seem highly pointed.

Rude boys and white staffs: the 1613–14 masques and sexual crisis

> Hold your tongues!
> And let your coarser manners seek some place
> Fit for their wildness.[27]

The Carr–Howard masques addressed directly the climate of rumour and the political libels in a strikingly explicit manner.[28] Using the sexual licence permitted within epithalamia these masques translate libellous bawdy into the more decorous language of fertility, countering imputations of sexual decadence and impotence with an image of a revitalized Jacobean union, extended in the *Irish Masque at Court* to include the 'civilising' project of the Irish plantation. These verbal translations acquire absolutist implications in the *Irish Masque* where Jonson deploys the ideal of decorum to differentiate between civil and uncivil speech about both marriage and plantation, dismissing the rebellious Irish and political libellers of the Carr–Howard match as barbarians.

At least superficially, however, the masques, tilts and ritualised hospitality marking the nuptials enacted a more reconciliatory politics to refound the Jacobean union. Chamberlain describes a 'late pacification of the court' and each event carefully deployed English and Scots, mixing members of opposing factions. Most importantly, Queen Anne was persuaded to countenance the nuptials:

> The marriage was thought should be celebrated at Audley End the next week and great preparation there was to receive the King, but I hear that the Queen beeing won and having promised to be present, it is put off till Christmas and then to be performed at Whitehall.[29]

The changed venue and timetable suggests that Anne sought to thwart the Howards of their greatest triumph (she was in dispute with Northampton over Greenwich Park at this time),[30] while also inconveniencing Carr with whom she intermittently feuded despite a formal reconcilation in 1612.[31]

Although observers noted a 'general reconcilement in this conjuncture' the queen's sponsorship of an alternative marriage, between her maid of honour Jean Drummond and Lord Roxburgh carefully distances her from her husband's behaviour:

> All the talk now is of masking and feasting at these towardly marriages, whereof the one is appointed on St. Stephen's day in Christmas, the other for Twelfthtide. The King beares the charge of the first, all saving the apparell, and no doubt the Quene will do as much of her side, which must be a maske of maides yf they may be found:

> and that is all the charge she meanes to be at, saving the brides wedding gown and the mariage bed, wheerin she will not exceed 500li: for she saith her maide Drummond is riche enough otherwise as well in wealth as in vertue and favor.[32]

In contrast to the 'magnificence' lavished by James on his bedchamber favourite, Anne salutes the marriage of her lady of the bedchamber with a parsimonious insistence upon 'vertue', and she pointedly invited the Earl of Essex to the feast.[33] These divergences, implicit in the 1614 presentation of Daniel's *Hymen's Triumph*, become explicit in its 1615 printing.[34] In effect, although the joint participation of James and Anne was supposed to stress the exemplary unity of the royal marriage, the entertainments created a gendered dialogue, focusing especially upon the roles of Cupid/Venus and Hymen as the tutelary deities of desire and marriage.

Campion's *Somerset Masque*, the linchpin of the debate, illustrates the defensive strategies and the implications of these gender politics. Campion's antimasque explicitly raised potential criticisms of the match through the enchanters and enchantresses Error, Rumour, Credulity and Curiosity, creators of the storms which have diverted the knight adventurers summoned by Fame to celebrate the marriage: 'these alone/turne all the world into confusion.'[35] Each of these figures wear costumes suitable to their distortions of truth: 'a deformed visard', 'a skin coate full of winged Tongues', 'a Cap like a tongue, with a large paire of wings to it', 'a skin coate full of eyes', 'a fantastick Cap full of Eyes' and a 'habit painted with eares, and an antick Cap full of eares.'[36] The prominence given to Error and Rumour suggests precisely the gossip and libels which surrounded the match, while Curiosity and Credulity embody the voyeurism which attended the annulment proceedings.

Anne's role develops this association of the libels with witchcraft. Invoked as 'Bel Anna', her presence (rather than the king's) validates the marriage and draws upon her powers depicted in the *Masque of Queens*. In *Queens*, Anne banished the 'envious' witches who 'Mix[ed] hell with heaven' and made 'Nature fight / Within herself.'[37] Like the witches of *The Somerset Masque* who create 'confusion',[38] the witches in *Queens* deployed 'Ignorance, Suspicion, Credulity'[39] to encourage 'Two-faced Falsehood', 'Murmur' and 'Malice', 'Slander', and finally 'black-mouthed Execration',[40] but whereas in Jonson's masque Anne merely embodies the virtue spread by Fame, in Campion's text she is the active participant. Thus in *The Somerset Masque*, Anne not only undoes the 'Knotted spels'[41] but in accepting the sacred tree brought in by the three Destinies she liberates the knights and releases the 'Good spels'.[42] The emphasis upon Anne's 'manifest' 'glory in th'effect' and the role of 'Vertuous Dames'[43] appropriates her female virtue to support this male-centred match as she both banishes the malicious and distinctly libel-like spells and releases the poetic energy for the celebrations.

Anne's agency is not contained by 'Men-making poets',[44] but is asserted in her acceptance of the 'Sacred Tree'. This marks the most striking formal innovation of the text as Anne not only substitutes for the king (the normal centre of the masque), but her actions break the bounds of the masque fiction as she was not actually performing in the masque. In this way she bridges the masque and court worlds, emphasising her political position as a consort queen rather than the masque or poetic fiction. As with the use of the 'arteficially presented' London and the Thames,[45] the first use of a 'realistic' setting in a court masque, it clearly links the masque's fictions to the contemporary political situation. It is a suitably transgressive gesture for a transgressive match.

In contrast to Anne's central and active role, James only features as the passive recipient of the 1st Squire's praises and this diversion away from the king's role and the insistence upon Anne's virtue may register some of the contemporary unease over James's connection with Carr. Yet, even amidst the repeated injunctions to and celebrations of heroic procreativity (suggested in the allusions to the marriage of Peleus and Thetis which produced Achilles), Carr's entanglements cannot be entirely suppressed.[46] Thus in the '4th Song, a Dialogue of three with a Chorus after the 2nd Dance':

I. Let us now sing of Loves delight,
For he alone is Lord to night.

II. Some friendship betweene man and man prefer,
But I th'affection betweene man and wife.

III. What good can be in life,
Whereof no fruites appeare?

I. Set is that Tree in ill houre,
That yields neither fruite nor flowre.

II. How can man Perpetuall be,
But in his own Posteritie?

CHORUS
That pleasure is of all most bountiful and kinde,
That fades not straight, but leaves a living Joy behind.[47]

Lindley argues that these lines show that Campion is 'self-evidently not concerned about any homosexual relationship which might have subsisted between Carr and the King or Carr and Overbury' and on one level they do continue the theme of fecundity, emphasising 'fruites' over 'pleasure'.[48] Yet this pleasure is not only between man and woman, but explicitly in the friendship of 'man and man' which some 'prefer'.

Although the decorum of the masque would not permit direct allusion to the precise connection between Carr and James (let alone the recognition of it as an alternative 'pleasure'), but the marriage – as we have seen – is founded upon male bonds and male power alliances. Indeed, Campion's text is oddly contradictory in this respect, dominated by 'Love's delight / For he alone is Lord tonight',[49] stressing the role of Cupid over Hymen, and the language of this song constantly pushes at the boundaries of the unsayable as the inter-male 'friendship' which some 'prefer' reminds the auditors of the connection between this preference and preferment. Later, the song which seems to celebrate fructification alludes both to 'posterity' and 'behind' almost as if recalling the libellers' puns on 'in-taileth'.

Rather, then, than effacement, these masques are centrally concerned with containment, echoing the bawdy discourse of gossip, refuting its truth, but also recuperating some of its language in order to restrict its implications. In particular, *The Somerset Masque* contains Carr's subversive potential, especially in the emphasis upon procreativity in marriage. Figuratively and verbally it makes the 'defence of a good prick' which Northampton had urged upon Carr by more violent means.

Whilst Campion only had to negotiate the debates around the marriage, Jonson had to circumvent his own past involvement in the celebrations for Frances Howard's first marriage. Yet, although the titles and headnotes of the implicated masques are sanitised in the 1616 folio, the texts themselves evidence more equivocal attitudes. Thus, *The Challenge* uses the debating cupids to gloss the marriage as the unification of two types of desire, just as its actual performance sought to unite the court. More controversially, *The Irish Masque*, while carefully distancing itself from the Howards, accepts Carr and his pre-eminence as the product of royal power. In fact, this is one of Jonson's most absolutist masques.

Like Campion's masque, *The Challenge at Tilt* pursued a dual strategy of containment and reconciliation stressing the reciprocity of love and continuing the court unity expressed during Carr's installation as an earl earlier in 1613. Yet the very occasion, a tilting, was fraught with problems, not least because it recalled the *Barriers at a Marriage* performed for Essex and Frances Howard in 1606. Moreover, Essex, the impugned party in the divorce, was a leading martial figure and many of the faction associated with him and Pembroke were exponents of military intervention against Catholicism in Europe, policies which the pro-Catholic Howards opposed. In the context of the marriage which had hinged on the unmanliness of one of the parties, to promote a tilt which focused on manly skills may have been, to say the least, tactless, especially if we bear in mind that Carr had gained his first real entrée into royal favour by falling off his horse in front of the king while tilting.

None of these embarrassments are registered in the text which reeks of sexual tension jokingly referring to unregulated sexual appetite and even sodomy.[50] In the dialogue, Eros and Anteros, representing Carr and Howard, struggle for precedence. Interestingly, Eros is characterised by his 'excellent beauty' is 'right worthy'[51] of his mother Venus, which recalls Carr's own handsomeness, while the second Cupid, standing for Lady Howard, refuses to give way: 'Thou cannot put modesty into me, to make me come behind you, thou I will stand for my inches with you, as peremptory as an ambassador.'[52] Both these allusions seem to court disaster reminding the participants of Carr's 'Male Beauty' which 'prevaileth' with the king, while the bawdy echoes the kinds of accusations about Frances Howard's indecorous behaviour and the language of the libels which depicted her as 'a lusty filly', 'growne so wide / theare is a passage for a Carre to ride.'[53] These bawdy Cupids relentlessly portray raging, even outrageous, desire 'playing in your bloods, like fishes in a stream, or diving like boys i'the bath, and then rising on end, like a monarch, and treading humour like water, bending those stiff pickardills of yours, under this yoke, my bow', sentiments which are regarded as 'most stiffly spoken, and fit for the sex you stand for!'[54]

Like the Campion masque with its strategy of containing the libellous innuendo around the Carr–Howard nuptials, the bawdy of this text corrals desire within the bounds of acceptable marriage and discourse, casting Carr, like Aeneas, as a Venusian figure. The concluding explanation by Hymen suggests that desire will now be regulated within marriage and that love and presumably the marriage will 'flourish and prosper' with children, a further dynastic extension of the implicit Carr–Aeneas parallel.[55] Hymen's intervention sanctions desire just as the text absorbs the bawdy of the libels and translates it into a more courtly setting and marriage. Even here, however, the dialogue negotiates the tensions created by the match:

> And may this royal court never know more difference in humours, or these well-graced nuptials more discord in affections, than what they presently feel and may ever avoid.[56]

The prayer-like conditionality of this closing sentiment marks how far the Carr–Howard match had stretched the harmony of the court. This closure, moreover, illustrates one of the problems in this strategy for, as in *The Irish Masque*, simply to turn the libels into fescenine verses and to translate the tensions within the court into 'difference in humours' belittles genuine concerns about the political implications of the alliance.

The appearance of the Cupids in *The Challenge* and the containment of desire within marriage is repeated in many of the masques and epithalamia surrounding the Carr–Howard match. Often the Carr–Howard marriage is depicted as expressing true love (as early as June 1613 Chamberlain recorded that 'the world speakes liberally that my Lord of Rochester and she be in love one with another'), against the failed dynastic Devereux–Howard marriage.[57] The emphasis upon Cupid in many of the masques, especially in *The Challenge* and Middleton's *Masque of Cupids* may register this aspect of the relationship.[58] Certainly, the reconciliatory role assigned to Hymen in Jonson's text continues the dialogue between the entertainments for the Somerset match over its tutelary deity, each text exploring the balance between Cupid and the restraining forces of social order. Campion's masque, for instance, stresses the roles of Cupid and Venus (the 'Sea-borne Godesse'), combining 'Hymen' with 'Amor', although the potentially disruptive qualities of desire are encased within choruses praising Hymen, 'charmes' which are 'enclosing' and 'closing'.[59]

An alternative view of this incorporation of desire within Hymen's realm is enunciated by Daniel's *Hymen's Triumph* whose 'unusual decorousness of subject-matter' contrasts pointedly with bawdry of Jonson's contributions.[60] The 'Prologue' added to the 1615 printed text establishes 'feminine' 'recreatiues' presided over by Cynthia 'Wherein no wild, no rude, no antique sport' is allowed,[61] and these echoes of Jonson's masque distance Daniel and his patroness from Jonson and his patron, even carving out a virtuous female space, the 'faire structure'

Denmark House, 'sacred to integrity' where 'honour keepes the doore.'[62] Indeed, the Prologue lavishly praises the queen's marital virtue and productivity.[63]

In Daniel's Prologue a disguised Hymen confronts '*Avarice*, *Envy* and *Jealousie*, the disturbers of quiet marriage' but, although these figures recall *The Somerset Masque*, this Hymen does not combine love and marriage, using instead a lowly habit and a 'white wand'[64] to shepherd lovers towards true, marital bliss. The symbolism of Hymen's 'white wand', substituted for the conventional torch, relegates the role of passion and is suggestive of the white staff carried by the Lord Chamberlain and which formed such a key part of Jonson's *Irish Masque at Court*. This symbolism, coming at the end of a series of entertainments which had sought to counter tales of lack of erection and over-heated sexual appetite, protracted political negotiations about the redistribution of royal offices and their associated official staves, a tilt which had urged unity on the participants by 'crack[ing] kisses not staves', and a masque which made great play of the position of the Chamberlain and his role in controlling behaviour, would have struck contemporary audiences. This Hymen, the god–shepherd–chamberlain of a household ruled by honour and integrity, contrasts sharply with the two last historical chamberlains, Suffolk and Somerset, who typified the 'newborn creations' celebrated in *The Irish Masque*.

The complex interweaving of intertextual details between the Carr–Howard marriage masques and Daniel's *Hymen's Triumph* suggest that, although modern criticism has depicted Jonson as only marginally concerned with the Carr–Howard nuptials, the *Irish Masque* may deal more directly with their political ramifications.[65] This is unsurprising as Carr's marriage was *the* pressing political event of 1614 and Carr's gravitation into the Howard aegis marked a significant realignment of power: now Suffolk would 'guide the rudder of the state.'[66] Although in Jonson's masque the epithalamic and Irish elements may seem in tension, the underlying connections can be seen in the parallels drawn between the renewal of the Anglo–Scots union and the wider Jacobean colonial project in the anonymous *Masque of Flowers*. The masque featured an elaborate garden, filled with fruit trees and flowers presided over by garden gods whose charm envisioned a renewed, fertile and civilised Britain, proffering not only marital fertility but an apocalyptic return to a new unionist world which reverses the 'rude and waste' and 'mends all things' making 'Britain fit to be / A seat for a fifth monarchy.'[67] This phrase, which echoes the *Irish Masque*'s 'civilising' process, suggests that mending the broken nuptials of the Devereux–Howard match promises a new golden age of civil plenty in a renewed Britain. Indeed, in the *Irish Masque*, if Ireland submits to the 'music of [...] peace', the king will 'in her all the fruits of blessing plant' the female pronoun applying as much to Frances Howard as to Ireland.[68]

Whereas, implicitly, *Flowers* voices the hope that some of the divisions occasioned by the match might now be resolved, Jonson's masque insists upon decorum in speech and behaviour, rejecting the scatological terms and sexual innuendo which have characterised the commentary surrounding the nuptials. This harsher view emerges from the opening of the antimasque with its derogatory depictions of the comic and disordered servants (Dennis, Donnell, Dermock and

Patrick) of the party of Irish ambassador–masquers who have come to mark the 'great bridal' of 'ty man Robin'.[69] According to their servants, the masquers have supposedly lost all their clothes ('te prishe of a cashtle or two upon teir backs'),[70] during a storm on the Irish sea so they must dance in their 'mantles',[71] a traditional Irish garb. In fact, 'a civil gentleman of the nation'[72] takes over the celebrations, introducing first a bard and then the masquers, who dance in their cloaks and then reveal 'their masquing apparel'. The bard's song informs us that they have been translated into 'newborn creatures all'[73] under the 'spring' of the king's 'presence'.[74]

The masque clearly alludes to the Jacobean project to 'civilise' Ireland and replace the Old Irish with the New Irish and, indeed, criticises the 'few rebelsh and knavesh'[75] who discredit the Irish nation with their recalcitrance. Much of the comedy stems from the mock-Irish accents of the antimasquers (who are more than just Irishmen as they also represent the labouring and middling sorts, including a citizen), and their gossipy overfamiliarity which echoes some of the libellous poetry which attacked the wedding. Thus, while their talk of 'ty man Robin' is merely and jokily over-familiar, their language and behaviour quickly becomes unacceptable in the 'civilised' court world . Their scatological puns (notably on 'shit' twice in lines 116 and 131), and the dance performed 'to the bagpipe and other rude music',[76] represent an unacceptable coarseness: 'let your coarser manners seek some other place / Fit for their wildness.'[77]

The contrast between the 'rude' and the 'civil' centres upon their speech, the very issue which occasioned so much anxiety around the Carr–Howard match. Most importantly, in the ordering of the masque the Lord Chamberlain fails to control these indecorous upstarts and it requires the king, his prophetic position and his ability to metamorphose, to foster both the civilisation of the Irish and the re-creation of the masquers. Here, one of the major complaints against James, the creation of baronets and peers, is defended as belonging to the necessary mystery of monarchy. More pointedly, given that the masque was danced by at least two of the bedchamber staff, Achmouty and Abercromby, in honour of the most prominent and successful member of the bedchamber, the very performance asserts the king's prerogative.[78] Carr, as a 'newborn creature' like the Irish ambassadors, is neither clotheless nor naked but, like the masquers, he is created in his new robes by royal intervention.

The comic portrayal of Suffolk ('tere is very much phoit stick here stirring tonight'),[79] may have been revenge upon the Chamberlain's exclusion of Jonson and his companion Sir John Roe from the masquing hall in 1604, but it also marks an important distinction between the power of the Howards and royal prerogative.[80] Indeed, the Howards are seen as inept and even potentially violent, a sentiment echoed by at least one near-contemporary satirist who noted 'when they are great / they emprison and beat.'[81] In contrast, the king wields power to 'end our country's most unnecessary broils.' The argument is that, like the plantation in Ireland, this match is designed to produce 'the fruits of blessing', and that this royal Orphism, the power to civilise and replace 'barbarism' with 'harmony', applies as much to England as to Ireland. The conclusion of the civil gentleman's speech places royal power at the centre of the masque:

Sing then some charm, made from his present looks,
That may assure thy former prophecies,
And firm the hopes of these obedient spirits,
Whose love, no less than duty, hath called forth
Their willing powers; who if they had much more,
Would do their all, and think they could not move
Enough to honor that which he doth love.[82]

Criticism of royal policy is a failure in obedience and it is the duty of loving subjects to both support the Irish plantation and the Carr–Howard nuptials. Moreover, not only must subjects 'do their all', not like the 'shubshects' of Ireland who carp at royal policy, but they must 'honour that which he [James] doth love.' 'That which' James 'doth love' is Carr and proper obedience lies in recognising that Carr's position is created by James's favour (his love) and to thwart or even question the favourite's position, a manifestation of royal power, is to fail to be a good subject and to become a barbarian: 'Obedience doth not well in parts.'[83] The insistence upon total rather than partial submission ('in parts') to royal power not only rejects the Irishman's defence of his partly rebellious nation, it also radically shifts the masque away from the language of the libels and their crude naming of body parts to a vision of loyal bodily wholeness. The concentration of the libellers upon sexual parts and 'in parts' is dismissed as uncivil.

Lindley's apt characterisation of this masque as 'complacent' underestimates Jonson's delegitimisation of any criticism of the monarch and his favourite. The masque is less concerned with effacement than with facing down opposition to the extent that, just as the queen in Campion's masque 'undid all knots' through her presence, so here James's 'gladding face' countenances and, therefore, legitimates the masque.[84] In this sense this masque and, to a lesser extent *The Challenge at Tilt*, are largely untroubled by the marriage, even if there are some reservations about the role of the Howards. The difference between the two masques lies, crucially, in the attitude to the 'opposition' to the masques. For Campion these are smoothed by the actions of the 'vertuous Dame', for Jonson the critics of the match, represented by the Irish, are buffoons and barbarians. For Jonson, the issue is not the immorality of the match or the sexual implications of Carr's rise, it is reduced to 'Obedience' and 'at once'.

'Virtuous Somerset': Jonson, patronage and the male erotic

May she whom thou for spouse today dost take
Out-be that wife in worth thy friend did make.[85]

After the Somerset trial Jonson celebrated the fall of the erstwhile favourite in *The Golden Age Restored* (1616), and began the process of negotiating with George Villiers the new favourite who seemed likely to prove the malleable tool of the Pembroke faction. Also in 1616 the sanitised masque-texts appeared, cleansing any evidence of Jonson's connection with either the Devereux–Howard or Carr–

Howard marriages. Thus far, Jonson's behaviour can be seen as having some consistency, negotiating an awkward situation with adroitness, distancing himself from the Howards, but still retaining his position as a royal masque-poet. This dexterity, however, belongs to the narrative which Jonson himself shaped through the 1616 texts, and the sense that he had survived implication in a distasteful business (his 'embarrassments' as it were) has been confirmed by modern critics. Yet evidence exists that Jonson was far more pragmatic about Carr.

In fact, a twenty-six line epithalamium for Carr 'most noble above his titles' has survived tipped into a 1640 folio of Jonson's *Workes*.[86] The praise of 'Virtuous Somerset', echoes the strategies found in the masques, replacing homosocial and potentially homoerotic relations with marriage in which 'every joy' 'turn a fruit' (line 18). Jonson's insistence on the veracity of his friendship and love (lines 1–6), against the 'face', 'clothes' and 'gifts' of others is accentuated not by his actual presence but by the 'early' salutation the poet offers. Most importantly, Jonson offered this poem not in print but in the more valued medium of manuscript, in this case in autograph, a mode Jonson chose to represent the aspiration towards intimacy or especially close, personal connection. A near contemporary note adds 'These verses were made by the aucthor of this booke, and were delivered to the Earle of Somersett vpon his lordshipps wedding day.'

Jonson's poem to Carr is interesting not simply because it exposes the poet's cynical manipulation of his texts and patrons, but because it offers a further instance of the complex interplay between heteroerotic, homosocial and, potentially, homoerotic relations which underpinned Jacobean court culture.[87] Not only is Frances to be measured in Overburian terms in the clear allusion to his poem *The Wife*, but the reference connects Jonson and Carr in shared intimacy as readers (and 'knowers') of Overbury. In this way Frances Howard again acts as the 'pot of glue' affirming the friendship between men, reducing her from living individual to textual symbol of a male wifely ideal. Indeed, throughout the poem she textually and verbally cements the patronage relationship between Carr and Jonson, itself physically demonstrated in the exchange of the private manuscript copy now glued into a copy of the printed text which belonged to Carr's relatives.

Jonson's own insistence on 'love not bought' encroaches into the complex arena of friendship, patronage and inter-male affectivity, which might explain why Jonson suppressed the poem, not simply because it associates him with the marriage, but because its rhetoric of love and friendship connects him too closely with Overbury and Carr and their questionable male connections. In this Jonson may not have forgotten Dekker's jibe in *Satiromastix* (1601) that he played the 'ningle' to the idiot patron, Asinus Bubo.[88] Indeed, the poem with its underpinnings of male patronage and power relations achieved through the symbolic exchange of women, in real and figurative form, suggests that the intimacy which Jonson claimed in the poem also provided the reason for its later suppression. As with the marriage masques, although modern critics have accepted Jonson's own self-narrativisation as embarrassed by Frances Howard, in fact, the masques themselves, like the relations Jonson seeks to erase in suppressing this poem, embody a troublesome, charged intimacy between men.

Notes

[1] Historical Manuscripts Commission, *Report on the Manuscripts of the Marquess of Downshire: Volume Four, Papers of William Trumbull the Elder, January 1613–August 1614*, ed. by A. B. Hinds (London: H. M. S. O., 1940), pp. 285 and 286.

[2] David Lindley, 'Embarrassing Ben: The Masques for Frances Howard' in *Renaissance Historicism: Selections from ELR*, ed. by Arthur F. Kinney and Dan S. Collins (Amherst: University of Massachusetts Press, 1987), pp. 248–64 (p. 250); and also David Lindley, *The Trials of Frances Howard: Fact and Fiction at the Court of King James* (London: Routledge, 1993), esp. pp. 123–44.

[3] Cambridge University Library, MS Dd.3.63, fol. 44 cited in Lindley, *Trials*, p. 85.

[4] *The Journal of Sir Roger Wilbraham, Solicitor-General in Ireland and Master of Requests, for the Years 1593–1616. Together with notes in another hand for the years 1642–1649*, ed. by Harold S. Scott, Camden Miscellany, 10 (London: Royal Historical Society, 1902), p. 115.

[5] For the term 'open secret', see Alan Sinfield, *Cultural Politics – Queer Reading* (London: Routledge, 1994), p. 47.

[6] William A. McClung and Rodney Simard, 'Donne's Somerset Epithalamion and the Erotics of Criticism', *Huntington Library Quarterly*, 50 (1987), 95–106.

[7] *The Irish Masque at Court*, line 166 in *Ben Jonson: The Complete Masques*, ed. by Stephen Orgel (New Haven: Yale University Press, 1969). All subsequent references are to this edition.

[8] *Journal of Sir Roger Wilbraham*, p. 115.

[9] George Calvert to Sir Thomas Edmondes, 1 August 1612, cited in Thomas Birch, *The Court and Times of James the First*, 2 vols (London: H. Colburn, 1848), I, 191.

[10] In what follows I have drawn on Linda Levy Peck's, 'Monopolizing Favour: Structures of Power in the Early Seventeenth-Century English Court', in *The World of the Favourite*, ed. by John H. Elliott and L. W. B. Brockliss (New Haven: Yale University Press, 1999), pp. 54–70.

[11] Neil Cuddy, 'The Revival of the Entourage: The Bedchamber of James I, 1603–1625', in *The English Court: From the Wars of the Roses to the Civil War*, ed. by David Starkey (London: Longman, 1987), pp. 173–225 (p. 208) and Peck 'Monopolizing Favour', p. 58.

[12] Cited in Peck, 'Monopolizing Favour', p. 59, and Peter R. Seddon 'Robert Carr, Earl of Somerset', *Medieval and Renaissance Studies*, 14 (1970), 48–68 (p. 51).

[13] Peck, 'Monopolizing Favour', p. 59 and A. R. Braunmuller, 'Robert Carr, Earl of Somerset, as Collector and Patron', in *The Mental World of the Jacobean Court*, ed. by Linda Levy Peck (Cambridge: Cambridge University Press, 1991), pp. 230–50, pp. 230–2 (esp. p. 230). Carr's paintings are discussed by Timothy Wilks, 'The Picture Collection of Robert Carr, Earl of Somerset (*c.*1587–1645), Reconsidered', *Journal of the History of Collections*, 1 (1989), 167–77. Writing in 1610 William Cecil advised a fellow nobleman that he should collect Italian art 'to increase your magnificence' (see Braunmuller, 'Collector and Patron', p. 231).

[14] Cuddy, 'The Revival of the Entourage', p. 181, and idem, 'The Conflicting Loyalties of a "vulger counselor": The Third Earl of Southampton, 1597–1624', in *Public Duty and Private Conscience in Seventeenth Century England*, ed. by John Morrill, Paul Slack and Daniel Woolf (Oxford: Oxford University Press, 1993), pp. 121–50 (p. 140).

[15] *Calendar of State Papers (Venetian), Volume XIII (1613–15)*, ed. by A. B. Hinds

(London: H. M. S. O., 1907), p. 219.

[16] *Letters of King James*, pp. 335–40, cit. Peck, 'Monopolizing Favour', p. 58.

[17] Bodleian Library, Oxford, Tanner MS 75, fol. 265 (1607), cit. Linda Levy Peck, *Northampton: Patronage and Policy at the Court of James I* (London: Allen & Unwin, 1982), p. 30.

[18] Alan Stewart, *Close Readers: Humanism and Sodomy in Early Modern England* (Princeton: Princeton University Press, 1997), pp. 161–87.

[19] *The Journal of Sir Roger Wilbraham*, p. 116 and Lisa Jardine and Alan Stewart, *Hostage to Fortune: the Troubled Life of Francis Bacon, 1561–1626* (London: Gollancz, 1998), p. 360.

[20] Stewart, *Close Readers*, pp. xxvii–xxviii and Alan Bray, 'Male Homosexuality and the Signs of Male Friendship', *History Workshop Journal*, 29 (1990), 1–19 also in *Queering The Renaissance*, ed. by Jonathan Goldberg (Durham, North Carolina: Duke University Press, 1994).

[21] Chester R.O., CR63.2.19, fol. 14 (commonplace book of William Davenport), cit. Lindley, *Trials*, p. 99.

[22] *Cobbett's Complete Collection of State Trials and Proceedings for High Treason and other Crimes and Misdemeanors from the earliest period to the present time,* ed. by William Cobbett, Thomas Bayly et al, 33 vols (London: Longman & Co.: London, 1809–26), II, 816, cit. David Lindley, *Thomas Campion* (Leiden: E. J. Brill, 1986), p. 222.

[23] Lindley, *Trials*, p. 71.

[24] Peck, 'Monopolizing Favour', p. 70, n. 55.

[25] Harvard MS 686, fol. 13ᵛ cited in James L. Sanderson, 'Poems on an Affair of State', *Review of English Studies*, n. s. 17 (1966), 57–61.

[26] William R. Chetwood, *Memoirs of the Life and Writings of Ben Jonson* (Dublin: W. R. Chetwood, 1756), p. iv.

[27] *Irish Masque*, lines 134–6, *Complete Masques*, p. 211.

[28] See Lindley, *Trials*, pp. 139–40 for a similar emphasis in Chapman's *Andromeda Liberata*.

[29] *The Letters of John Chamberlain*, I, 496 and 487.

[30] Peck, *Northampton*, pp. 73–4.

[31] Carr and Overbury apparently referred to her as Agrippina in their coded letters: see Anne Somerset, *Unnatural Murder: Poison at the Court of James I* (London: Weidenfeld and Nicolson, 1997), p. 98.

[32] *Letters of John Chamberlain*, I, 487.

[33] Historical Manuscripts Commission, *Report on the Manuscripts of the Duke of Portland*, ed. by J. J. Cartwright and R. F Isaacson (London: H. M. S. O., 1923), IX, 31 (Holles Letter Book).

[34] John Pitcher has pointed out that *Hymen's Triumph* was probably in preparation by mid-1613, and mainly intended for celebrations to mark the completion of the rebuilding of Somerset House and its re-naming by the Queen, but the text was also adapted to suit the nuptial occasion and Anne's entertainment of her husband: see Samuel Daniel, *Hymen's Triumph*, ed. by John Pitcher, Malone Society Reprints (Oxford: Oxford University Press for the Malone Society, 1994), pp. viii–x.

[35] *The Description of a Maske: Presented in the Banquetting roome at Whitehall, on Saint Stephens night last, At the Marriage of the Right Honourable the Earle of Somerset:*

And the right noble the Lady Frances Howard (hereafter *Somerset Masque*) in *The Works of Thomas Campion: Complete Songs, Masques, and Treatises with a Selection of the Latin Verse*, ed. by Walter R. Davis (London: Faber and Faber, 1969), pp. 263–84, p. 270.

[36] *Somerset Masque*, in *The Works of Thomas Campion*, p. 271.

[37] *The Masque of Queens*, lines 123, 135–6, *Complete Masques*, pp. 126–7.

[38] *Somerset Masque*, in *Works of Thomas Campion*, p. 270.

[39] *The Masque of Queens*, lines 15–16, *Complete Masques*, p. 123.

[40] *The Masque of Queens*, lines 111–17, *Complete Masques*, p. 126.

[41] *Somerset Masque*, in *Works of Thomas Campion*, p. 272.

[42] *Somerset Masque*, in *Works of Thomas Campion*, p. 274.

[43] *Somerset Masque*, in *Works of Thomas Campion*, pp. 272 and 273.

[44] *The Masque of Queens*, line 362, *Complete Masques*, p. 135.

[45] *Somerset Masque*, in *Works of Thomas Campion*, p. 273.

[46] *Somerset Masque*, in *The Works of Thomas Campion*, p. 276.

[47] *Somerset Masque*, in *The Works of Thomas Campion*, pp. 274–5.

[48] Lindley, *Trials*, pp. 125–26.

[49] *Somerset Masque*, in *The Works of Thomas Campion*, p. 274.

[50] David Riggs, *Ben Jonson: A Life* (Cambridge, Massachusetts: Harvard University Press, 1989), p. 203.

[51] *The Challenge at Tilt, At a Marriage*, lines 179–80, *Complete Masques*, p. 204.

[52] *The Challenge at Tilt, At a Marriage*, lines 9–11, *Complete Masques*, p. 198.

[53] Lindley, *Trials*, pp. 116–17.

[54] *The Challenge at Tilt, At a Marriage*, lines 97–100, 154, *Complete Masques*, pp. 201, 203.

[55] *The Challenge at Tilt, At a Marriage*, line 195, *Complete Masques*, p. 205.

[56] *The Challenge at Tilt, At a Marriage*, lines 206–9, *Complete Masques*, p. 205.

[57] *Letters of John Chamberlain*, I, 461.

[58] Although little survives of Middleton's lost *Masque of Cupids* its plural title suggests it may have responded directly to Jonson's text. It clearly continues the emphasis upon love and desire: see *The Masque of Cupids*, ed. by M. T. Jones-Davies and A. J. Hoenselaars in *The Complete Works of Thomas Middleton*, ed. by G. Taylor et al (Oxford: Clarendon Press, forthcoming).

[59] *Somerset Masque*, in *The Works of Thomas Campion*, pp. 275, 267 and 274.

[60] *Hymen's Triumph*, ed. Pitcher, p. xi.

[61] Samuel Daniel, *Hymen's Triumph. A Pastorall Tragicomaedie. Presented at the Queenes Court in the Strand at her Maiesties magnificent entertainment of the Kings most excellent Maiestie, being at the Nuptials of the Lord Roxborough* (London, 1615), 'Prologue', lines 15, 18–21, in *The Complete Works in Verse and Prose of Samuel Daniel*, ed. by Alexander B. Grosart, 5 vols (London: Hazell, Watson and Viney, 1865–96, repr. New York: Russell & Russell, 1963), III, 331.

[62] *Hymen's Triumph*, 'Prologue', lines 49, 51, in *Complete Works in Verse and Prose*, III, 331. John Peacock, 'Ben Jonson's Masques and Italian Culture', in *Theatre of the English and Italian Renaissance*, ed. by J. R. Mulryne and M. Shewring (Basingstoke: Macmillan, 1991), pp. 73–94 provides an important discussion of the divergences between Campion, Daniel and Jonson over masque theory.

[63] *Hymen's Triumph*, 'Prologue', lines 20–39, in *Complete Works in Verse and Prose*,

III, 331–2.

[64] *Hymen's Triumph*, 'Prologue', line 22, in *Complete Works in Verse and Prose*, III, 332.

[65] Thus one of the best studies passes over the 'incriminating aspects of the scandal' to study the Irish contexts in detail: see James M. Smith, 'Effaced History: Facing the Colonial Contexts of Ben Jonson's *Irish Masque at Court*', *English Literary History*, 65 (1998), 297–321.

[66] *HMC, Downshire*, IV, 285.

[67] *The Masque of Flowers*, lines 376–84 in *A Book of Masques*, ed. by Stanley Wells (Cambridge: Cambridge University Press, 1967).

[68] *Irish Masque*, lines 143, 149, *Complete Masques*, p. 211.

[69] *Irish Masque*, lines 52–4, *Complete Masques*, p. 208.

[70] *Irish Masque*, line 69, *Complete Masques*, p. 205.

[71] *Irish Masque*, line 74, *Complete Masques*, p. 209.

[72] *Irish Masque*, line 127, *Complete Masques*, p. 211.

[73] *Irish Masque*, lines 166–7, *Complete Masques*, p. 212.

[74] *Irish Masque*, line 164, *Complete Masques*, p. 212.

[75] *Irish Masque*, lines 105–6, *Complete Masques*, p. 210.

[76] *Irish Masque*, line 121, *Complete Masques*, p. 210.

[77] *Irish Masque*, lines 134–5, *Complete Masques*, p. 211.

[78] Some of the surrounding documentation for this masque makes this explicit: 'his Majestie is determyned to have a maske this Christmas performed by some gentlemen of his owne servants' (Public Record Office, SP 14/75/53).

[79] *Irish Masque*, line 59, *Complete Masques*, p. 208.

[80] Alvaro Ribiero, 'Sir John Roe: Ben Jonson's Friend', *Review of English Studies*, n. s. 24 (1973), 153–64.

[81] G. P. V. Akrigg, 'The Curious Marginalia of Charles, Second Earl Stanhope', in *John Quincy Adams Memorial Studies,* ed. by James G. MacManaway, Giles E. Dawson and Edwin E. Willoughby (Washington: Folger Shakespeare Library, 1948), 785–801.

[82] *Irish Masque*, lines 150–6, *Complete Masques*, p. 211.

[83] *Irish Masque*, line 160, *Complete Masques*, p. 212.

[84] *Irish Masque*, line 138, *Complete Masques*, p. 211.

[85] 'To the Most Noble, and Above His Titles, Robert, Earl of Somerset', in *Ben Jonson*, ed. by Ian Donaldson (Oxford: Oxford University Press, 1985), p. 449 (lines 11–12).

[86] British Library, C.28.m.11. Jonson, *Workes* (1640), contains a tipped-in sheet in two hands: Jonson's neat italic copy of the verses to Carr, and, second, a note in a near-contemporary hand about authorship and provenance. The volume contains a fragment of leather binding with the armorial stamp of the earls of Lothian.

[87] For Eve Sedgwick's conception of the 'homosocial triangle', see *Between Men: English Literature and Male Homosocial Desire* (New York: Columbia University Press, 1985), pp. 35 and 38.

[88] Thomas Dekker, *Satiromastix*, 1.2.21, in *The Dramatic Works of Thomas Dekker*, ed. by Fredson T. Bowers, 4 vols (Cambridge: Cambridge University Press, 1953), I, 317.

Civil War in 1614: Lucan, Gorges and Prince Henry*

Jonathan Gibson

Anna Beer has recently challenged the view that Sir Walter Ralegh's abortive patronage relationship with Prince Henry is at the heart of the *History of the World*. Arguing that the *History* should be read as a piece of 'public' writing rather than as a patronage text distorted by the death of its intended patron, she links its appearance in 1614 to roughly simultaneous publications by three out-of-favour writers associated with Ralegh: the verse translation of Lucan's *Pharsalia* by Ralegh's cousin and close friend Sir Arthur Gorges, a collection of sermons by Dr John Hoskins and John Selden's *Titles of Honour*. 1614 was a crucial year for these writers, Beer suggests, as it marked the point at which they began to use the public medium of print to express their grievances. Michelle O'Callaghan has made a similar argument about an 'oppositional' group of 'Spenserian' Inns of Court writers (William Browne, George Wither and Christopher Brooke), who moved into print at about the same time.[1] Beer and O'Callaghan's research suggests that 1614 marked an important stage in the development of a potentially subversive, print-based 'public sphere' in English culture. In this essay I gloss this thesis by reverting to the Henry-centred view of the *History of the World* challenged by Beer. Focusing on Arthur Gorges's translation of Lucan's Stoic epic, I argue that both Ralegh's *History* and Gorges's *Pharsalia* were written in the first instance for Henry and politically radicalised by the Prince's death in 1612.[2] I also argue that some key features of 'Henrician' ideology need to be reassessed.

Gorges and Ralegh were close associates over a period of many years and their writings share many themes and strategies.[3] *The History of the World* and Gorges's translation of Lucan belong together, as part of a single 'Neostoic' project for Henry undermined – and 'subversively' pushed into the public domain – by his death.

Lucan and Henry

Seneca's nephew and Nero's favourite, Lucan was condemned to death for his participation in the Pisonian conspiracy. His account of the civil war between

* I would like to thank Lorna Hutson, Gillian Wright, Rosalind Davies, Mandy Green, Michelle O'Callaghan, Anna Beer and Carlo Bajetta for help with previous drafts of this article.

Cæsar and Pompey in the *Pharsalia* juxtaposes aggressive republicanism with the gaudy flattery of Nero. As the 'one leading Roman poet who could become a focus for republican loyalties' – sympathetic to Pompey and the republic; hostile to Julius Cæsar – Lucan is central both to Andrew Shifflett's recent radical reading of renaissance Neostoicism and to David Norbrook's painstaking excavation of the seventeenth-century English republican tradition.[4] Norbrook argues that Gorges's translation has republican leanings and is thus oppositional: it made, he says, 'a political statement', registering 'discontent with the current direction of royal policies', and offering readers a teasingly ambiguous view of Roman politics. Colin Burrow and Carlo M. Bajetta, more conservatively, suggest that 'the fear of tyrannical injustice and its consequences, not love of the Republic, underlies [the] translation.' Burrow has linked Gorges's translation to other texts for which the *Pharsalia* 'became a vehicle for articulating unease at arbitrary distributions of honours, rewards, and offices.' 'Between about 1590 and 1615', he argues, 'Lucan assisted the emergence of honour-conscious heroes who believed they had been wronged by unjust monarchs.'[5] Despite their differences these critics agree in emphasising Gorges's opposition to the Jacobean status quo.

These arguments are persuasive and I would not want to deny their relevance to Gorges's text. There is little doubt that in 1614 Gorges saw himself as a man of honour wronged by the crown. He had been a client of Prince Henry and was a cousin and close associate of Ralegh. An unsuccessful courtier with literary and naval interests, he had spent many years in Elizabeth's reign as a Gentleman Pensioner. Out of favour with James, he had been briefly held in custody in 1603 in connection with the Bye plot. A number of manuscript texts by Gorges directly criticise the Jacobean court. Unsurprisingly, it is not hard to find oppositional elements in Gorges's Lucan. Gorges plays up the parallels between Rome and England. Twice in the first book, added first person plural forms ('us', 'our') smuggle Gorges's Jacobean readers into corrupt, pre-war Rome.[6] Here much of Gorges/Lucan's text (the law's loss of 'sacred freedome', clashes between consuls and tribunes, the prevalence of bribery and '*Usuryes* moth-eating trade', a sidenote, original with Gorges, deploring '*Honors* bought and sold, and not conferred by merit')[7], would have had troubling contemporary resonances. Several episodes must have seemed particularly relevant in 1614: Lucan's reference to 'suffrage bought and priz'd' recalls the 'undertaking' scandal; Cæsar's plundering of the Roman treasury (3.97–168), can be linked to James's financial demands. Faction and rivalry are key themes both in Lucan and in the 'Addled Parliament'. Strikingly, Gorges amplifies Lucan's praise of the Neronian peace, turning it into an in implicit homage to James *rex pacificus*: 'Multum Roma tamen debet civilibus armis / Quod tibi res acta est' (1.44), becomes 'And yet thou *Rome* shalt be in debt / Unto these wrackes, that did beget / This happy peace, wherein we live, / And to our toyles an end did give.'[8] To Lucan's optimistic anticipation of a universal peace presided over by Nero (1.60–2), Gorges adds a hope for 'Trades increase', an important element in James's pacifism.[9] He also expands on Lucan's praise of national unity, adding to Lucan's text (and italicising) the aphorism '*Divided Kingdomes staggring stand, / One Scepter fits one soveraigne hand.*'[10] Lucan's praise of Nero translates into implicit praise of James: does this mean James is /

will be like Nero?[11] In uneasy juxtaposition with all this is Gorges's straightforward translation of key republican passages. He faithfully renders Lucan's republican apostrophe to non-Romans (7.449–51)[12], and is equally unflinching when confronting Lucan's anger at Pompey's murder (10.526–9).[13] Translating Lucan's anticipation of the death of Cæsar (7.451), he swerves from Lucan in calling Cæsar a 'Tyrant',[14] and a little later adds a sidenote registering Lucan's 'derision' of the belief in imperial deification.[15] Gorges is also consistently friendly to Brutus: the Latin note to 2.234, 'Bruti constantia', is expanded to '*Brutus* constancy and courage',[16] whilst Gorges faithfully translates a laudatory apostrophe to Brutus which includes a bitter evocation of Cæsar's pride (7.588–95).[17]

There is much to be said, then, for the 'oppositional' sort of reading advocated, with differing emphases, by Norbrook, Burrow and Bajetta. Even so, an analysis of Gorges's *Pharsalia* in relation to Gorges's other writings suggests that originally the translation was designed for presentation to Prince Henry, Gorges's patron, and that its initial aim was to provide Henry with advice that would help him grow into a wise and powerful monarch.

Both 'oppositional' and 'Henrician' elements in Gorges's translation can be characterised as 'Neostoic'. Several writers have highlighted the 'Neostoic' tinge of Prince Henry's circle, though there has been a tendency to overstress its oppositional side. J. H. M. Salmon's analysis has set the tone for many other discussions:

> Gerhard Oestreich has described the European Neostoic movement as an ideology of statesmen, soldiers and scholars, providing 'the theory behind the powerful military and administrative structure of the centralised state of the seventeenth century.' This is not a judgement that can readily be applied to Stuart England, where Neostoicism had a far less positive role to play. The reason for this is partly that the English disciples of Seneca and Tacitus were usually members of circles soured by suspicion and defeat, and partly that the Senecan and Tacitean ideas they took from Lipsius and his continental disciples contained ambiguities that allowed a more negative application to English politics.

Salmon stresses the connection between the Essex circle and subversive Tacitean 'politic history' and argues that after Essex's fall oppositional Taciteans gathered around Prince Henry. As James was unsympathetic to Neostoicism, Tacitean Neostoicism became a means of articulating discontent with the status quo.[18]

My feeling, *contra* Salmon, is that Oestreich's 'state-building' Neostoicism – christened 'Counter-Reformation Anti-Machiavellianism' by Robert Bireley and 'Princely Theory' by Debora Shuger – was of considerable importance to many members of Prince Henry's circle and underpins much 'Henrician' writing.[19]

The chief aim of the 'anti-Machiavellian' tradition was to provide renaissance princes with an ethically acceptable way to build up their power. Tacitus's editor, the leading renaissance Neostoic, Justus Lipsius, followed Giovanni Botero in using material from Tacitus to help advise early modern princes on political and military policy or 'reason of state'. 'Anti-Machiavellian' writers stressed the need for princes to behave virtuously in order to win power-enhancing reputation. Princely intervention in economic development and the military was also important: wealth and a disciplined soldiery were conceived of as key components in a state's strength. Botero stressed the importance of governmental involvement in economic policy. Lipsius linked Stoic ethics to military reforms imitated from ancient Roman practice and rooted in the virtue of a Neostoic prince.

Within the terms set by this intellectual tradition, a variety of issues relating to Henry were debated by his and James's clients: whether or not he should make war in Europe; how trade should be encouraged to build up the state's wealth; military tactics and strategy; martial discipline; the role of colonisation in state-building; the place of ethics in politics; the importance of a strong navy; how a prince should choose his officers and servants.[20]

All the writing undertaken by Ralegh and Gorges for Prince Henry engages with these themes. One of the cousins' major aims seems to have been to guide Henry towards a wise and virtuous military heroism, geared to the fighting of a war against Spain. The key text here is Gorges's narrative account of the 'Islands Voyage' of 1597, presented to Henry in 1607 along with a revised text of a tract on the navy originally written by Ralegh for Queen Elizabeth. A later manuscript tract by Gorges dedicated to Henry yokes together the two key 'princely theory' themes of economic strength and military strength and caps its argument with an unacknowledged quotation from Botero. Ralegh's vision of England as the centre of a world empire is derived from Botero. Ralegh echoes Botero's emphasis on the importance of riches in his *Discourse of the Invention of Ships* (written between 1604 and 1616), and may have translated Botero's treatise on the greatness of cities.[21] Ralegh's brief unfinished treatise 'On the Seat of government' (probably written in 1609–10 for Prince Henry), which analyses the means of holding and maintaining royal power, is strongly reminiscent of the 'princely theory' tradition. The providentialist framework of *The History of the World* reflects a popular tactic of the 'anti-Machiavellians' ('providentialist pragmatism' is Bireley's term for it), which is particularly important to Lipsius.[22] As Pierre Lefranc has shown, Ralegh engaged in a complex and comprehensive way with the thought of Machiavelli. Several highly Machiavellian texts are among the Ralegh apocrypha and *The History of the World* is sprinkled with attacks on Machiavellian 'policy'.[23]

Gorges's treatises and Ralegh's *History* make significant use of Roman example in writing about military practice. Lipsius's work on Tacitus and Polybius directly influenced Maurice of Nassau in his celebrated reform of the Dutch army. As Maurice was one of Prince Henry's heroes and Dutch military practice was emulated by several of Henry's servants, it seems *prima facie* feasible that Henry's English followers should deliberately invoke in their writings for Henry the programme recommended by Lipsius for Maurice.[24]

The closeness of the association between Gorges and Ralegh strongly suggests that Gorges's translation of Lucan was from the first conceived of as a pendant to the *History*, another 'Henrician' text. Concluding his narrative in 168 BC, Ralegh looks forward to the decay of Rome, soon to face many 'stormes of ambition'. Gorges's Lucan, a text published like the *History* by the stationer Walter Burre, can be read as a bleak sequel to Ralegh's narrative.[25]

Gorges's translation is a rough-hewn, unscholarly piece of work, peppered with misreadings. He seems to have been working from a Lyon edition of 1561, a sparsely annotated text which included only simple sidenotes.[26] His aim would have been to produce not a scholarly version of Lucan's poem but a text that Henry would find helpful in considering questions of political and martial behaviour and policy. Rich – like Ralegh's *History* – in material on strategy and tactics, rousing speeches, descriptions of battles and analyses of heroic virtue and leadership, the *Pharsalia* would have appealed strongly to Henry's military interests and his related enthusiasm for the study of history, at the same time providing him with a sobering account of the less glamorous side of warfare.[27] The unusually large amount of naval warfare would have picked up on one of Henry's strongest enthusiasms. In effect, Henry would have received a commonplace book of military, political and moral wisdom held together in an exciting narrative framework, clearly designed to furnish him with a storehouse of Neostoic *exempla* and *sententiæ* to ponder and to deploy in speech and action.[28] Many *sententiæ* are marked, in a departure from the practice of the Lyon edition. Quite often, too, Gorges turns non-sententious moments in Lucan's text into *sententiæ* (see, for example, 'And those most soundly take their ease, / Whom lowly poverty can please', adapting 5.505–6).[29] Gorges's sidenotes, meanwhile, frequently mint new Neostoic *sententiæ*: 'True valor increaseth with mis-fortune';[30] 'The remembrance of former felicities is grievous in adversitie';[31] 'Opportunity in martiall affaires once lost is hardly recovered.'[32] Gorges's sidenotes cut most of the technical rhetorical material in the Lyon edition's apparatus, focusing attention instead on potentially useful elements of martial lore.[33] Gorges scrupulously annotates Cæsar's, Pompey's and Cato's speeches to their troops, though without using rhetorical terms. He registers the speeches' strengths and weaknesses and notes the troops' reactions. At several points Gorges compares moments in Lucan's narrative to recent military history: the Spaniards' use of a 'stockado' before Antwerp;[34] the sinking of the *Mary Rose*.[35] Implicit reference is made in some sidenotes to Gorges's own military experience on the Islands Voyage of 1597.[36] Military topics highlighted in added sidenotes include the treatment of veteran soldiers,[37] the importance of armies in preventing idleness,[38] 'The cruelty of fire in a sea-fight',[39] the way in which 'Confused fighting in Troopes; obscures particular valour',[40] and the Roman practice of 'fighting in an orbe [...] in extremity.'[41] Gorges is full of admiration for the courage and dedication of Cæsar's men,[42] and the affection[43] and awe[44] with which they regarded their general. He also approves of the Romans' thirst for 'future fame'[45] and honour,[46] and individual heroism such as 'The resolution of *Vulteius*.'[47] Many of Gorges's original sidenotes register individual acts of bravery (e.g. the Massilians in Book 3). He makes much of Lucan's Stoicism, italicising all of the long passage in Book 9 in which Cato refuses to ask an oracle about the future, and heightening the Stoicism of other speeches. He adds to Pompey's speech in Book 7 praising the man who is able to delay action in the face of danger the phrase 'setled patience'. All of this material fits well with 'Lipsian' ideology.

At the centre of the *Pharsalia* is the heroic but problematic figure of Cæsar. Much of Cæsar's behaviour would have been considered worthy of Henry's emulation. The figure of Cæsar was strongly associated with Henry, in part because James had specifically recommended the study of him to his son. Dedicating to Henry a volume of observations on Cæsar's *Commentaries* (1604), Clement Edmondes explained that he had returned to his unfinished work on this text after having read James's praise of Cæsar in *Basilicon Doron*. In 1609 Edmondes's commentary on Cæsar's *Civil Wars*, again dedicated to Henry, appeared, making liberal use of Lucan and accompanied by a commendatory poem by Joshuah Sylvester identifying Henry as 'a CÆSAR of our owne'. The title-page engraving shows Cæsar and Pompey facing each other across an archway surmounted by a portrait of Prince Henry. George Chapman's *Cæsar and Pompey*, a relatively even-handed dramatisation of the civil war, possibly written at about the same time as Gorges's translation of Lucan, was, it has been suggested, originally composed for Henry. The texts by Edmondes and Chapman both cover the same events as Lucan, and both involve the juxtaposition of Cæsar's good and bad qualities with the good and bad qualities of Pompey and Cato. Perhaps the sort of issues raised by the events of the civil war were being actively discussed at Henry's court, and Chapman's, Edmondes' and Gorges's texts were designed to feed that discussion.[48] Ralegh's *History of the World* depicts Cæsar as the most heroic figure of history and is much concerned with the discussion of this sort of topic.

Henry's court would have been an ideal arena for airing such themes. It would have been possible for writer–clients presenting Henry (a young prince under instruction) with accounts of Pompey, Cato and Cæsar to argue that he should emulate some of these figures' actions and avoid others. The conventional identification of Henry with Cæsar need not, of course, have prevented his clients from criticising some of Cæsar's actions. Many renaissance treatments of the civil war assigned blame equally to Pompey and Cæsar, at the same time recognising the 'worthiness' of both.[49]

A context such as this would help to explain Gorges's consistent generosity to Cæsar. Though registering much of Lucan's hostility to 'the tyrant', Gorges's translation consistently plays down Cæsar's evil and accentuates his heroism. Translating Lucan's first major attack on Cæsar, Gorges censors the suggestion that Cæsar 'rejoices' ('gaudet' (2.439)) in slaughter. 'Cæsar in arma furens nisi sanguine fuso / Gaudet habere vias' (439–40), becomes '*Cæsar* in Armes with furies sway / Not without bloud will shape his way.'[50] Unflattering adjectives are regularly doctored. The 'unjust ('iniqui' (7.40)) victor's weapons' become simply 'the hand / Of him that doth the victor stand.'[51] At 7.503 the blades of the swords of Cæsar's soldiers are 'guilty' only in Latin ('nocens').[52] Gorges also detaches 'furor' and 'rabies' from Cæsar: 'Hic furor, hic rabies, hic sunt tua crimina, Cæsar' (7.551) becomes the more neutral 'Here rage and furie now exceeds, / Here *Cæsar* are thy hainous deeds.'[53] At 7.386, Gorges omits the 'fear of tyranny' animating Pompey's army: 'metus hos regni, spes excitat illos' thus becomes 'Feare doth one side to courage straine, / The others hope to rule and raigne.'[54] Latin sidenotes hostile to Cæsar are suppressed, and Cæsar is described as 'noble' (5.301) and 'manly' (7.248–9),[55] in departures from Lucan.[56] Gorges amplifies Cæsar's boldness by wrongly stating that his reputation was not as great as Pompey's.[57] At numerous other points in the text he emphasises Cæsar's courage and nobility. At

7.701–2 ('Quo pectore Romam / Intrabit factus campis felicior istis?'), for example, he doctors Lucan to present the reader with the image of an implausibly compassionate Cæsar:

Thinke what remorse will straine his breast
When he shall enter *Rome*, opprest
With griefe, for her deare people lost,
Gain'd to *Pharsalia* at her cost.[58]

He mollifies the impact of Cæsar's wicked defiance on crossing the Rubicon (1.225–7) by making it into part of a rallying speech to his troops. Gorges's sidenotes add complimentary adjectives (e.g. 'mercifull' and 'pious')[59] not found in the Latin sidenotes they translate.[60] In the storm in Book 5 (5.654–71), Gorges adds sidenotes which play down Cæsar's foolhardiness and highlight his bravery. Where Gorges's notes register hostility to Cæsar it is usually marked as being Lucan's own opinion only ('The Authors bitternesse in taxing *Cæsar*')[61]; 'The Authors love to Pompeys merit').[62] Bias towards Cæsar is accompanied by bias against Pompey, so that, for example, at 1.131–3 Gorges adds a sidenote censuring Pompey's courting of the people as 'popular affectation'.[63]

The ideological core of Gorges's translation comes in Book 8, in a remarkably extensive addition to Lucan's text. Young King Ptolemy's court debate whether or not to keep faith with the fleeing Pompey. Old Acoreus's proposal of aid is opposed by Pothinus in a gleefully cynical speech. Pothinus argues that, as the law of the jungle makes it necessary to act amorally, Pompey must die (8.483–535: 'exeat aula / qui vult esse pius' (lines 493–4)). Lucan's failure to give Acoreus's speech is rectified by Gorges who, in more than a hundred lines, supplies his own idea of what Acoreus might have said.[64] Gorges's addition performs three functions simultaneously: it debates a central 'anti-Machiavellian' theme, praises Cæsar's virtue and sings the praises of the Roman republic.

The self-defeatingly 'politic' murder of Pompey by Ptolemy's henchmen was used by some writers in the 'anti-Machiavellian' tradition to support the argument that princes ought to keep their word.[65] Attacking Pothinus as '*Machiauels* maister',[66] Gorges supplies in the speech he gives Acoreus a concise summary of 'anti-Machiavellian' political ethics. Acoreus's key argument is that amorality in government leads to rebellion. If princes do not keep faith, how are subjects to behave?

All Kings by Ceremonies stand,
By lawes they rule with powerfull hand.
But if those lawes they vioalate, [*sic*]
They weaken then their owne estate.[67]

Gorges's sidenote strengthens the message: 'Order and justice [are] the support of regall power.'[68] A king's lawlessness invites violent opposition from overmighty subjects:

When Kings themselves lawlesse grow,

They hazard then to overthrow
Their owne estate; and teach that mind
That is ambitiously enclind,
How to aspire by fraud or might,
To reave away their soveraignes right.[69]

One of the things Gorges is doing by giving Acoreus a voice is implicitly lending support to Lucan's sympathetic portrayal of the republican Pompey: Pompey should be supported, not Cæsar. At one point Acoreus says that Ptolemy should not count on Rome's continued support for imperial rule:

[...] *Rome* doth Monarchie disdaine,
And her brave spirits that still liv'd free,
To vassallage will not agree.[70]

This, the closest Gorges comes to the advocacy of republican rule, echoes Botero's admiration for republics.[71] The speech also praises Cæsar. Acoreus argues correctly that treacherous behaviour will be frowned on by Cæsar (he will 'condemne thy mind / As most disloyall and unkind').[72] Cæsar's nobility is stressed at length.

Just as Gorges was a virtuous elderly advisor to Prince Henry, so Acoreus is a virtuous elderly advisor to the young King Ptolemy. It is striking, then, that Acoreus's advice should be rejected by Ptolemy, who sides with the vicious Pothinus. There are echoes here of texts by Gorges which express anxiety about Henry's future. In *The Olympian Catastrophe*, Gorges's long narrative elegy for Henry, Atropos justifies the Prince's death by arguing that, had he lived, he might have gone to the bad, as Nero did after his promising *quinquennium*.[73] A similar anxiety informs Acoreus's speech:

Be well advised and stand in awe,
The worlds defame on thee to draw
In thy yong yeares, for such a staine
Will all thy life on thee remaine.
The vessell alwayes holdeth fast
The sent whereof it first did tast.[74]

At the ideological core of his translation, then, Gorges confronts the possibility that his project will be useless. Acoreus's speech to Ptolemy stages in little Gorges's original intentions for his book and writes into them an acute awareness of the possibility of failure.

Lucan in 1614

As a text dedicated to Henry, a young prince interested in learning about martial affairs, Gorges's *Pharsalia* need not have been viewed as 'oppositional'. It is easy to imagine the sort of dedication Gorges would have written for it, linking its themes to his and Ralegh's other 'Neostoic' writings. Henry's death in 1612, howver, would have rendered that strategy redundant. With the Howards ascendant at Court, no patron hospitable to Gorges's or Ralegh's 'state-building' brand of Neostoicism was available. Instead, like the texts written by the disappointed 'Henricians' discussed by O'Callaghan and Beer, Gorges's translation appeared in print in an experimentally 'anti-patronage' form and its 'oppositional' qualities came to the fore.[75]

O'Callaghan stresses the way in which the Spenserians forged links between themselves, constructing a 'print community' in lieu of patronage ties. Gorges deployed a related, more explicitly 'Neostoic', strategy: a Senecan stress on the ability of the wise man to find an authoritative source of virtue within himself.[76] The potentially radical implications of this form of Stoic individualism, a key element in Lipsian thought, have been recently highlighted by Shifflett, who argues that in the early seventeenth century they provided martial 'men of honour' with a personal centre of authority which enabled them to defy the Crown. In Shifflett's reading of Senecan withdrawal, 'retirement could itself be a decisive act of political rhetoric and a tacit but hard to ignore plea for a return to virtue-centred politics' – a way of opposing tyranny. This meant that early modern Stoicism often entailed a paradoxical form of publication: 'the publication of privacy, the commercialisation of the withdrawn personality.'[77] Publication of this type performs, in Gorges's Lucan of 1614, the same role as O'Callaghan's 'print community': it attempts to construct a point of authority for the writer outside the patronage system and, in a rather bizarrely paradoxical way, looks forward to the emergence of the 'public sphere'.[78] At the same time, Henry's absence meant that anti-tyrannical, republican elements in Gorges's translation – which would have appeared relatively innocuous in the context of a *Pharsalia* dedicated to the education of Prince Henry – approached the status of political subversion.[79]

Gorges provides no author's dedication for his translation, and at no point, either in the preliminaries or in the main text, explains why he undertook the translation or what he thinks about Lucan or any of the issues his text raises.[80] The dedication to the Countess of Bedford is not written in the voice of Gorges himself but in the voice of Carew, Gorges's ten-year old son. Attributing the dedication to his son allows Gorges to dramatise his work's marginal status. 'Carew' makes hardly any reference to the contents of his father's translation:

> The least good documents, which we learne in our youth, may in some part of our life serue us to use. I remember this sentence in my *Pueriles, Voluntas, ubi desunt vires, est laudanda*: Where power is wanting the good will is to be accepted. Which I presume will be my warrant in presenting your Ladyship with this Poeme, which by chance I did see in my fathers study, amongst many other of his manuscripts. And because it lay idly there, I desired him to give it me. Who then asking what I would do with it, I told him that I would present it to my Lady my Mistresse. Which humor of mine he seemed very well to like: but he answered, that it was not faire enough written for her reading. Whereunto I replied, that if I might have it, I would amend that fault, and get it printed by the helpe of my Schoole-maister, and in that sort offer it[.] Whereto my father said, that he liked so well of my devotion to so noble a mistresse, as that he would freely give it mee. The which now (as mine

owne) I do humbly recommend to your honourable acceptance, as some testimony of my devoted zeale, untill yeares, and ability shall second my indevors with parts more answerable to my desire. And in the meane season I will perswade myselfe that this poore present is the more aptly offered, knowing that the reading of Heroicall actions do as properly belong to noble and vertuous Ladies, as the acting of them to worthy and valorous Knights. Besides that, your Ladiship is an honourable lover and Patronesse of learning and the Muses, an instinct naturally ingrafted in your excellent spirit, by that worthy blood of the *Sydneyes*, wherewith you do so nearely participate, and whose perfections did so eminently shine in that hopefull yong Lord your late brother, one of the mirrours of our Age. Now if this may but receive your honourable applause, as some pledge of my Devotion, I will never thinke that I need to be ashamed to flutter with my Fathers feathers.[81]

There is an implicit contrast between Carew and another boy: Prince Henry, probably the original intended reader of the translation.[82] Unable, unlike Henry, to translate Lucan/Gorges's *sententiæ* into virtuous action, Carew deploys a schoolbook *sententia* emphasising his lack of power. And as his patron is female, she too is unable, as Carew makes clear, to put Lucan's precepts into action. Publicising Gorges's self-imposed, virtuous exclusion from the patronage system, the dedication constructs a deliberately feeble, *ersatz* replacement for Gorges's clientage relationship with the Prince. Gorges's absence from his preliminaries protects him from the public world in which its publication landed his text, enabling his life to remain focused in the virtuous *vita contemplativa* of his study. Meanwhile, other people – 'Carew', the writers of commendatory poems – contextualise Gorges's translation. The choice of the Countess of Bedford as dedicatee hints at an allegiance to the old Elizabethan 'war party'.[83] The commendatory poems, meanwhile, make links between Gorges and Lucan, identifying Gorges as a virtuous, truth-telling opponent of tyranny. The well-known poem by W. R. (almost certainly Ralegh) links Lucan's pursuit of 'truth' to Gorges's refusal to revere 'worthlesse men':

Had *Lucan* hid the truth to please the time,
He had been too unworthy of thy Penne:
Who never sought, nor ever car'd to clime
By flattery, or seeking worthlesse men.
For this thou hast been bruis'd: but yet those scarres
Do beautifie no lesse, then those wounds do
Receiv'd in just, and in religious warres;
Though thou hast bled by both, and bearst them too.
Change not, to change thy fortune tis too late.
Who with a manly faith resolves to dye,
May promise to himselfe a lasting state,
Though not so great, yet free from infamy.
Such was thy *Lucan*, whom so to translate
Nature thy Muse (like LUCANS) did create.[84]

Casting Gorges as a latter-day Lucan, disappointed in life and out of key with the time, W. R. counsels a Stoic endurance. The time for action is past – Gorges has been a virtuous man and that ought to be enough to satisfy him. The only test left is the encounter with death. Gorges expresses his virtue, his independence from the need to flatter the great, by simply, like Lucan, telling it as it is.[85] Stoicism is deployed as a way to escape the patronage system, a way of vindicating failure as a client and rewriting the failed client's sense of self. The setbacks offered by Gorges as a result of his refusal to kow-tow to 'worthlesse men' are equated with the wounds of battle: thus Gorges's Stoic defiance is part of his martial identity as a man of honour.[86] In another commendatory poem, S. S. contrasts the truthfulness of Lucan with the fabling of Homer and Virgil. T. W., meanwhile, links Gorges's and Lucan's truthfulness and unfanciful way of writing to opposition to tyranny.[87] These poems echo the association made several times in Gorges's prose treatises between Roman historians' brave telling of truth and their hatred of tyrants.[88] Gorges is empowered as an angry Stoic out of tune with the times and the patronage system.[89]

The stress on 'Truth' in these commendatory poems is paralleled in the work of O'Callaghan's Spenserians as are Gorges's and Ralegh's 'patriotic' militarism and their 'anti-Machiavellianism'.[90] Clearly, Gorges, Ralegh and the Spenserians all belong together in the same general ambit. All these writers shared 'oppositional' qualities which seem to have been largely produced by the death of Henry and which heralded in a complex way the emergence of more publicly-oriented ways of writing.

Notes

1 Anna R. Beer, *Sir Walter Ralegh and his Readers in the Seventeenth Century: Speaking to the People* (Basingstoke: Macmillan, 1997), Chapter 2; Michelle O'Callaghan, *The 'Shepheard's Nation': Jacobean Spenserians and Early Stuart Political Culture 1612–1625* (Oxford: Clarendon Press, 2000). For O'Callaghan's definition of 'oppositional' see p. 234. See also James Doelman, 'Born with Teeth: Christopher Brooke's *The Ghost of Richard the Third* (1614)', *Seventeenth.Century*, 14 (1999), 115–29.

2 For the importance of Henry's death to 'oppositional' writers see Christopher Hill, *Intellectual Origins of the English Revolution* (Oxford: Clarendon Press, 1965); David Norbrook, *Poetry and Politics in the English Renaissance* (London: Routledge & Kegan Paul, 1984), Chapter 8; William Hunt, 'Spectral Origins of the English Revolution: Legitimation Crisis in Early Stuart England', in *Reviving the English Revolution: Reflections and Elaborations on the Work of Christopher Hill*, ed. by Geoff Eley and William Hunt (London: Verso, 1988), pp. 305–32; O'Callaghan, *Jacobean Spenserians*, pp. 13–15. Ralegh says in the preface to his *History* that the work had originally been intended for Henry.

3 Helen Estabrook Sandison, 'Arthur Gorges, Spenser's Alcyon and Ralegh's Friend', *PMLA*, 43 (1928), 645–74; Jonathan Gibson, 'Arthur Gorges (1557–1625) and the Patronage System' (unpublished doctoral thesis, London University, 1997).

4 Andrew Shifflett, *Stoicism, Politics and Literature in the Age of Milton: War and Peace Reconciled* (Cambridge: Cambridge University Press, 1998); David Norbrook, *Writing the English Republic: Poetry, Rhetoric and Politics, 1627–1660* (Cambridge: Cambridge University Press, 1999). The quotation is from Norbrook's earlier study of Lucan, 'Lucan, Thomas May, and the Creation of a Republican Literary Culture', in *Culture*

and Politics in Early Stuart England, ed. by Kevin Sharpe and Peter Lake (London: Macmillan, 1994), pp. 45–66 (p. 46).

[5] Norbrook, 'Lucan', pp. 51, 52; Norbrook, *Writing*, pp. 41–3; Colin Burrow, *Epic Romance: Homer to Milton* (Oxford: Clarendon Press, 1993), pp. 188, 189; Carlo M. Bajetta, *Sir Walter Ralegh: poeta di corte elisabettiano* (Milan: Mursia, 1998), pp. 346–49. For other radical readings see Gerald M. Maclean, *Time's Witness: Historical Representation in English Poetry, 1603–1660* (Madison: University of Wisconsin Press, 1990), pp. 39–41; Hill, *Intellectual Origins*, p. 150.

[6] Arthur Gorges, *Lucan's Pharsalia: containing the Civill Warres betweene Cæsar and Pompey* [...] *Translated into English verse by Sir A. Gorges.* [...] *Whereunto is annexed the life of the Authour, collected out of divers Authors.* (London, 1614), sig. B5^r; *M. Annei Lvcani de bello civili libri decem, Nunc recèns post omnium editiones sedulò recogniti, ac scholijis illustrati Lvgduni apvd haered. Seb. Gryphii* (Lyon, 1561), sig. C3^r. The parenthetic references in the text refer to book and line numbers in the Loeb edition.

[7] Gorges, *Pharsalia*, sig. C3^r.

[8] Gorges, *Pharsalia*, sig. B5^v.

[9] Gorges, *Pharsalia*, sig. B5^v.

[10] Gorges, *Pharsalia*, sig. B6^v.

[11] Though Gorges follows tradition in believing that the first part of the poem was written as a patronage text for Nero during the virtuous beginning of his reign (Gorges, *Pharsalia*, sig. B5^v), he glosses Lucan's hyperbolic vision of the deified Nero as too heavy for the heavens (1.53–5), as 'meere Ironicall flatttery' (Gorges, *Pharsalia*, sig. B5^v). His note to 1.60 *et seq.*. – 'In this he teacheth NERO how he should governe, by an Imagination of what is' – suggests that he imagined Lucan as having combined panegyric with instruction.

[12] Gorges, *Pharsalia*, sig. 2B6^v.

[13] Gorges, *Pharsalia*, sig. 2Q5^r.

[14] Gorges, *Pharsalia*, sig. 2C1^r.

[15] Gorges, *Pharsalia*, sig. 2C1^r.

[16] *De bello civili*, sig. C2^r, Gorges, *Pharsalia*, sig. F6^v.

[17] Gorges, *Pharsalia*, sig. 2C4^v.

[18] J. H. M. Salmon, 'Seneca and Tacitus in Jacobean England', in *The Mental World of the Jacobean Court*, ed. by Linda Levy Peck (Cambridge: Cambridge University Press, 1991), pp.169–88 (pp. 169–70). For another version of this article see 'Stoicism and Roman Example: Seneca and Tacitus in Jacobean England', *Journal of the History of Ideas*, 50 (1989), 199–225. Salmon cites Gerhard Oestreich, *Neostoicism and the Early Modern State*, ed. by Brigitta Oestreich and H. G. Koenigsberger, trans. by David McLintock (Cambridge: Cambridge University Press, 1982).

[19] I owe this idea to Lorna Hutson. Robert Bireley, *The Counter-Reformation Prince: Anti-Machiavellianism or Catholic Statecraft in Early Modern Europe* (Chapel Hill: University of North Carolina Press, 1990); Debora Shuger, 'Castigating Livy: The Rape of Lucretia and *The Old Arcadia*', *Renaissance Quarterly*, 51 (1998), 526–48. Key texts in this tradition included Giovanni Botero's *Della Ragione di Stato* (Venice, 1589) and Justus Lipsius's *Politicorum* (Leiden, 1589). Other writers find more common ground than Bireley does between Machiavelli and the 'anti-Machiavellians'. Lipsius, in particular, allows the prince considerable ethical leeway). See, among many others, Peter Burke, 'Tacitism, Scepticism, and Reason of State', in *The Cambridge History of Political Thought 1450–*

1700, ed. by J. H. Burns (Cambridge: Cambridge University Press, 1991), pp. 479–98; Richard Tuck, *Philosophy and Government 1572–1651*, Ideas in Context, 26 (Cambridge: Cambridge University Press, 1993); Maurizio Viroli, *From Politics to Reason of State: The Acquisition and Transformation of the Language of Politics 1250–1600* (Cambridge: Cambridge University Press, 1992); Adriana McCrea, *Constant Minds: Political Virtue and the Lipsian Paradigm in England, 1584–1650* (Toronto: University of Toronto Press, 1997). See also Blair Worden's bracingly sceptical review of Oestreich ('Constancy', *London Review of Books*, 20 January–2 February 1983, 13–14).

[20] Within these broadly 'Neostoic' parameters there were disagreements which have been registered by several critics. Perhaps the most significant involved the question of whether or not Henry should pursue a militant Protestant foreign policy: for discussions of this, see J. W. Williamson, *The Myth of the Conqueror. Prince Henry Stuart: A Study of 17th Century Personation* (New York: AMS Press, 1978); John Pitcher, *Samuel Daniel: The Brotherton Manuscript. A Study in Authorship*, Leeds Texts and Monographs, n.s. 7 (University of Leeds, 1981), pp. 20–37; Roy Strong, *Henry, Prince of Wales and England's Lost Renaissance* (London: Thames & Hudson, 1986), pp. 141–51; 155–7; 160–74; Richard Badenhausen, 'Disarming the Infant Warrior: Prince Henry, King James, and the Chivalric Revival', *Papers on Language and Literature*, 31 (1995), 20–37. McCrea stresses another conflict, between more and less 'Machiavellian' or 'Tacitist' advisers to Henry, Ralegh being an anti-Machiavellian (*Constant Minds*, Chapter 1).

[21] Trinity College, Cambridge, MS R. 7.23*, fol. 23^{v} (quoting Botero's definition of 'stato' in Latin translation); Tuck, *Philosophy and Government*, pp. 116–17; Markku Peltonen, *Classical Humanism and Republicanism in English Political Thought 1570–1640* (Cambridge: Cambridge University Press, 1995), p. 200; Pierre Lefranc, *Sir Walter Ralegh, écrivain: l'œuvre et les idées* (Paris: Colin, 1968), p. 66; Steven W. May, *Sir Walter Ralegh*, Twayne's English Authors Series, 469 (Boston: Twayne, 1989), pp.174–5. As Tuck says, Ralegh's writings are 'full of arguments drawn from the Tacitists' (*Philosophy and Government*, p. 116).

[22] Bireley, *Anti-Machiavellianism*, p. 31.

[23] Lefranc, *Sir Walter Ralegh*, Appendix G. See also McCrea, *Constant Minds*, Chapter 1.

[24] Oestreich, *Neostoicism*, p. 50; Strong, *England's Lost Renaissance*, pp. 68–70, 73.

[25] Walter Ralegh, *The Historie of the World* (London, 1614), sig. 6T4^{r}; May, *Sir Walter Ralegh*, p. 104. Gorges's Lucan echoes material in Ralegh's fragmentary *A Discourse of the Original and Fundamental Cause of [...] War* (written in 1614, according to May (*Sir Walter Ralegh*, pp. 106–9)), much of which concentrates on ambition in great men as a cause of civil war.

[26] Published by the heirs of Sebastianus Gryphius (see note 6). For more detail on Gorges's translation, see Gibson, 'Arthur Gorges', pp. 251–80.

[27] Cf. Charles G. Salas, 'Ralegh and the Punic Wars', *Journal of the History of Ideas*, 57 (1996), 195–215 (p. 199).

[28] *Sententiæ* were crucial to Neostoic writing. In Gorges's translation they hit home in a punchy style which can be linked to Lipsius's staccato 'Tacitist' Latin prose.

[29] Gorges, *Pharsalia*, sig. S4^{r}.

[30] Gorges, *Pharsalia*, sig. L5^{v}.

[31] Gorges, *Pharsalia*, sig. 2E1^{v}.

[32] Gorges, *Pharsalia*, sig. 2Q2^{v}.

[33] Cf. Gabriel Harvey's martially-oriented 'reading' of Livy for Philip Sidney (Lisa

Jardine and Anthony Grafton, '"Studied for Action": How Gabriel Harvey Read His Livy', *Past & Present*, 129 (1990), 30–78 (pp. 36–7)).

[34] Gorges, *Pharsalia*, sig. H6r.

[35] Gorges, *Pharsalia*, sig. L6v.

[36] See, for example, Gorges, *Pharsalia*, sig. T1r.

[37] Gorges, *Pharsalia*, sig. D2v.

[38] Gorges, *Pharsalia*, sig. K5v.

[39] Gorges, *Pharsalia*, sig. M1v; sig. 2Q4r.

[40] Gorges, *Pharsalia*, sig. O4v.

[41] Gorges, *Pharsalia*, sig. P6v.

[42] Gorges, *Pharsalia*, sig. M5r.

[43] Gorges, *Pharsalia*, sig. O5r.

[44] Gorges, *Pharsalia*, sig. R6r; sig. V6r.

[45] Gorges, *Pharsalia*, sig. O5r.

[46] Gorges, *Pharsalia*, sig. 2I4v.

[47] Gorges, *Pharsalia*, sig. O5v.

[48] Rolf Soellner, 'Chapman's *Cæsar and Pompey* and the Fortunes of Prince Henry', *Medieval and Renaissance Drama in England*, 2 (1985), 135–51; Williamson, *Myth of the Conqueror*, Chapter 2; *The Basilicon Doron of King James VI*, ed. by James Craigie, 2 vols (Edinburgh: Edinburgh University Press, 1944–50), I, 151; Clement Edmondes, *Observations Upon Cæsars Commentaries* (London, 1604), sig. A3r; idem, *Observations Upon Cæsars Commentaries* (London, 1609), sig. A3r. For the discussion of historical topics at Henry's court see Strong, *England's Lost Renaissance*, p. 145. Botero's *Prencipe* (translated in 1602), is also ambivalent about Cæsar.

[49] See, for example, Edmondes, *Observations* (1609), sig. B1v–B2r.

[50] Gorges, *Pharsalia*, sig. G6r.

[51] Gorges, *Pharsalia*, sig. 2A2r.

[52] Cf. Gorges, *Pharsalia*, sig. 2O2r.

[53] Gorges, *Pharsalia*, sig. 2C3v.

[54] Gorges, *Pharsalia*, sig. 2B5r.

[55] Gorges, *Pharsalia*, sig. 2B1v.

[56] The note 'Cæsaris impietatem, imprudentiamque taxat' (D3v; note to 3.73), is omitted. 'Cæsarem metuebant civitates, non amabant' (*De bello civili*, sig. D3v; note to 3.78), is toned down into '*Cæsar* not applauded by the Citties, as he past towards *Rome*.' (Gorges, *Pharsalia*, sig. I4r).

[57] Gorges, *Pharsalia*, sig. C2r, mistranslating 1.143.

[58] Gorges, *Pharsalia*, sig. 2D1r.

[59] Gorges, *Pharsalia*, sig. 2B3v and sig. 2B3r respectively.

[60] *De bello civili*, sig. I3v.

[61] Gorges, *Pharsalia*, sig. 2H1v.

[62] Gorges, *Pharsalia*, sig. 2I1r.

[63] Gorges, *Pharsalia*, sig. C1v.

[64] Burrow was the first to notice this (*Epic Romance*, p. 188).

[65] For an English example, dedicated to Henry, see Sir George More's *Principles for yong princes* (London, 1611), sigs. B3v–B8r. Cf. Bireley, *Anti-Machiavellianism*, p. 59.

[66] Gorges, *Pharsalia*, sig. 2G4r.

[67] Gorges, *Pharsalia*, sig. 2G2r.

[68] Gorges, *Pharsalia*, sig. 2G2^{r}.

[69] Gorges, *Pharsalia*, sig. 2G2^{r}.

[70] Gorges, *Pharsalia*, sig. 2G2^{v}.

[71] Bireley, *Anti-Machiavellianism*, p. 52.

[72] Gorges, *Pharsalia*, sig. 2G^{v}.

[73] *The Poems of Sir Arthur Gorges*, ed. by Helen Estabrook Sandison (Oxford: Clarendon Press, 1953), lines 937–48. See also Trinity College, Cambridge MS R. 7.23*, fols. 23^{r}–23^{v}.

[74] Gorges, *Pharsalia*, sig. 2G2^{r}.

[75] It could be argued that Henry's death is also behind the other 1614 'print acts' listed by Beer (*Sir Walter Ralegh*, pp. 31–5). For all the writers Beer lists, Henry could, when alive, have provided patronage that would have obviated the appeals to print audiences they made in 1614.

[76] This strategy was also used by the Spenserian Wither. Lipsius concentrated on this 'Senecan' aspect of Neostoicism in his *De constantia* (1584). See Tuck, *Philosophy and Government*, pp. 62–3, for an interesting account of the relationship between the personal and the political strands in renaissance Neostoicism.

[77] Shifflett, *Stoicism, Politics and Literature*, pp. 3, 4.

[78] As O'Callaghan stresses, though, patronage remained crucially important for all the Spenserian writers (and the same is true for Gorges and Ralegh). It is very tempting to read the anti-patronage rhetoric used by all these authors as a gambit *within* the patronage system: an attempt to win the approval of potential patrons by stressing the Stoic writer's incorruptible virtue.

[79] The *Pharsalia* itself is, in Annabel Patterson's phrase, 'functionally ambiguous' (*Censorship and Interpretation: The Conditions of Writing and Reading in Early Modern England* (Madison: University of Wisconsin Press, 1984)). Patterson derived the concept of functional ambiguity from Frederick M. Ahl's *Lucan: An Introduction* (Ithaca: Cornell University Press, 1976).

[80] Gorges supplies a life of Lucan (sig. B1^{r}–B3^{v}) put together from *vitae* in contemporary editions of Lucan, but he is careful to leave out the most politically contentious parts.

[81] Gorges, *Pharsalia*, sigs. A3^{r}–A4^{r}.

[82] The dedication also mentions a third boy, a once 'hopefull' scion of 'the worthy blood of the *Sydneyes*': John, second Baron Harington of Exton, the Countess's brother and Prince Henry's best friend, who had died in 1614. The Sidney connection is important. Gorges's verse elegy for 'the Young lord *Harrington*' follows one of his elegies for Henry in echoing Ralegh's poem on the death of Sidney (*Poems*, pp. 130–1, 229–30).

[83] Norbrook, 'Lucan', p. 52.

[84] Gorges, *Pharsalia*, sig. A4^{v}.

[85] It is perhaps no accident that in the *Pharsalia* virtuous victims of tyranny are given speeches of considerable length and rhetorical force.

[86] Ralegh refers to wounds suffered by Gorges on the Islands Voyage of 1597. Gorges himself referred to his wounds in a similar way in a legal case of 1615 (Gibson, 'Arthur Gorges', pp. 52–4). Cf., too, Lucan's use of wounds in the *Pharsalia*. Ralegh's poem echoes contemporary poems by Gorges himself (Bajetta, pp. 348–49; Gibson, 'Arthur Gorges', n. 28, p. 275). As May points out, Ralegh's poem 'is unusual in its neglect of the work itself' (*Sir Walter Ralegh*, p. 104).

[87] Both poems also look like attacks on Chapman's Homer, a translation initially undertaken for Prince Henry then appearing volume by volume. MacLean argues that T.W.'s poem is 'directed against James's attempt to legitimate his reign by recourse to a classicising style that permits exaggeration and fable' (*Time's Witness*, p. 40). Cf. Norbrook, 'Lucan', pp. 52–3. In a fourth poem, A.I. stresses the 'modesty' with which Gorges presents Lucan to the public.

[88] See, for example, Helen Estabrook Sandison, 'Manuscripts of the *Islands Voyage* and *Notes on the Royal Navy* (In Relation to the Printed Versions in Purchas and in Ralegh's *Judicious Essayes*)', in *Essays and Studies in Honor of Carleton Brown* (New York: New York University Press, 1940), pp. 242–52 (p. 250).

[89] In this period Gorges also used 'anti-patronage' strategies in prose dedications (Beer, *Sir Walter Ralegh*, p. 26).

[90] Norbrook, *Poetry*, Chapter 8; O'Callaghan, *Jacobean Spenserians*, p. 18. See also Norbrook's '"The Masque of Truth": Court Entertainments and International Protestant Politics in the Early Stuart Period', *Seventeenth Century*, 1 (1986), 81–110. There are other links. A cousin of Gorges's was married to Sir Robert Phelips, an associate of the Spenserians. Ralegh features in Browne's *Britannia's Pastorals*. In 1611/12, Gorges's business venture, 'The Public Register for Public Commerce', operated from the Middle Temple, one of the Spenserians' bases (Gibson, 'Arthur Gorges', pp. 46–9; for a related Inns of Court community see Tom Cain, 'Donne and the Prince D'Amour', *John Donne Journal*, 14 (1995), 83–111). The style of Gorges's elegy for Henry, *The Olympian Catastrophe* (in *Poems*), is more 'Spenserian' than the work of the Spenserians. For a strongly 'anti-Machiavellian' work by a Spenserian writer, see Brooke's *The Ghost of Richard the Third* (London, 1614).

13

Robert Cotton's *A Short View of the Life of Henry the Third*, and its Presentation in 1614

Stephen Clucas

Shortly after the anonymous publication of *A Short View of the Long Life and Raigne of Henry the Third of England, presented to King James* in 1627 a contemporary observed that:

> There is a little booke published comprising severall passages of state historically related, as they were carried in the long raigne of King Henrie the 3rd with some observations of application to our state at this present which by reason of favourites and discontented peeres resembles in many things that ancient government.[1]

Printed as it was at a time when George Villiers, the Duke of Buckingham was at the height of his influence, the topicality of the manuscript to the political situation is not to be questioned. The question which does emerge, however, is the topicality of the text at the time when (as its subtitle suggests) it was originally 'presented to King James.' William A. Jackson in his 1950 article on Cotton's *A Short View* observed that 'all of the surviving manuscripts' (and there are at least thirteen surviving manuscripts of this text) 'which are dated bear the date 29 April 1614,' while Kevin Sharpe noted that a Cambridge University Library manuscript of the work tells us that it was 'written by Sir Robert Cotton Knight Baronett in anno 1614 and by him presented to his Majestie the same year.'[2] In his article, Jackson suggested that Cotton's work was 'applicable to the political situation of 1627,' and Kevin Sharpe in his 1979 monograph takes a similar view, observing that 'Much of the content points to George Villiers, Duke of Buckingham,' adding that 'If Robert Cotton wrote the history in 1614, he or another clearly saw its relevance to 1627' and it is its 1627 topicality on which Sharpe concentrated his efforts.[3] What I propose to consider here is what the topical relevance of Cotton's history was at the time of its composition in 1614, and to suggest that the historical parallels were far more pertinent to the parliamentary difficulties of 1614 than they were to Buckingham in 1627.[4]

Kevin Sharpe, Linda Levy Peck, and Harold Love have in their various ways established the political contexts for Cotton's historical and antiquarian researches, and his predilection for scribal publication.[5] Love has emphasised that Cotton's 'conception of himself was as an author solely for the scribal medium.'[6] For this reason, and because there are serious doubts whether Cotton was involved in the decision to publish the printed version, the disproportionate attention to the circumstances surrounding the 1627 publication seems a little unwarranted, and says little about Cotton's designs for its scribal publication.[7] Jackson's article suggested that the number of manuscript copies could be explained by the fact that it had been 'circulated among Cotton's friends, as was customary with most of his treatises.'[8] This view of Cotton's textual production as an informal coterie distribution based on disinterested friendship has been corrected by Sharpe, Peck and Love, who stress the tactical political deployment of his antiquarian texts. Harold Love noted that Cotton's works (many of which concerned the 'powers and functions of the great officers of the crown') had a 'vital tactical role to play with regard to questions of procedure' in parliament, 'providing precedents to support claims for parliamentary privilege against the exercises of Royal prerogative,' looking to mediaeval and ancient sources for 'the conduct of contemporary affairs.'[9] Cotton's 'most characteristic form of writing,' Love says was the short essay summarising the historical precedents relevant to some contemporary administrative question: Sharpe has illuminatingly compared them to the kind of position paper that today might be prepared by a civil servant for a minister.[10]

Peck, following Sharpe, also talks of Cotton's pieces as 'position papers,' comparing his role to that of the modern 'technocrat' or 'speechwriter,' and if these comparisons are a little anachronistic in terms of the more fluid political structures of the Jacobean period, they do in part reflect the view of Cotton's patron the Earl of Northampton, who referred to him as an 'industrous servant' and 'active and sufficient minister'.[11] As Peck has suggested Cotton used his antiquarian researches 'both to support government policy and to reform government practice,'[12] and in both these respects scribal publication was a necessity as well as a desideratum. As Love says in his thumbnail sketch of Cotton's output, his works often contained 'privileged information that would have to be carefully guarded from the press.'[13] This is certainly true of Cotton's *A Short View*, which was designed to function as a critical historical parallel to the uncomfortable and tense political interlude between the parliaments of 1610 and 1614, and to suggest a way forward for Jacobean crown policy.

'The surfett of long peace': *A Short View* and historical parallelism.

Cotton's *A Short View* begins with the 'sodaine fall of a licentious Soveraigne' and the accession of the young Henry, 'mild, and gracious but easie of Nature', invoking the sudden hopes for preferment and advancement which had attended the accession of James in 1603, after the office-starved reign of Elizabeth: 'all men stood at gaze expecting the event of their long desires [...] and easie of their new hopes [...] ffor in everie shift of Princes, there are few [...] that please not themselves with some probable object of Preferment.'[14] The 'distempers' of the early Jacobean state, the parallel argues, were kept in check by the king's reliance on experienced council: 'These vapours did ever and easily vanish soe long as the helme was guided by temperatt spiritts and the King tied his actions to the Rule of good Councell, and not to young, single or passionate advice.'[15]

However, in the figure of the elder statesman De Burgo, we can see the sketchy outlines of a critique of the predominance of single counsel in government. De Burgo is described as:

> a man in whome nothing of worth was wanting, but Moderation, whose length of daies geving him the advantage of sole power, did owne Ambition and Age gave him desire and Art to keepe out others: This bredd to him the fatall Envy of most, with the proud title of Earle and Offices then bestowed on him much encreased.[16]

Beneath this description is a clear parallel with the position of Robert Cecil, who was created Baron Cecil of Essendine in 1603, and Viscount Cranborne in 1604, before being created Earl of Salisbury in 1605. Having served as Principal Secretary to Queen Elizabeth and having (together with the Earl of Northampton) smoothed the path for James's accession in 1603, Cecil was retained as Principal Secretary, and after being granted his earldom, became Lord Lieutenant of Hertfordshire, and three years later, after the death of the Earl of Dorset, was chosen to succeed as Lord Treasurer in May 1608.

The first part of *A Short View* also alludes obliquely to the discontent caused by James's promotion and preferment of his Scottish subjects.[17] Cotton describes how having brought down De Burgo, Peter Des Roches, Bishop of Winchester 'displaceth the Natives' from important Court offices, replacing them with Frenchmen. This, he says, 'draweth [...] the king into evill opinion of his people; ffor nothing is more against the Nature of the English then to have straungers to rule over them.'[18] Charges laid against the French courtiers in Cotton's history closely echo those laid against the Scots in the middle years of James's reign:

> They fill upp the places of Justice and trust with their countreymen straungers, put out the English, Exact of whome, and how they please, wast the Treasure and Crowne lands on themselves and followers; sett price on all offences; and reyne the lawe within the rule of their owne breast [...] Yet least the Kings should heare the groanes and greediness of his Ministers, which good and able men would tell him, they barr all access.[19]

If we compare this, for example, with a speech by Sir John Holles during the 1610 parliament, the parallel seems quite clear: '[T]he Scottish monopolize his princely person', Holles told the house:

> standing like mountains betwixt the beams of his grace and us; yet we most humbly beseech his Majesty his Bedchamber may be shared as well to those of our nation as to them, that this seven years' brand of jealousy, distrust or unworthiness, may at the last be removed from us [...]. From this inequality proceeds a twofold unequal distribution of benefits [and] of favors, for not only they possess the royal presence, they be warm within, while the best of ours starve without. Hence as from a fountain, is fed that great and daily renewing overplus of their nation, which surrounding the whole court devours the royal hospitality and trebles the ordinary expense.[20]

Foremost among a number of Scottish courtiers who enjoyed the favours of James was, of course, Robert Carr (other favoured Scottish courtiers included the Earls of Lennox, Holderness, and Dunbar, the Duke of Lennox and Lord Kinlosse). The figure of Simon de Mountford in Cotton's history, whom Sharpe sees as clearly alluding to the Duke of Buckingham, would seem (bearing in mind the French/Scots parallel developed by the text) to have been originally intended to represent Robert Carr:

> ffor Mountford a ffrenchman became the next object of the Kings delight, a gentleman of choice bloud, education and features. On this mans content the headie affection of the Soveraigne did soe much doate; that at his first entry of grace, in Envy of the Nobillitie he made him Earle of Leicester [...]. Mountford made wanton with the dalliance of his maister, forgetteth Moderation, for seldome discretion in youth attendeth greate and sodain ffortune: he draweth all affaires publique into his hands; all ffavours must pass from him, Preferments by him, all suites addressed to him.[21]

While the critique of court favouritism and monopoly was relevant enough be re-deployed later to attack Buckingham, the parallel more nearly fits the case of Carr who was created Viscount Rochester in March 1611, and Earl of Somerset in November 1613, and whose position in the Royal Bedchamber ensured him a virtual monopoly of James's favours until late 1614, or early 1615, when George Villiers was beginning his meteoric rise in James's estimation. Besides his influence as part of the king's bedchamber, Carr obtained a series of influential offices. In 1612 he was made a Privy Councillor, and when Cecil died later that year, it was Carr who was asked to act as the king's Principal Secretary. After the death of Northampton in 1614, Carr also took over as acting Privy Seal, thus embodying within himself two of the most important offices of the Crown. The clinching detail which marks Simon de Mountford as a representation of Carr is the reference to Henry's 'offence of the cleargie' by marrying his favourite to his 'vowed, vailed sister.'[22] This transgressive act I would argue is intended to allude to the active role James had played in the controversial annulment of Frances Howard's marriage to the Earl of Essex so that she was free to marry Carr on 25 September 1613.

Cotton makes the lesson to be drawn from these parallels quite clear: the blame for allowing the Scots to monopolise and abuse court offices, and reliance on the 'young, single or passionate' council of Robert Carr, was to be laid at the feet of James himself, whose mismanagment of the distribution of court favour, like Henry's, amounted to 'incapacitie of governement'. James had fallen 'prey to [...] lawless Minions' and his ill judgement had laid the 'ground of infinite corruption in all members of his State,' which he condemns as 'Princes weakenes of licentious libertie'.[23]

Cotton's *A Short View* and the 'Parliament of love'

The fruition of Henry's 'licentious libertie' according to Cotton's history, was a disastrous parliament, summoned to resolve the religio-political wranglings of 'factious Bishops' and to 'supplie the Kings Extremities.'[24] The ensuing debates expose the king to the fierce and unseemly attacks of his subjects:

> jere they begann to him that he had wronged the publique state in takeing to his private election, the Justice, Chancellor and Treasurer that should be only by the comon counsell of the Realme [...] They blame him to have bestowed the best places of trust and benefitt in his gift on straungers, and to leave the English unrewarded, To have undone the trade of Merchaunts by bringing in [...] heavie customes, and to hurt the comon libertie by *Non obstantes*, [... and in] his Pattents to make good Monopolies for private ffavourites, That he hath taken from his Subjects *quicquid habuerunt*.[25]

The two parliaments which form the central part of Cotton's narrative of Henry III's mismanagement of kingship have clear parallels with the Jacobean parliaments of 1610 and 1614. This first parliament has identifiable parallels with the 1610 assembly, which was called to settle the matter of episcopacy, and to satisfy the parlous debts and deficits of the royal household. The 'jeering' of the Commons in Cotton's history, with their attacks on monopolies, impositions[26] and unequal access to Royal Bounty, clearly recall the critical speeches of 1610, which James told his Privy Council, he considered to be injurious to his honour and reputation:

> Our fame and actions have been daily tossed like tennis balls amongst them, and all that spite and malice durst do to disgrace and infame us hath been used. To be short, this Lower House by their behaviour have perilled and annoyed our health, wounded our reputation, emboldened all ill-natured people, encroached upon many of our privileges, and plagued our purse with their delays.[27]

This last point refers to the ignominious defeat of the Great Contract, designed to establish public subsidy of the royal purse. Members of the house were extremely outspoken in their refusal, one speaker, for example, 'wished the King would be pleased to live of his own, and to remove his pensions and lessen his charge.' It was 'unfit and dishonourable' he said, 'that those should waste the treasure of the State who take no pains to live of their own, but spend all in excess and riot, depending wholly upon the bounty of the Prince.'[28] The defeat of the Contract and the acrimony which surrounded it is clearly echoed in Cotton's history, in the jeers of Henry's subjects, who 'wonder [... that the King] should now demaunde reliefe from his [...] pilled and polled Comons.' Henry, like James in 1610, was (according to Cotton), criticised for his 'needles expences,' which he is told, would more fitly be drawn 'from his favouritts, who had gleaned the Treasure of the Kingdome, and shared the old lands of the crowne.'[29] Cotton has the commons refer to a particular favourite who was a '*Clericus Militaris*, that in short space had [...] growne to the possession of an Earledome,' which seems a clear allusion to Carr, who had risen from the rank of Royal Page to Earl in the space of ten years. Like James in 1610, the Commons offer Henry 'a moderate supplie [...] to performe soe farr reliefe in obedience as the desert of his carriage should meritt towards them.'[30] 'Parliaments that before were ever a medicine to heale upp any rupture in the Princes fortune,' Cotton concludes (slipping momentarily into a significant present tense), 'are now growne worse then the malladie, sithence malignant humours begann more to rule in them then well composed tempers.'[31] Henry, stung by the rejection of his 'rebellious subjects' who used his 'want of treasure' as 'a way whereby they enthralled his Majestie,' responds by beginning to 'play the good husband, closeth his hand of waste, and resolved himself (too late) to stand alone.'[32]

In the aftermath of the Great Contract, as we know, James pressed his ministers to investigate a variety of alternative means to improving his fiscal situation, and Cotton himself was commissioned by his patron to write a tract on the 'Means to repair the Kings Estate.'[33] Every conceivable method of extracting profit from the royal prerogative was implemented, and unnecessary expenditure curtailed wherever possible. Many of the available means were inadequate to the task of servicing the increasing royal debts: the sale of royal lands, whilst providing a quick fix, decreased revenues from rent, parliamentary subsidies were insufficient, and the selling of patents to projectors, and farming out various parts of the royal prerogative while reasonably lucrative, barely kept pace with interest and inflation.[34] Borrowing from London merchants was plagued by crippling interest, compounded by rescheduling, and provided no hope of long-term financial stability. Cecil's and Howard's attempts to reform the royal household and shore up Crown revenues, in the period between 1608 and 1614, as Peck has noted, 'were founded on, and ultimately foundered on, the assumption that James was seriously willing to curtail his spending and cut off new grants'[35] – he was not. Cotton's Henry, likewise, is not able to curb his spending, 'yet still alas such was his flexibility when he came to be pressed by his french Minions, that he could not hold his any longer from their vast desires and endless wast.'[36]

As Lamar Hill has said, the 'sure mark of the failure of the [Treasury] Commissioners to achieve anything of significance was the necessity, in 1614, of summoning another Parliament,'[37] and in Cotton's *A Short View*, the inability of Henry to curb spending leads directly to the summoning of another parliament:

> Seeing that Majestie and right subsist not, without meanes and Power, And himself had of neither soemuch as would stopp the present breach in his owne want, or his subjects loialties; he flieth to the bosome of his people for reliefe and counsell.[38]

James opened the 1614 Parliament with a determination that he should not suffer the ignominious wranglings which he felt had marred the last parliament. While he explicitly told the Commons that 'this parliament is principally called to relieve my wants', he also insisted that he had not come prepared to bargain with them as he had with the Contract:

> I will not deal with you by way of bargain as at our last meeting but will tell you what I will grant you, the which things shall be such fruits as appertain unto a just prince. For if I should, like a merchant, treat with you, where a contract begins affection ceases.[39]

He also began in a conciliatory fashion, regretting what he called the 'misunderstanding between you and me which was in the last parliament.'[40] 'A King knows his subjects,' he told them in a speech delivered on the 5 April, they 'can never have so good access unto him, speak so freely and safely, and have means to lay open the just complaints and griefs of his subjects as in parliament; and this parliament, I hope, shall be called the parliament of love.'[41]

As we now know, this fond wish was to be frustrated by subsequent events, and if James emphasised parliament's 'duty to retribute to [his] necessity,'[42] the members of the House were equally determined to emphasise the role of parliament as a means by which the grievances of subjects could be addressed, reminding him in early May, that:

> It was the resolution of the last parliament that it is in the King's power to call a parliament, but when they are assembled it is freely to consult of what they shall determine themselves; for if they should be bound to treat of what the King list, there is no freedom. No parliaments have begun with subsidies; it ought to be in the last place.[43]

If we bear in mind that Cotton's text was composed some time between Carr's creation as Earl of Somerset in November 1613 and 29 April 1614, the outcome of Henry's second parliament in the *A Short View* seems peculiarly prophetic. 'At Oxford they mett in Parliament', Cotton says, 'where his Necessities mett soe many undutifull demaunds that he was forced to render upp to their rebellious wills his regal power.'[44] While James was not obliged to yield up power to the extent of Cotton's Henry, the general question of the 'forever restriccions of regall power' which Cotton raises in his historical narrative were obviously at the heart of the debates in the parliaments of 1610 and 1614, with their tense negotations of the boundaries between royal prerogative and the rights and interests of the subject. Cotton's political acumen led him to foresee that the 1614 session was liable to see a continuation of the disputes surrounding the Great Contract. By late April discussions in the house were already moving in this direction, with a return to the controversial grounds of impositions, with Christopher Brooke, for example, arguing that: 'If the King may impose by this absolute power, then no man [can be] certain what he has, for it shall be subject to the King's pleasure. [... We must resolve not] to leave our posterity in worse case then our ancestors have left us.'[45]

John Hoskins demanded that the issue of impositions be settled 'before consideration of [the king's] supply', and John Whitson called for a petition to the king to remove all impositions, so that 'A means [be found] to supply the King without grievance to any subject.'[46] It was at this moment of accumulating tension that Cotton undertook the scribal publication of his *A Short View*. Shortly after Hoskins's and Whitson's demands, the session deteriorated, with the king arguing on 4 May that 'the impositions were a great flower of his prerogative', and that he would 'die a 100 deaths before he would infringe his prerogative.'[47] In spite of the king's refusal to allow a discussion of impositions, the Commons formed a committee on impositions whose views were reported by Sir Edwin Sandys on 12 May, when it was stated that, contrary to the king's opinion, 'no King in Christendom has power to impose without consent of the 3 estates,' and the committee therefore requested a conference on the issue, despite James's express desire not to proceed by way of conference.[48] In the committee's view it was no 'diminishing of regal prerogative to bind him' to parliamentary consent, on the grounds that 'no prince ever had power of imposing originally in the right of their crown but by consent of the subject.'[49]

This was not necessarily a view shared by the whole house, and Cotton's *A Short View* takes a critical view of the sorts of arguments being advanced in the 1610 and 1614 parliaments. Cotton's Henry, bound by the 'hard bargaine' of the Commons through his financial wants, is obliged to 'loose to them the knott of legall dutie,' leaving him with 'noe part of his Soveraignetie left but the bare title.'[50] The limitation of regal power by the king's subjects, Cotton seems to conclude from his historical example, is no solution to the problem of royal mismanagement:

> Chaungeing sole power into the rule of many and those by popular elections, made the State beleeve, that by this forme of lymited pollicie, they had utterly suppressed the mind of mankind for ever dreameing upon the imaginarie humours of licentious Soveraignetie: but it fell out nothing soe, for now every one begann to estimate his owne worth, and to hammer his head on all designes that might enlarge his power and commaund.[51]

The encroachment on royal power meant an increase in the destructive emulation of the nobility, which (in the history) results in a bloody civil war – 'the common wealth turned againe the sword into her owne bowells.' While Cotton did not necessarily imply in this that the 1614 parliament was likely to foment civil unrest, this was certainly the view taken by a number of foreign ambassadors, who watched the growing divide between king and parliament with some interest.[52] Cotton's narrative stresses the role of factious nobles in urging the king to convene parliaments which they knew to be imprudent in order to serve their own 'ambitious designes'.[53] These 'tumultuous Barons', 'young and noble spiritts, warme and overweening' were not, Cotton seems to be suggesting, unlike those younger Jacobean courtiers who, frustrated by Cecil's grasp on the the reins of power, criticised James's government at every step, and deluded themselves with republican designs:

> Holding certeyne Imaginarie and fantastick formes of common wealthes, flatter[ing] their owne beliefs and Abillities, that they could mould any estate to those generall Rules, which in particular applicacion will prove them gross and idel absurdities.[54]

Having clearly adumbrated the outlines of James's own problems in the guise of those of Henry III, Cotton's narrative goes on to suggest, in its account of the subsequent reversal in Henry's fortunes, some possible ways in which the king could attempt to deal with his difficulties.

'The entrance of his regayned rule': palliatives for Jacobean reform

In the 'happie accident' which topples the usurper Leicester from his position of power and gives Henry III the liberty to reflect on his mistakes and 'search the ground of his former misery', Cotton anatomises what he sees to be the malaise of James's reign:

> Here he finds his wastfull hand had bene to[o] quick both over the persons and estates of his people, The griping avarice of his Civill injustices, and lawless liberty of his martiall followers, the neglect of grace and breach of his word to have lost the Nobillytye at home, and Necessitie his reputation abroad [...] geveing over himself to a sensuall securitie, and referring all to base greedie and unworthy Ministers.[55]

But in his representation of 'the entrance of [... Henry's] regayned Rule', Cotton also sets out a pattern for future Jacobean reforms, including the rejection of 'Immoderate liberality,' in favour of 'Reward and Reprehension justly laid,' and a tight control on royal expenditure: 'Expence of house service [...] measured by the just Rule of his owne propre Revenue.'[56] It is significant, given Cotton's own involvement in the investigation of Naval Corruption in 1608, that he identifies the investigation of corruption as a vital part of Henry's revival of fortunes: 'The Rigor and Corruption of his Judiciall offices he examineth and redresseth by strict commission.'[57] Along with these reforms of the king's excesses, Cotton counsels a closer reliance on noble council, rather than the empowerment of arbitrarily elected favourites:

> The Seate of Judgement and Counsell, he filled upp with men nobly borne, for such attract with less offence the generous spiritts to respect and Reverence; Their abilityes he measureth not by favour or private Informacion as before, but generall voice [...] Counsellors be they never soe wise, or worthy, are but as accessaries, not principalls in sustenacion of the State. Their office must be subjection, not fellowshipp in consultacions of moment, and to have ability to advise, not authoritie to resolve.[58]

Henry's reformed reign is seen as 'exact grounds of discipline and pollicy for his best successour to rule by,'[59] a template for the future of Stuart government. There is no hard evidence, outside the inscription of some of the manuscripts, and the subtitle of the printed version of a *A Short View*, that the work was ever actually presented to James, and perhaps given the tense political climate in late April 1614, it seems unlikely that it was. We do, however, have evidence of a presentation in the aftermath of the disastrous parliament to one of James's most trusted and senior officials. On 1 October 1614 Sir Julius Caesar, who had been

Chancellor and Under-Treasurer of the Exchequer since 1607, formally took over as Master of the Rolls from Sir Edward Phillips (having been offered the reversion by James in 1610), and resigned his other offices. Shortly after taking up his new position in James's government (in late 1614 or early 1615), Caesar received a presentation manuscript from one 'Wa[lter] Jeffes'.[60] This manuscript, which remains amongst the Caesar Papers in the British Library, comprised three short discourses, in consecutively numbered folios: Sir Robert Cotton's 'A Short Viewe of the liffe of Henry the third', Henry Percy's 'Conceipt concerning ffriends and ffriendshipp', and an anonymous translation from the Spanish (possibly by Jeffes himself), 'Whence proceedeth the litle security of ffavouritts.'[61] Thus while Cotton's advice may not have reached the royal ear until its controversial publication thirteen years later, it certainly reached some of the highest levels of Jacobean government.

In conclusion I would like to suggest some of Cotton's possible motivations for composing and distributing *A Short View* during the 1614 parliament. Unlike most of Cotton's works, which were composed to answer particular briefs, and to provide precedents to guide his patron in presenting particular policies, *A Short View* was devised to diagnose a more general political problem – the decline of the Privy Council's powers in comparison with an increasingly smaller group of royal favourites. Cotton's patron the Earl of Northampton had been ailing since the early months of 1614, and by the time the session opened he was too sick to participate.[62] On 15 June, eight days after the parliament was dissolved, he was dead. Northampton had vigorously opposed the calling of the parliament from the outset and although his direct political involvement had effectively ended in late February 1614 (the last time he was well enough to attend Privy Council was on 22 February),[63] this did not prevent him from taking indirect action, and it is in this light that I think we should view Cotton's tract. Northampton had been the dominant figure of the Privy Council in the period 1612–14, but increasingly found the Council's functions compromised by James's reliance on private consultations with Carr, Sir Thomas Lake and other favourites.[64] Cotton's *A Short View*, with its emphasis on the conciliar role of the old nobility of the Privy Council rather than rule by 'favour or private Informacion' – which gave too much 'authoritie' (and too much familiarity) to the inner sanctum of the king's personal advisers – was clearly a document which spoke to the concerns of the Earl of Northampton. As a work which attacked the role of royal favourites, and called for the reform and regulation of royal revenue, it was obviously a document which was intended to promote the views of Cotton's dying patron.[65] The dedication of the Jeffes manuscript to another prominent Privy Councillor after Northampton's death suggests that the concerns about the waning influence of the Council on royal policy outlived the death of its original paymaster. During the course of the parliament James impatiently dismissed those 'good chroniclers' and 'nimble wits' who 'hunt after precedents what kings had done or might do',[66] it seems likely that he had scholars like Cotton at the forefront of his mind. The antiquarian researches of Cotton, and others like him, were not so much disinterested historical research as highly-charged contributions to contemporary political life. In this troubled moment in James's reign when his claims to prerogative brought him into open conflict with parliament, Cotton's chronicles sought ancient precedents for oiling the rusty wheels of conciliar diplomacy.

Notes

[1] *The Diary of Thomas Crosfield, M.A., B.D., Fellow of Queen's College Library*, ed. by Frederick S. Boas (London: Oxford University Press, 1935), cited in Fred J. Levy, *Tudor Historical Thought* (San Marino, California: Huntington Library, 1967), pp. 269–70.

[2] William A. Jackson, 'Sir Robert Bruce Cotton's *A Short view of the long life and raigne of Henry the third*', *Harvard Library Bulletin*, 4 (1950), 28–37 (at p. 28); Kevin Sharpe, *Sir Robert Cotton 1586–1631: History and Politics in Early Modern England* (Oxford: Oxford University Press, 1979), p. 238, n. 89.

[3] Jackson, 'Cotton's *A Short view*', p. 33; Sharpe, *Sir Robert Cotton*, p. 238, n. 89.

[4] This is a view also espoused by Graham Parry in *The Trophies of Time: English Antiquarians of the Seventeenth Century* (Oxford: Oxford University press, 1995), pp. 85–90.

[5] Sharpe, *Sir Robert Cotton*, *passim*. Linda Levy Peck, *Northampton: Patronage, Policy and the Court of James I* (London: George Allen & Unwin, 1982), pp. 103–17; Harold Love, *Scribal Publication in Seventeenth Century England* (Oxford: Oxford University Press, 1993), pp. 83–9.

[6] Love, *Scribal Publication*, p. 87.

[7] During his legal examination in 1627, Cotton admitted having composed the work but denied responsibility for its publication (Public Record Office, State Papers 14/54/4, p. 5). See Sharpe, *Sir Robert Cotton*, p. 142.

[8] Jackson, 'Cotton's *A Short view*', p. 28.

[9] Love, *Scribal Publication*, p. 85.

[10] Love, *Scribal Publication*, p. 88.

[11] Peck, *Northampton*, pp. 113, 104.

[12] Peck, *Northampton*, p. 104.

[13] Love, *Scribal Publication*, p. 88.

[14] Robert Cotton, 'A Short Viewe of the Long Life and Raigne of Henry the Third of England', British Library, Additional MS 12504, fol. 47^{r}.

[15] 'A Short Viewe', BL Add. MS 12504, fol. 47^{v}.

[16] 'A Short Viewe', BL Add. MS 12504, fol. 47^{v}.

[17] On the promotion of the Court Scots, and the anti-Scottish feelings which it caused see Neil Cuddy, 'The Revival of the Entourage: the Bedchamber of James I, 1603–1625', in *The English Court. From the Wars of the Roses to the Civil War*, ed. by David Starkey (London: Longmans, 1987), pp. 173–225, and Jenny Wormald, 'James VI and I: Two Kings or One?', *History*, 68 (1983) 187–209.

[18] 'A Short Viewe', BL Add. MS 12504, fol. 49^{r}.

[19] 'A Short Viewe', BL Add. MS 12504, fol. 50^{v}.

[20] Historical Manuscripts Commission, *The Manuscripts of his Grace, the Duke of Portland, Preserved at Welbeck Abbey*, ed. by F. H. Daniell *et al.*, 10 vols (London: HMSO, 1891–1931), IX, 113.

[21] 'A Short Viewe', BL Add. MS 12504, fol. 50^{r}.

[22] 'A Short Viewe', BL Add. MS 12504, fol. 49^{v}.

[23] 'A Short Viewe', BL Add. MS 12504, fol. 50^{v}.

[24] 'A Short Viewe', BL Add. MS 12504, fol. 51^{r}.

[25] 'A Short Viewe', BL Add. MS 12504, fol. 51^{v}.

[26] James's re-introduction of impositions on virtually all merchantable goods except foodstuffs and ships stores in June 1608, was according to Lamar Hill, the 'catalyst that drew together the opposition to the crown's financial program in 1610.' Lamar M. Hill, *Bench and Bureaucracy: The Public Career of Sir Julius Caesar 1580–1636* (Stanford: Stanford University Press, 1988), pp. 148–9.

[27] James to Privy Council, 7 December 1610, *Letters of King James*, Letter 150, pp. 318–19.

[28] Samuel R. Gardiner, *England from the accession of James I to the outbreak of the Civil War, 1603–1642*, 10 vols (London: Longmans, Green & Co., 1883–84), II (1607–1616), 108.

[29] 'A Short Viewe', BL Add. MS 12504, fol. 51^{v}.

[30] 'A Short Viewe', BL Add. MS 12504, fol. 51^{v}.

[31] 'A Short Viewe', BL Add. MS 12504, fol. 52^{r}.

[32] 'A Short Viewe', BL Add. MS 12504, fol. 52^{r}.

[33] See Hill, *Bench and Bureaucracy*, pp. 179–91; Peck, *Northampton*, pp. 94–100, 113.

[34] Peck, *Northampton*, pp. 95–6; Hill, *Bench and Bureaucracy*, p. 180.

[35] Peck, *Northampton*, p. 114.

[36] 'A Shorte Viewe', BL Add. MS 12504, fol. 52^{r}.

[37] Hill, *Bench and Bureaucracy*, pp. 191–2.

[38] 'A Shorte Viewe', BL Add. MS 12504, fols 52^{v}–53^{r}.

[39] *Proceedings, 1614*, 5 April 1614, p. 17.

[40] *Proceedings, 1614*, 5 April 1614, p. 18.

[41] *Proceedings, 1614*, 5 April 1614, p. 19.

[42] *Proceedings, 1614*, 9 April 1614, p. 44.

[43] *Proceedings, 1614*, 4 May 1614, p. 159.

[44] 'A Short Viewe', BL Add. MS 12504, fol. 53^{r}.

[45] *Proceedings, 1614*, 18 April 1614, p. 95.

[46] *Proceedings, 1614*, 18 April 1614, pp. 96–7.

[47] *Proceedings, 1614*, 4 May 1614, p. 138.

[48] *Proceedings, 1614*, 12 May 1614, p. 224. On James's stipulation that the House not proceed by conferences, see *Proceedings, 1614*, 5 April 1614, p. 19.

[49] *Proceedings, 1614*, 12 May 1614, p. 224.

[50] 'A Short Viewe', BL Add. MS 12504, fol. 54^{r}.

[51] 'A Short Viewe', BL Add. MS 12504, fol. 53^{v}.

[52] See *Proceedings, 1614*, pp. xiii–xvi.

[53] See 'A Short Viewe', BL Add. MS 12504, fol. 51^{r}: 'A parliament was called much to the likeing of these Lords, who as little meant to relieve the King, as they did desire to acquitt the State.' Cf. also fol. 52^{v}: 'the Rebellious Lords desire nothing more than to see the Kings extremeitie constraine a Parliament [...] To hasten on the tyme [...] there are sowen certaine seditious Runours that the Kings necessitie must repaire it self upon the fortune and libertie of his people.'

[54] 'A Short Viewe', BL Add. MS 12504, fols 53^{v}, 54^{r}.

[55] 'A Short Viewe', BL Add. MS 12504, fol. 55^{v}.

[56] 'A Short Viewe', BL Add. MS 12504, fols 55^{v}, 56^{r}.

[57] 'A Short Viewe', BL Add. MS 12504, fol. 56^{v}. On the Naval Commission of 1608 see Linda Levy Peck, *Court Patronage and Corruption in Early Stuart England* (London: Routledge, 1993), pp. 106–33, on Cotton's role in the Commission see pp. 114–15, 126.

[58] 'A Short Viewe', BL Add. MS 12504, fol. 56^{v}.

[59] 'A Short Viewe', BL Add. MS 12504, fol. 57^{r}.

[60] So far my attempts at uncovering details of Walter Jeffes and his involvement in this document have been unsuccessful. Dr Christopher Thompson has kindly drawn my attention to Norfolk Record Office, Hare MS 2723, in which a 'Walter Jeffes' appears as a signatory witness to a deed of release by Sir Thomas Barrington, Sir William Marsham, Sir Nathaniel Rich, John Pym, and Peter Phesaunt to Sir John Hare of the manor and estate of Shouldham in Norfolk. This might indicate that Jeffes was a lawyer to one of the parties. The document is dated 1632.

[61] BL Add. MS 12,504, fols 45^{r}–65^{r}. The presentation can be dated by its reference to Caesar as 'Master of the Rolls, and one of his Maj*esties* most honourable Privy Counsell.'

[62] Peck, *Northampton*, p. 208.

[63] Peck, *Northampton*, pp. 205, 208.

[64] Peck, *Northampton*, pp. 84–5.

[65] On Northampton's views on the reform of Royal expenditure see Peck, *Northampton*, pp. 94–100.

[66] *Proceedings, 1614*, 30 May 1614, p. 383.

Bibliography

Acts of the Privy Council of England, 1613–1614 (London: HMSO, 1921).

Adams, S. L., 'The Road to La Rochelle: English Foreign Policy and the Huguenots, 1610–1629', *Proceedings of the Huguenot Society of London* (London: Huguenot Society of London, 1970–76), XXII, 419–29.

A Proclamation against Private Challenges and Combats: With Articles annexed for the better directions to be used therein, and for the more judiciall proceeding against Offenders (London: Robert Barker, 1613).

A Publication of his Majesties Edict, and severe Censure against Private Combats and Combatants (London: Robert Barker, 1613).

Akrigg, G. P. V. (ed.), *Letters of King James VI and I* (Berkeley & London: University of California Press, 1984).

Akrigg, G. P. V., 'The Curious Marginalia of Charles, Second Earl Stanhope', in James G. MacManaway, Giles E. Dawson and Edwin E. Willoughby (eds.), *John Quincy Adams Memorial Studies* (Washington: Folger Shakespeare Library, 1948), 785–801.

Alexander, Julius, *Ob secundum et felicem eventum conjugij ... Frederici 5. Electoralis palatinatus principis ... et ... Elizabethæ filiæ ... regis magnæ Britanniæ ... Carmen* (London, 1614).

Alsop, J. D., 'The Privy Council Debate and Committees for Fiscal Reform, September 1615', Bulletin of the Institute of Historical Research, 68 (1995), 191–211.

Alston, Robin, *Books with Manuscript: A Short-title Catalogue of Books with Manuscript Notes in the British Library* (London: The British Library, 1994).

Alting, Henricus, *A votive oration for the auspicial government of Fredericke the V. Palatine of Rhene* (London, 1614).

Andrewes, Lancelot, *A Sermon preached before His Maiestie, at Whitehall on Easter day last, 1614* (London, 1614).

Andrewes, John, *Christ his crosse* (London, 1614).

Anon., *The Wars in Germany, with the taking of the severall townes by the Marquesse Spynola, and the present estate of the whole armie now on foote, in sight of the Emperour ... Together with the present estate of the contrary armie, conducted by Graue Maurice of Nassau ... Truely translated out of Dutch and French into English.* (London, 1614).

Arber, Edward (ed.), *A Transcript of the Registers of the Company of Stationers of London: 1554–1640*, 5 vols (London and Birmingham: privately printed, 1875–1894).

Atherton, Ian, *Ambition and Failure in Stuart England: The Career of John, First Viscount Scudamore* (Manchester: Manchester University Press, 1999).

Atherton, Ian, '"The Itch Grown a Disease": Manuscript Transmission of News in the Seventeenth Century', in *News, Newspapers, and Society in Early Modern Britain*, ed. by Joad Raymond (London: Franck Cass, 1999), pp. 39–65.

Bacon, Francis, *The Charge of Sir Francis Bacon Knight, his Majesties Attourney Generall, touching Duells, upon an information in the Star-chamber against Priest and Wright. With The Decree of the Star-chamber in the same cause* (London: Robert Wilson, 1614).

Baker, J. H., *An Introduction to English Legal History*, 3rd ed. (London: Butterworths, 1990).

Barnard, John, 'The Stationers' Stock 1663/4 to 1705/6: Psalms, Psalters, Primers and ABCs', *The Library*, 6th ser., 21 (1999), 369–75.

Barnes, John, *An act or decree of the Court of Parliament of Paris, made the 26. and executed the 27. of Iune. 1614. Against a booke ... intituled Francisci Suares ... Defensio fidei Catholicæ & apostilicæ, adversus Anglicanæ sectæ errores: containing diuers principles and propositions repugnant to the soueraigne power of kings ... translated out of the French copie, etc.* (London, 1614).

Baumann, Wolf-Rüdiger, *The Merchants Adventurers and the Continental Cloth-trade (1560s–1620s)* (Berlin and New York: Walter de Gruyter, 1990).

Beal, Peter, *In Praise of Scribes: Manuscripts and their Makers in Seventeenth-Century England* (Oxford: Clarendon Press, 1998).

Beer, Anna R., *Sir Walter Ralegh and His Readers in the Seventeenth Century: Speaking to the People* (London: Macmillan, 1997).

Bell, Maureen, 'Entrance in the Stationers' Register', *The Library*, 6th ser., 16 (1994), 50–54.

Bell, Maureen, and Barnard, John, 'Provisional Count of *STC* Titles 1475–1640', *Publishing History*, 31 (1992), 48–64.

Bell, Maureen, and Barnard, John,'Provisional Count of *Wing* Titles 1641–1700', *Publishing History*, 55 (1998), 89–97.

Bellany, Alistair, '"Raylinge Rymes and Vaunting Verse": Libellous Politics in Early Stuart England, 1603–1628', in *Culture and Politics in Early Stuart England*, ed. by Kevin Sharpe and Peter Lake (Basingstoke and London: Macmillan, 1994), pp. 285–310.

Bellany, Alistair, '"Mistress Turner's Deadly Sins": Sartorial Transgression, Court Scandal, and Politics in Early Stuart England', *Huntington Library Quarterly*, 58 (1996), 179–210.

Berners, Juliana, *A Jewell for Gentrie. Being an exact Dictionary, or true Method, to make any Man understand all the Art, Secrets ... belonging to Hawking, Hunting, Fowling and Fishing ... now newly published, and beautified* (London, 1614).

Birch, Thomas, *The Court and Times of James the First*, 2 vols (London: H. Colburn, 1848).

Birch, Thomas, *The Life of Henry, Prince of Wales, Eldest son of King James I* (London, 1760).

Black, Joseph Laurence, 'Pamphlet Wars: The Marprelate Tracts and "Martinism", 1588–1688' (University of Toronto, Ph.D. thesis, 1996).

Blayney, Peter W. M., 'The Publication of Playbooks', in *A New History of Early English Drama*, ed. by John D. Cox and David Scott Kastan (New York: Columbia University Press, 1997), pp. 383–422.

Boas, Frederick S. (ed.), *The Diary of Thomas Crosfield, M.A., B.D., Fellow of Queen's College Library* (London: Oxford University Press, 1935).

Booth, Robert, *A Relation of all matters passed, especially in the Low-Countries, touching the causes of the warre now in Cleveland. Together with such occurrences of note as have happened in Spain, Italie, England, Germany, Hungarie and Transylvania since March last to this present, 1614. Translated according to the originall of Mercurius Gallo-Belgicus* (London, 1614).

Braddick, Michael J., *Parliamentary Taxation in Seventeenth-Century England: Local Administration and Response* (London: Boydell, 1994).

Brathwaite, Richard, *A Strappado for the Divell. Epigrams and Satyres alluding to the time, with diuers measures of no lesse Delight* (London, 1615).

Braunmuller, A. R., 'Robert Carr, Earl of Somerset, as Collector and Patron', in *The Mental World of the Jacobean Court*, ed. by Linda Levy Peck (Cambridge: Cambridge University Press, 1991), pp. 230–250.

Bray, Alan, 'Male Homosexuality and the Signs of Male Friendship', *History Workshop Journal*, 29 (1990), 1–19.

Brenner, Robert, *Merchants and Revolution. Commercial Change, Political Conflict, and London's Overseas Traders, 1550–1653* (New Jersey: Princeton University Press, 1993).

Bretnor, Thomas, *A new almanacke and prognostication* (London, 1614).

Breton, Nicholas, *I Would, and would not* (London, 1614).

Browne, William, *The Shepheards Pipe* (London, 1614).

Burgess, Glenn, 'The Impact on Political Thought: Rhetorics for Troubled Times', in *The Impact of the English Civil War*, ed. by John Morill (London: Collins & Brown, 1991), pp. 67–83.

Calendar of State Papers, Venetian 1610–13, ed. by H. F. Brown and A. B. Hindes, 38 vols (London; HMSO, 1864–1947).

Calendar of State Papers Domestic Series, of the Reign of James I. 1611–1618, Preserved in the State Paper Department of Her majesty's Public Record Office ed. by Mary Anne Everett Green (London: Longman, Green, Longmans and Robert, 1858).

Campion, Thomas, *The Works of Thomas Campion*, ed. by W. R. Davis (London: Faber, 1969).

Campion, Thomas, *The Description of a Maske: presented in the Banqueting Roome at Whitehall ... at the Mariage of the ... Earle of Somerset and ... the Lady Frances Howard. Whereunto are annexed divers choyse Ayres composed for this Maske that may be sung with a single voyce to the Lute or Base-Viall* (London, 1614).

Chapman, George, *Andromeda Liberata. Or the nuptials of Perseus and Andromeda* (London, 1614).

Chapman, George, *A Free and offenceles justification of a lately publisht and most maliciously misinterpreted Poeme: Entituled Andromeda Liberata* (London, 1614).

Chapman, George, *The Poems of George Chapman*, ed. by Phyllis Brooks Bartlett (New York: Modern Language Association; London: Oxford University Press, 1941).

Chartres, J. A.,'Road Carrying in England in the Seventeenth Century: Myth and Reality', *Economic History Review*, 30 (1977), 73–94.

Chetwood, William R., *Memoirs of the Life and Writings of Ben Jonson* (Dublin: W. R. Chetwood, 1756).

Clark, Peter, 'Josias Nicholls and Religious Radicalism 1553–1639', *Journal of Ecclesiastical History*, 28 (1977), 133–50.

Clegg, Cyndia Susan, *Press Censorship in Elizabethan England* (Cambridge: Cambridge University Press, 1997).

Clucas, Stephen, '"Noble virtue in extremes" : Henry Percy, ninth Earl of Northumberland, patronage and the politics of stoic consolation', *Renaissance Studies*, 9:3 (1995), 267–291.

Cogswell, Thomas, *Home Divisions: Aristocracy, the State and Provincial Conflict* (Manchester: Manchester University Press, 1998).

Cogswell, Thomas, *The Blessed Revolution: English Politics and the Coming of War, 1621–1624* (Cambridge: Cambridge University Press, 1989).

Cogswell, Thomas, 'Underground Verse and the Transformation of Early Stuart Political Culture, in *Political Culture and Cultural Politics in Early Modern England*, ed. by Susan D. Amussen and Mark A. Kishlansky (Manchester and New York: Manchester University Press, 1995), pp. 277–300.

Coiro, Anne Baynes, 'Milton and class identity: the publication of *Areopagitica* and the 1645 *Poems*', *Journal of Medieval and Renaissance Studies*, 22 (1992), 269–75.

Coke, Edward, *A Booke of Entries* (London: Societie of Stationers, 1614).

Coke, Edward, *The Third Part of the Institutes of the Laws of England Concerning High Treason, and other Pleas of the Crown, and Criminall causes* (London: M. Flesher for W. Lee and D. Pakeman, 1644).

Coke, Edward, *The Third Part of the Institutes of the Laws of England*, 4th edn (London: A. Crooke et al., 1669).

Colclough, David, '"Of the alleadging of authors": The Construction and Reception of Textual Authority in English Prose' (unpublished doctoral thesis, University of Oxford, 1996).

Colclough, David, '*Parrhesia*: The Rhetoric of Free Speech in Early Modern England', *Rhetorica*, 17 (1999), 177–212.

Collins, Douglas C., *A Handlist of News Pamphlets 1590–1610* (London: South West Essex Technical College, 1943).

Conrad, F. W., '"A Preservative Against Tyranny": Sir Thomas Elyot and the Rhetoric of Counsel', in Gordon J. Schochet, Patricia E. Tatspaugh and Carol Brobeck (eds.), *Reformation, Humanism, and 'Revolution'. Papers Presented at the Folger Institute Seminar 'Political Thought in the Henrician Age, 1500–1550'* (Washington: Folger Institute, 1990), pp. 191–206.

Conrad, F. W., 'The Problem of Counsel Reconsidered: The Case of Sir Thomas Elyot', in Paul A. Fideler and T. F. Mayer (eds.), *Political Thought and the Tudor Commonwealth. Deep Structure, Discourse and Disguise* (London: Routledge, 1992).

Coquillette, Daniel R., *Francis Bacon* (Stanford CA: Stanford University Press, 1992).

Coughlan, Patricia, *Spenser and Ireland: An Interdisciplinary Perspective* (Cork: Cork University Press, 1989).

Cramsie, John, *Kingship and crown finance under James VI & I, 1603–1625* (London: Boydell, forthcoming 2002).

Cramsie, John, 'Commercial Projects and the Fiscal Policy of James VI & I', *Historical Journal* 43:2 (2000), 345–364.

Cressy, David, *Travesties and Transgressions in Tudor and Stuart England* (Oxford: Oxford University Press, 2000).

Croft, Pauline, 'English Commerce with Spain and the Armada War, 1558–1603', in M. J. Rodriguez Salgado and Simon Adams (eds.), *England, Spain and the Gran Armada: essays from the Anglo-Spanish conferences, London and Madrid 1988*. (Edinburgh: John Donald Publishers, 1991), pp. 236–63.

Croft, Pauline, 'The Reputation of Robert Cecil: Libels, Political Opinion and Popular Awareness in the Early Seventeenth Century', *Transactions of the Royal Historical Society*, 1 (1991), 43–69.

Cromartie, Alan, 'The Constitutionalist Revolution: the Transformation of Political Culture in Early Stuart England', *Past & Present*, 163 (1999), 76–120.

Cromartie, Alan, 'The Printing of Parliamentary Speeches in November 1640–July 1642', *Historical Journal*, 33 (1990), 23–44.

Crum, Margaret (ed.), *First-Line Index of English Poetry 1500–1800 in Manuscripts of the Bodleian Library Oxford*, 2 vols (Oxford: Oxford University Press, 1969).

Cuddy, Neil, 'The Revival of the Entourage: the Bedchamber of James I, 1603–1625', in *The English Court. From the Wars of the Roses to the Civil War*, ed. by David Starkey (London: Longmans, 1987), pp. 173–225.

Cuddy, Neil, 'The Conflicting Loyalties of a "vulger counselor": The Third Earl of Southampton, 1597–1624', in John Morrill, Paul Slack and Daniel Woolf (eds.), *Public Duty and Private Conscience in Seventeenth Century England* (Oxford: Oxford University Press, 1993), pp. 121–50.

Cust, Richard, *The Forced Loan and English Politics, 1626–1628* (Oxford: Clarendon Press, 1987).

Cust, Richard, 'News and Politics in Early Seventeenth-Century England', *Past & Present*, 112 (1986), 60–90.

Dahl, Folke, *A Bibliography of English Corantos and Periodical Newsbooks 1620–1642* (London: Bibliographical Society, 1952).

Dalrymple, David, *Memorials and Letters Relating to the History of Britain in the Reign of James the First* (Glasgow: Robert and Andrew Foulis, 1762).

Daly, James, 'The Idea of Absolute Monarchy in Seventeenth-Century England', *The Historical Journal*, 21 (1978), 227–50.

Daniel, Samuel, *Hymen's Triumph*, ed. by John Pitcher (Oxford: Oxford University Press [Malone Society Reprints], 1994).

Darnton, Robert, *The Literary Underground of the Old Regime* (Cambridge, Mass. & London: Harvard University Press, 1982).

Davies, John, *The Poems of Sir John Davies*, ed. by Robert Krueger (Oxford: Clarendon Press, 1975).

Deakins, Roger, 'The Tudor Prose Dialogue: Genre and Anti-Genre', *Studies in English Literature*, 20 (1980), 1–23.

Dean, David, *Law-making and Society in Late Elizabethan England: The Parliament of England 1584–1601* (Cambridge: Cambridge University Press, 1996).

Dekker, Thomas, *The Dramatic Works of Thomas Dekker*, ed. by Fredson T. Bowers 4 vols (Cambridge: Cambridge University Press, 1953).

Dietz, Frederick C., *English Public Finance 1558–1641* (New York: Century, 1932).

Dzelzainis, Martin, 'Milton and the Protectorate in 1658', in *Milton and Republicanism*, ed. by David Armitage, Quentin Skinner, and Armand Himy (Cambridge: Cambridge University Press, 1995), 181–205.

Elton, G. R., *The Parliament of England 1559–1581* (Cambridge: Cambridge University Press, 1986).

Elton, G. R., 'A High Road to Civil War?' in *From Renaissance to the Counter-Reformation: Essays in honour of Garrett Mattingly*, ed. by C. H. Carter (London: Jonathan Cape, 1966), pp. 325–47.

Est, William, *Two sermons* (London, 1614).

Fisher, F. J., 'Some Experiments in Company Organisation in the Early Seventeenth Century', in *London and the English Economy, 1500–1700* ed. by P. J. Corfield and N. B. Harte (London & Ronceverte: The Hambledon Press, 1990), pp. 43–60.

Foster, Elizabeth Read (ed.), *Proceedings in Parliament 1610*, 2 vols (New Haven and London: Yale University Press, 1966).

Fox, Adam Peter, 'Rumour, News and Popular Political Opinion in Elizabethan and Early Stuart England', *Historical Journal*, 40 (1997), 597–620.

Fraser, Nancy, 'Rethinking the Public Sphere: A Contribution to the Critique of Actually Existing Democracy', in *Habermas and the Public Sphere*, ed. by Craig Calhoun (Cambridge, Mass, & London: M.I.T. Press, 1996).

Friis, Astrid, *Alderman Cockayne's Project and the Cloth Trade* (Copenhagen: Levin & Munksgaard & London: Oxford University Press, 1927).

Gardiner, Samuel Rawson, *England from the accession of James I to the outbreak of the Civil War, 1603–1642*, 10 vols (London: Longmans, Green & Co., 1883–84).

Gardiner, Samuel Rawson (ed.), *Parliamentary Debates in 1610*, (London: Camden Society, 1862).

Gardiner, Samuel Rawson (ed.), *Narrative of the Spanish Marriage Treaty*, (London: Camden Society, 1869).

Girtin, Thomas, *The Golden Ram: A Narrative History of the Clothworkers Company 1528–1958*, second edition (Aylesbury: The Worshipful Company of Clothworkers, 1958).

Girtin, Thomas,'Mr Hakluyt, Scholar at Oxford', *Geographical Journal*, 119 (1953), 208–12.

Goldberg, Jonathan, (ed.), *Queering The Renaissance* (Durham, North Carolina: Duke University Press, 1994).

Goldie, Mark, 'The Revolution of 1689 and the Structure of Political Argument: An Essay and an Annotated Bibliography of Pamphlets on the Allegiance Controversy', *Bulletin of Research in the Humanities*, 83 (1980), 473–564.

Graves, Michael A. R., and Kyle, Chris R., '"The Kinge's most Excellent majestie out of his Gracious Disposition": The Evolution of Bills of Grace in English Parliaments 1542–1642', *Parliaments, Estates and Representatives*, 18 (1998), 27–51.

Greg, W. W., *Some Aspects and Problems of London Publishing Between 1550 and 1650* (Oxford: Clarendon Press, 1956).

Grundy, Joan, *Spenserian Poets: A Study in Elizabethan and Jacobean Poetry* (London: Edward Arnold, 1969).

Guy, John, 'The Henrician Age', in J. G. A. Pocock, et al. (eds.) *The Varieties of British Political Thought, 1500–1800* (Cambridge: Cambridge University Press, 1993), pp. 13–46.

Guy, John, 'The Rhetoric of Counsel in Early Modern England', in *Tudor Political Culture* ed. by Dale Hoak (Cambridge. Cambridge University Press. 1995), pp. 292–310.

Hakluyt, Richard, *The Principal Navigations, Voiages and Discoveries of the English Nation* (London: George Bishop & Ralph Newberie, 1589).

Hakluyt, Richard, *The Principal Navigations, Voiages, Traffiques and Discoveries of the English Nation*, 3 vols (London: George Bishop, Ralph Newberie & Robert Barker, 1598–1600).

Hakluyt, Richard, *Principal Navigations*, ed. by D. B. Quinn and R. A. Skelton, 2 vols (Cambridge: Cambridge University Press, 1965).

Harrison, William, *The Difference of Hearers. Or, an Exposition of the parable of the sower. Deliuered in certaine sermons at Hyton in Lancashire* (London, 1614).

Hayden, J. Michael, *France and the Estates General of 1614* (Cambridge: Cambridge University Press, 1974).

Hill, Lamar M., *Bench and Bureaucracy: The Public Career of Sir Julius Caesar 1580–1636* (Stanford: Stanford University Press, 1988).

Hirst, Derek, *Authority and Conflict: England 1603–1658* (London: Edward Arnold, 1986).

Historical Manuscripts Commission, *The Manuscripts of his Grace, the Duke of Portland, Preserved at Welbeck Abbey*, ed. by F. H. Daniell et al., 10 vols (London: HMSO, 1891–1931).

Historical Manuscripts Commission, *Report on the Manuscripts of the Marquess of Downshire: Volume Four, Papers of William Trumbull the Elder, January 1613–August 1614*, ed. by A. B. Hinds (London: HMSO, 1940).

Horne, Robert, *Gods gentle remembrance* (London, 1614).

Hotine, Margaret, '*Richard III* and *Macbeth* – Studies in Tudor Tyranny', *Notes and Queries*, 236 (1991), 480–86.

Hunt, Arnold, 'Book Trade Patents, 1603–1640', in *The Book Trade and its Customers 1450–1900: Historical Essays for Robin Myers*, ed. by Arnold Hunt, Giles Mandelbrote and Alison Shell (Winchester: St Paul's Bibliographies, 1997), pp. 27–54.

Hughes, John and Kennett, White (eds.), *A complete History of England: with the lives of all the kings and queens thereof; from the earliest account of time, to the death of his late Majesty King William III*, 3 vols (London, 1719).

Isocrates, 'To Nicocles' in *Isocrates, With an English translation by George Norlin*, 3 vols. (London: William Heinemann, 1928–45), I, 40–71.

Jackson, William A., 'Sir Robert Bruce Cotton's *A Short view of the long life and raigne of Henry the third*', *Harvard Library Bulletin*, 4 (1950), 28–37.

Jackson, William A., 'Counterfeit Printing in Jacobean Times', *The Library*, 15 (1934–35), 364–76.

James, Mervyn, *Society, Politics and Culture: Studies in Early Modern England* (Cambridge: Cambridge University Press, 1986).

Jansson, Maija (ed.), *Proceedings in Parliament, 1614, House of Commons* (Philadelphia: American Philosophical Society, 1988).

Jansson, Maija,'Dues Paid', *Parliamentary History*, 15:2 (1996), 215–20.

Jones, Norman, 'Parliament and the Political Society of Elizabethan England', in *Tudor Political Culture*, ed. by Dale Hoak (Cambridge: Cambridge University Press, 1995).

Jonson, Ben, *Ben Jonson: The Complete Masques*, ed. by Stephen Orgel (New Haven: Yale University Press, 1969).

Jonson, Ben, *Ben Jonson*, ed. by Ian Donaldson (Oxford: Oxford University Press, 1985).

Kaplan, M. Lindsay, *The Culture of Slander in Early Modern England* (Cambridge: Cambridge University Press, 1997).

Kiernan, V. G., *The Duel in European History: Honour and the Reign of Aristocracy* (Oxford: Oxford University Press, 1988).

King, John, *Vitis Palatina. A sermon appointed to be preached at Whitehall upon the Tuesday after the mariage of the Ladie Elizabeth her Grace* (London, 1614).

Knafla, Louis, *Law and Politics in Jacobean England: The Tracts of Lord Chancellor Ellesmere* (Cambridge, 1977).

Knott, John R., *Discourses of Martyrdom in English Literature, 1563–1694*(Cambridge: Cambridge University Press, 1993).

Lake, Peter, 'Deeds against Nature: Cheap Print, Protestantism and Murder in Early Seventeenth-Century England', in *Culture and Politics in Early Stuart England*, ed. by Kevin Sharpe and Peter Lake (Basingstoke and London: Macmillan, 1994), pp. 257–83.

Lake, Peter, 'Popular Form, Puritan Content? Two Puritan Appropriations of the Murder Pamphlet from Mid-Seventeenth-Century London', in *Religion, Culture and Society in Early Modern Britain: Essays in Honour of Patrick Collinson*, ed. by Anthony Fletcher and Peter Roberts (Cambridge: Cambridge University Press, 1994), pp. 313–34.

Lambert, John James (ed.), *Records of the Skinners of London, Edward I to James I* (London: Sir Joseph Clauston & Sons, 1933).

Larkin, James F., and Hughes, Paul L., (eds.), *Stuart Royal Proclamations, vol 1, Royal Proclamations of King James I 1603–1625* (Oxford: Clarendon Press, 1973).

Lefranc, Pierre, *Sir Walter Ralegh, ecrivain, l'oeuvre et les idees* (Paris: Librarie Armand Colin, 1968).

Lehmberg, Stanford E., 'The Role of Parliament in Early Modern England – A Reconsideration', in *The Swedish Riksdag in an International Perspective*, ed. by Nils Stjernquist (Stockholm: Olaf Palme Gotta, 1989), pp. 75–87.

Levy, Fred J., *Tudor Historical Thought* (San Marino, California: Huntington Library, 1967).

Lindley, David, 'Embarrassing Ben: The Masques for Frances Howard' in *Renaissance Historicism: Selections from ELR*, ed. by Arthur F. Kinney and Dan S. Collins (Amherst: University of Massachusetts Press, 1987), pp. 248–64.

Lindley, David, *The Trials of Frances Howard: Fact and Fiction at the Court of King James* (London: Routledge, 1993).

Lindley, David, *Thomas Campion* (Leiden: E. J. Brill, 1986).

Lipsius, Justus, *Sixe Bookes of Politics or Civil Doctrine*, trans. by William Jones (London, 1594).

Lithgow, William, *A most delectable, and true discourse, of an admired and* painefull peregrination from Scotland to the most famous Kingdomes in Europe, Asia, and Affricke (London, 1614).

Loftie, W. J., *The Inns of Court and Chancery* (Southampton: Ashford Press, 1985).

Love, Harold, *Scribal Publication in Seventeenth-Century England* (Oxford: Clarendon Press, 1993).

Lumisden, Alexander, *A heavenly portion* (London, 1614).

McClung, William A., and Simard, Rodney, 'Donne's Somerset Epithalmion and the Erotics of Criticism', *Huntington Library Quarterly*, 50 (1987), 95–106.

McClure, N. E. (ed.) *Letters of John Chamberlain*, 2 vols (Philadelphia: The American Philosophical Society, 1939).

McCullough, Peter E., *Sermons at Court: Politics and Religion in Elizabethan and Jacobean Preaching* (Cambridge: Cambridge University Press, 1998).

McKenzie, D. F., 'The London Book Trade in 1644', in *Bibliographia: Lectures 1975–1988 by recipients of The Marc Fitch Prize for Bibliography*, ed. by John Horden (Oxford: Leopard's Head Press, 1992), pp. 131–52.

McKenzie, D. F., 'The Economies of Print, 1550–1750: Scales of production and Conditions of Constraint' in *Produzione e commercio della cara e del libro secc. XIII–XVIII* (Prato, 1992; Istituto Internazionale di Storia Economica 'F. Datini' Prato. Serie II – Atti delle 'Settimane di Studi' e altri Convegni 23), pp. 389–425.

Marotti, Arthur, *Manuscript, Print, and the English Renaissance Lyric* (Ithaca and London: Cornell University Press, 1995).

Marshall, Joseph, 'Reading and Mis-reading King James 1622–1642: Responses to the *Letter and Directions Touching Preaching and Preachers*', in *Royal Subjects: Essays on the Writings of James VI and I*, ed. by Daniel Fishlin and Mark Fortier (Detroit: Wayne State University Press, forthcoming).

Marshall, Joseph, 'Recycling and Originality in British Pamphlets, 1640–48', unpublished paper, delivered at Cambridge University Library, 25 February 2000.

Middleton, Thomas, *The Masque of Cupids*, ed. by M. T. Jones-Davies and A. J. Hoenselaars, in *The Complete Works of Thomas Middleton*, ed. by G. Taylor et al. (Oxford: Clarendon Press, forthcoming 2001).

Milton, Anthony, 'Licensing, Censorship, and Religious Orthodoxy in Early Stuart England', *The Historical Journal*, 41 (1998), 625–51.

Milton, John, *Complete Prose Works of John Milton*, general ed. Don M. Wolfe, 8 vols (New Haven and London: Yale University Press, 1953–82).

Mocket, Richard, *God and the King: Or, a Dialogue showing that our Soveraigne Lord King James, being immediate under God within his Dominions, Doth rightfully claime whatsoever is required by the Oath of Allegeance* (London, 1615).

Moir, Thomas L., *The Addled Parliament of 1614* (Oxford: Clarendon Press, 1958).

Moran, Bruce T. (ed.), *Patronage and Institutions. Science, Technology, and Medicine at the European Court 1500–1750* (Woodbridge: The Boydell Press, 1991).

Morrill, John, 'Reconstructing the History of Early Stuart Parliaments', *Archives*, 21:91 (1994), 67–72.

Morrill, John,'Paying One's D'Ewes', *Parliamentary History*, 14:2 (1995), 179–86.

Morrill, John, 'Getting Over D'Ewes', *Parliamentary History*, 15:2 (1996), 221–30.

Nedham, Marchamont, *The excellencie of a free state: or, the right constitution of a Commonwealth ... With some errors of government, and rules of policie. Published by a well-wisher to posterity* (London, 1656).

Norbrook, David, *Poetry and Politics in the English Renaissance* (London: Routledge & Kegan Paul, 1984).

Notestein, Wallace, Relf, Frances Helen and Simpson, Hartley (eds.) *Commons Debates in 1621*, 7 vols (New Haven: Yale University Press, 1935).

O'Callaghan, Michelle, *The 'Shepheards Nation' : Jacobean Spenserians and Early Stuart Political Culture* (Oxford: Clarendon Press, 2000).

O'Callaghan, Michelle, '"Talking Politics": Tyranny, Parliament, and Christopher Brooke's *The Ghost of Richard the Third* (1614)', *The Historical Journal*, 41 (1998), 97–120.

O'Callaghan, Michelle, 'Literary Commonwealths: A 1614 Print Community, *The Shepheards Pipe* and *The Shepherds Hunting*', *Seventeenth Century*, 13 (1998), 103–23.

Parkin-Speer, Diane, 'Freedom of Speech in Sixteenth Century English Rhetorics', *Sixteenth Century Journal*, 12:3 (1981), 65–72.

Parry, Graham, in *The Trophies of Time: English Antiquarians of the Seventeenth Century* (Oxford: Oxford University press, 1995).

Patterson, Annabel, *Censorship and Interpretation: The Conditions of Writing and Reading in Early Modern England* (Madison: University of Wisconsin Press, 1984).

Peacock, John, 'Ben Jonson's Masques and Italian Culture', in *Theatre of the English and Italian Renaissance*, ed. by J. R. Mulryne and M. Shewring (Basingstoke: Macmillan, 1991).

Peck, Linda Levy, *Court Patronage and Corruption in Early Stuart England* (London: Routledge, 1993).

Peck, Linda Levy, *Northampton: Patronage, Policy and the Court of James I* (London: George Allen & Unwin, 1982).

Peck, Linda Levy, 'Kingship, Counsel and Law in Early Stuart Britain', in *The Varieties of British Political Thought, 1500–1800*, ed. by J. G. A. Pocock et al. (Cambridge: Cambridge University Press, 1993), pp. 80–115.

Peck, Linda Levy, 'Monopolizing Favour: Structures of Power in the Early Seventeenth-Century English Court', in *The World of the Favourite*, ed. by John H. Elliott and L. W. B. Brockliss (New Haven: Yale University Press, 1999), pp. 54–70.

Pocock, J. G. A., *The Machiavellian Moment. Florentine Political Thought and the Atlantic Republican Tradition* (Princeton: Princeton University Press, 1975).

Pocock, J. G. A., Gordon J. Schochet and Lois G. Schwoerer (eds.) *The Varieties of British Political Thought, 1500–1800* (Cambridge: Cambridge University Press, 1993).

Pocock, J. G. A., *Essays on Political Thought and History* (London: Methuen, 1972).

Pocock, J. G. A., 'James Harrington and the Good Old Cause: A Study of the Ideological Context of his Writings', *Journal of British Studies*, 10 (1970), 38–9; *Political Works of James Harrington*, ed. by J. G. A. Pocock (Cambridge: Cambridge University Press, 1977), pp. 13–14, 34–40.

Pollard, A. W., and G. R. Redgrave, G. R., *A Short-Title Catalogue of Books Printed in England, Scotland and Ireland: And of English Books Printed Abroad 1475–1640,* revised ed., 3 vols (London: Bibliographical Society, 1976–1991).

Powell, William S., *John Pory 1572–1636: The Life and Letters of a Man of Many Parts* (Chapel Hill, NC: University of North Carolina Press, 1977).

Prescott, Anne Lake, 'Evil Tongues at the Court of Saul: the Renaissance David as Slandered Courtier', *The Journal of Medieval and Renaissance Studies*, 21 (1991), 163–86.

Prestwich, Menna, *Cranfield: Politics and Profits under the Early Stuarts* (Oxford: Clarendon Press, 1966).

Price, Daniel, *Prince Henry, his second anniversary* (Oxford, 1614).

Prideaux, John, *Ephesus backsliding considered and applyed to these times, in a sermon* (London, 1614).

Pritchard, Allan, '*Abuses Stript and Whipt* and Wither's Imprisonment', *Review of English Studies*, 14 (1963), 337–45.

Questier, Michael C. (ed.), *Newsletters from the Archpresbyterate of George Birkhead,* Royal Historical Society, Camden 5th Series: (London: Cambridge University Press, 1998).

Quinn, David B. (ed.), *The Hakluyt Handbook*, 2 vols (London: The Hakluyt Society, 1974).

Rabb, Theodore K., *Jacobean Gentleman: Sir Edwin Sandys, 1561–1629* (Princeton: Princeton University Press, 1998).

Racin, John, *Sir Walter Ralegh as Historian: An Analysis of The History of the World*, Salzburg Studies in English Literature, 2 (Salzburg: Institut fur Englische Sprache und Literatur, 1974).

Ralegh, P., *The Art of War by Sea. Page references are to the edition in An Abridgement of Sir Walter Ralegh's History of the World. To which is added, his Premonition to Princes. With some genuine remains, published by P. Ralegh* (London, P. Ralegh, 1698).

Raleigh, Walter, *Dialogue betweene a Counsellor of State and a Justice of the Peace* (1615; Midelburge [London], 1628).

Ramsay, G. D., 'Industrial Discontent in Early Elizabethan London: Clothworkers and Merchants Adventurers in Conflict', *The London Journal*, 1:2 (1975), 227–39.

Ramsay, G. D. 'Clothworkers, Merchants Adventurers and Richard Hakluyt', *English Historical Review*, 92 (1977), 504–21.

Raymond, Joad, *The Invention of the Newspaper: English Newsbooks, 1641–1649* (Oxford: Clarendon Press, 1996).

Raymond, Joad, *Pamphlets and Pamphleteering in Early Modern Britain* (Cambridge: Cambridge University Press, forthcoming).

Records of the Stationers' Company, 1602 to 1640, ed. by William A. Jackson (London: The Bibliographical Society, 1957).

Ribiero, Alvaro, 'Sir John Roe: Ben Jonson's Friend', *Review of English Studies*, n. s. 24 (1973), 153–64.

Rich, Barnaby, *The Honestie of this Age. Proouing by good circumstance that the world was never honest till now.* (London, 1614).

Riggs, David, *Ben Jonson: A Life* (Cambridge, Massachusetts: Harvard University Press, 1989).

Roberts, Clayton, and Duncan, Owen, 'The Parliamentary Undertaking of 1614, *English Historical Review*, 93 (1978), 481–98.

Rolte, John, *A full declaration of the faith and ceremonies professed in the dominions of ... Fredericke, 5. prince elector palatine ... Translated into English by Iohn Rolte* (London, 1614).

Roskell, J. S., *The Commons and their Speakers in English Parliaments 1376–1523* (Manchester: Manchester University Press, 1965).

Russell, Conrad, *The Addled Parliament of 1614: The Limits to Revision*, The Stenton Lecture 1991 (Reading: University of Reading, 1992).

Russell, Conrad, *Unrevolutionary England, 1603–1642* (London: Hambledon Press, 1990).

Russell, Conrad, *Parliaments and English Politics 1621–1629* (Oxford: Clarendon Press, 1979).

Russell, Conrad, *The Fall of the British Monarchies 1637–1642* (Oxford: Clarendon Press, 1991).

Sanderson, James L., 'Poems on an Affair of State', *Review of English Studies*, new series, 17 (1966), 57–61.

Savage, James E. (ed.), *The 'Conceited Newes' of Sir Thomas Overbury and his Friends*, (Gainesville, Florida: Scholars' Facsimiles and Reprints, 1968).

Sawyer, Edmund (ed.), *Memorials of Affairs of State ... from the Original Papers of Sir Ralph Winwood*, 3 vols (London, 1725).

Scott, Harold S. (ed.), *The Journal of Sir Roger Wilbraham, Solicitor-General in Ireland and Master of Requests, for the Years 1593–1616. Together with notes in another hand for the years 1642–1649* in *Camden Miscellany*, 10 (London: Royal Historical Society, 1902).

Seddon, Peter R., 'Robert Carr, Earl of Somerset', *Medieval and Renaissance Studies*, 14 (1970), 48–68.

Sedgwick, Eve Kosofsky, *Between Men: English Literature and Male Homosocial Desire* (New York: Columbia University Press, 1985).

Shaaber, M. A., 'The Meaning of the Imprint in Early Printed Books', *The Library*, fourth series, 24 (1943–4), 120–41.

Sharpe, Kevin, *Politics and Ideas in Early Stuart England: Essays and Studies* (London: Pinter, 1989).

Sharpe, Kevin (ed.), *Faction and Parliament: Essays on Early Stuart History*, (Oxford: Clarendon Press, 1978).

Sharpe, Kevin, *Sir Robert Cotton 1586–1631: History and Politics in Early Modern England* (Oxford: Oxford University Press, 1979).

Simmons, Judith, 'Publications of 1623', *The Library*, 5th ser., 21 (1966), 207–22.

Sinfield, Alan, *Cultural Politics – Queer Reading* (London: Routledge, 1994).Skinner, Quentin, 'The Greek and Roman Classics as the Cause of the English Civil War', Neale Lecture, University College London, 3 March 2000 (unpublished).

Skinner, Quentin, 'John Milton and the Politics of Slavery', *Prose Studies*, 23:1 (2000), 1–22.

Sloane, Thomas O., *On the Contrary: The Protocol of Traditional Rhetoric* (Washington D.C.: The Catholic University of America Press, 1997).

Smith, James M., 'Effaced History: Facing the Colonial Contexts of Ben Jonson's *Irish Masque at Court*', *English Literary History*, 65 (1998), 297–321.

Smith, Logan Pearsall (ed.), *The Life and Letters of Sir Henry Wotton*, 2 vols (London: Oxford University Press, 1907).

Smith, Samuel, *Davids Repentance, or, a plaine and familiar Exposition of the 51. Psalme* (London, 1614).

Somerset, Anne, *Unnatural Murder: Poison at the Court of James I* (London: Weidenfeld and Nicolson, 1997).

Sommerville, Johann P., 'English and European Political Ideas in the Early Seventeenth Century: Revisionism and the Case of Absolutism', *Journal of British Studies*, 35 (1996), 168–94.

Sommerville, Johann P., *Politics and Ideology in England 1603–1640* (London and New York: Longman, 1986).

Spedding, James (ed.), *The Letters and Life of Francis Bacon*, 7 vols (London: Longman, 1861–1874).

Squibb, G. D., *The High Court of Chivalry: A Study of the Civil Law in England* (Oxford: Clarendon Press, 1959).

Stewart, Alan, *Close Readers: Humanism and Sodomy in Early Modern England* (Princeton: Princeton University Press, 1997).

Stock, Richard, *The Churches Lamentation for the loss of the Godly ... delivered in a Sermon at the funeral of John Lord Harington* (London, 1614).

Stone, Lawrence, 'Elizabethan Overseas Trade', *Economic History Review*, second series, 2 (1949–50), 30–58.

Strong, Roy, *Henry, Prince of Wales and England's Lost Renaissance* (London: Thames and Hudson, 1986).

Strong, Roy, 'England and Italy: The Marriage of Henry, Prince of Wales' in *For Veronica Wedgwood These: Studies in Seventeenth-Century History*, ed. by Richard Ollard and Pamela Tudor-Craig (London: Collins, 1986), pp. 84–6.

Supple, Barry E., *Commercial Crisis and Change in England 1600–1642* (Cambridge: Cambridge University Press, 1959).

Sylvester, Joshua, *The Parliament of vertues royal* (London, [1614?]). Whitlock, Baird W., *John Hoskyns, Serjeant-at-Law* (Washington DC: University Press of America, 1982).

Wright, Leonard, *A Display of dutie, dect with sage sayings, pythie sentences, and* proper similies: Pleasant to reade, delightfull to heare, and profitable to practice (London, 1614).

Tacitus, *Tacitus*, trans. by John Jackson, 5 vols (Cambridge, Mass.: Harvard University Press; London: William Heinemann, 1920).

Tailor, Robert, *The Hogge hath lost his Pearle. A Comedy* (London, 1614).

Taylor, E. G. R., (ed.), *The Original Writings and Correspondence of the Two Richard Hakluyts*, 2 vols (London: The Hakluyt Society, 1935).

Taylor, John, *The Nipping or Snipping of Abuses: or the woolgathering of Witte. With The Muses Taylor, brought from Parnassus by land, with a paire of Oares* (London, 1614).

Tillotson, Kathleen, 'Drayton, Browne, and Wither', *Times Literary Supplement*, 27 November 1937, p. 911.

Walker, William, *A sermon preached at the funerals of the right honourable, William, Lord Russell, Baron of Thorbaugh ... the 16 of September 1613.* (London, 1614).

Wells, Stanley (ed.), *A Book of Masques* (Cambridge: Cambridge University Press, 1967).

Wilks, Timothy, 'The Picture Collection of Robert Carr, Earl of Somerset (c.1587–1645), Reconsidered', *Journal of the History of Collections*, 1 (1989), 167–77.

Willson, David Harris (ed.), *The Parliamentary Diary of Robert Bowyer 1606–1607* (Minneapolis: University of Minnesota Press, 1931).

Wilson, Thomas, *Christs farewell to Jerusalem, and last prophesie* (London, 1614).

Wither, George, *The Shepherds Hunting: Being, Certain Eglogs written during the time of the Authors Imprisonment in the Marshalsey* (London, 1615).

Wither, George, *Abuses Stript, and Whipt* (London, 1615).

Wither, George, *A Satyre: Dedicated to his Most Excellent Majestie* (London, 1614).

Wormald, Jenny, 'James VI and I: Two Kings or One?', *History*, 68 (1983) 187–209.

Wormald, Jenny,'James VI and I, *Basilikon Doron* and the *Trew Law of Free Monarchies*: The Scottish Context and the English Translation', in *The Mental World of the Jacobean Court*, ed. by Linda Levy Peck (Cambridge: Cambridge University Press, 1991), pp. 36–54.

Wormald, Jenny, *Court, Kirk, and Community: Scotland 1470–1625* (London: Arnold, 1981).

Worship, William, *Earth raining upon Heaven. A sermon preached at the Assises at Nottingham, August 5, 1614.* (London, 1614).

Woudhuysen, H. R., *Sir Philip Sidney and the Circulation of Manuscripts 1558–1640* (Oxford: Clarendon Press, 1996).

Index